Hauula
Kahana
Waikane
Kaneohe Bay
Mokapu Pt.
Heeia
Kailua Bay
Kaneohe
Kalauao
Aiea
Waimanalo Bay
Pouloa
Waimanalo
Maunalua
Kahala
HONOLULU
Diamond Head
Koko Head



# Y & LAND CO.

# MILLSTONES AND MILESTONES
## THE CAREER OF B. F. DILLINGHAM

Benjamin Franklin Dillingham. Portrait painted in 1912 by George Burroughs Torrey.

# MILLSTONES AND MILESTONES
## THE CAREER OF B. F. DILLINGHAM 1844–1918

PAUL T. YARDLEY

Published for The B. F. Dillingham Company, Ltd.
*by*
The University Press of Hawaii
*Honolulu*

*Library of Congress Cataloging in Publication Data*

Yardley, Paul T., 1917–
Millstones and milestones.

Bibliography: p.
Includes index.
1. Dillingham, Benjamin Franklin, 1844–1918.
2. Businessmen—Hawaii—Biography. 3. Hawaii—
Industries—History. I. Title.
HC107.H3Y37 338'.04'0924 [B] 81–11506
ISBN 0–8248–0761–8 AACR2

*To my dear wife Maili*
*without whom this book*
*would not even have begun*
*to be possible*

*If one advances confidently in the direction of his dreams, and endeavors to live the life which he has imagined, he will meet with a success unexpected in common hours.*

Henry David Thoreau, *Walden*

# CONTENTS

# PREFACE

As the author of this book, I think it fair that its readers should know that Mr. Dillingham's descendants commissioned me to write it. At no time, however, has any one suggested that I should write anything but the truth as I see it, nor would I have complied if I had been asked to distort the record.

Also, I have spent a good deal of my adult life in the ownership and management of various businesses, and I believe in a system of private enterprise. I also believe in facts. Without some years of business experience, I would have been ill-equipped to assimilate the facts of Mr. Dillingham's life.

Mr. Dillingham was too big a man to need either panegyric or apologies. Let the facts speak for themselves.

In uncovering the facts on which this book is based, I have been immeasurably aided by many individuals.

Mr. Dillingham's descendants, and in particular Mrs. Edward O'Neill, have been generous in sharing whatever material remains in their hands. Those who have custody of other materials have been most helpful in making them available; in particular I wish to thank Mr. John C. Wright and Mrs. Cynthia Timberlake of the Bishop Museum, and Mrs. David Larsen of the Hawaiian Mission Children's Society. Miss Agnes Conrad, the state archivist, not only provided material but also read the manuscript and made valuable suggestions, as did Mrs. Sophie Cluff. Mr. Harold Dillingham, Jr., has given generously of his time in finding and obtaining photographs to illustrate this book.

Among others to whom I am particularly grateful for various favors are Mrs. Carl Ahlstrom, Mrs. Caroline Brown, Mr. E. H. Bryan, Mr. C. W. Carlsmith, Mr. E. R. Champion, Ms. Lynn Davis, Mr. Ernest S. Dodge, Miss Mary K. Dugar, Mr. Harold Eichelberger, Mrs. Kathleen Hasselman, Miss Katherine Hulme, Mrs. Betty Kam, Colonel Harold W. Kent, Mr. Francis B. Lothrop, Mr. Thomas J. O'Brien, and Mr. Barnes Riznik. Mahalo!

# Part I
# THE STAR AND THE ANCHOR

# CHAPTER 1

*Sailors . . . are notoriously unfamiliar with horses.*

B. F. Dillingham

ON a July afternoon in 1865 Benjamin Franklin Dillingham, first mate on the sailing packet *Whistler,* went horseback riding with other young officers from ships in Honolulu harbor. Up the broad valley behind the little town they rode, where Pacific Heights and Alewa Heights stood bare, dry, and uninhabited. As they reached Judd Street they could feel the cool breeze moving down Nuuanu Valley and hear the rustling of Nuuanu Stream and the singing of birds among the trees. Ahead of them lay an enchanted land of waterfalls and mountain pools, of clumps of coconut trees and patches of taro, and finally at the far head of the valley the great Nuuanu Pali, where the men of Kamehameha had pushed the warriors of Oahu to their death over the thousand-foot cliff some seventy years before.

Home for Frank Dillingham lay half a world away, five thousand miles as the crow flies and five months on a sailing ship around Cape Horn. The granite hills of Massachusetts were as different from the volcanic cliffs of Nuuanu as the careful, silent New Englanders were from the laughing, half-clad Hawaiians splashing in the mountain pools. Instead of oaks and elms and maples, Frank saw around him the lovely *kukui,* whose oily nuts the Hawaiians used for candles, the blossoming *'ōhi'a,* and the stately *koa.* Frank's every sense must have strained to take in this strange, mysterious world in which he found himself.

Frank Dillingham was short, stocky, and well muscled, and the firmness of his jaw and the direct glance of his blue eyes told the world that he could take care of himself. But underneath his rough sailor's exterior lay a nature that was generous, inquisitive, and affectionate. His mind never stood still, but was always weaving dreams, hatching schemes, and conceiving ambitions. While others aboard

As a young man B. F. Dilllingham was both forceful and handsome. This photograph was evidently taken not long after he settled in Honolulu. Throughout his life Mr. Dillingham was called Frank by his family and oldest friends. (Bishop Museum photo)

ship slept or spun yarns, he read and studied and memorized poetry. In terms of the New England stereotype of caution and reserve, he was a biological sport, an inexplicable mutation to romance and adventure.

Now almost twenty-one, Frank had followed the sea for six years since shipping out of Boston as a boy on one of the great Yankee clippers. Boys became men young in that life, and Frank, as second in command of the *Whistler,* was already nearing the top of his vocation. He had to his credit five passages around Cape Horn and three around the Cape of Good Hope; after those experiences his present berth under the redoubtable Captain John Paty seemed like a pleasure cruise.

This trip to Honolulu was his third aboard the *Whistler,* which plied regularly back and forth from San Francisco. He made friends easily and already knew quite a scattering of people in Honolulu; some of them from the services at Bethel Union Church and some who had taken passage on the *Whistler.* He had begun to feel at home in the little city.

After a leisurely ride up the valley, the band of young officers turned their horses homeward. As they reached the upper bridge in Nuuanu, just below Judd Street, they met an open carriage coming the other way. Frank lost control of his horse, collided with the carriage, fell to the ground, and felt a sudden sharp pain in his right leg.

Frank's friends carried him into the nearby home of C. C. Harris, chief justice of the Hawaiian Kingdom. Dr. Ford arrived and pronounced the injury a compound fracture of the lower leg. Frank was carried to the U. S. Marine Hospital, maintained by the United States Government for the benefit of American sailors in Hawaii, where he lay helpless and no doubt restless and fuming.

Frank's convalescence was slow and painful. The *Whistler* sailed without him, leaving him "on the beach" with time on his hands to think about the future.

Possibly he saw in the accident the hand of God. Ever since his ordeal when the clipper ship on which he was third mate was captured by a Confederate raider during the Civil War, he had felt a growing desire to leave the life of a sailor. Now his injury had given a sudden turn to his affairs. With the unfailing optimism that was perhaps his strongest trait, he accepted the new direction and never looked back. Overnight, Benjamin Franklin Dillingham became a resident of Hawaii.

# CHAPTER 2

*Farming was not to my taste for a livelihood.*

B. F. Dillingham

BENJAMIN Franklin Dillingham was born in the village of West Brewster, Cape Cod, Massachusetts, on 4 September 1844, in the "new" Dillingham home, a handsome eighteenth century colonial structure, which at that time stood immediately adjacent to the "old" Dillingham house. The old house, a seventeenth century two-story Cape Cod salt box with its back to the wind and its face to the highway, still stands in its original spot, a tribute to the integrity of its builders; the new house has in recent years been moved a few miles down the road to Barnstable.

Cape Cod, even in 1844, was an old country, and the Dillinghams an old family. Frank belonged to the eighth generation of his family in Massachusetts. By 1865, when he broke his leg and settled in Honolulu, his forebears had lived in Massachusetts well over two hundred years.

John Dillingham, the first of the family in America, came to Massachusetts with Governor Winthrop in 1630. He was a wealthy man whose estate took ten years and more than £900 to settle, the chief executor being Sir Richard Saltonstall. But John had no sons, and the Dillinghams in America descend from his brother Edward, who arrived a couple of years later.

Like his brother John, Edward was called "Mr. Dillingham," a sign of respect. Like him, he had land and cattle and horses. He left three or four children to divide his property, and they in turn heeded the biblical injunction to be fruitful and multiply. His son John Dillingham I had four children; John II had ten; John III at least six; John IV seven; and John V eleven. By the time of Benjamin Clark Dillingham, son of John V, the family wealth had fragmented and drifted away, leaving behind the two beautiful homes in West Brewster and patches of land worth more in prestige than in dollars.

The Dillingham houses at West Brewster, Cape Cod, Massachusetts. The handsome house on the left, where Benjamin Franklin Dillingham was born, has since been moved to Barnstable. The old Dillingham house on the right still stands in its original location. This picture is thought to have been taken in the early 1920s. (Courtesy of the Dillingham family)

But if the family became poor, they had plenty of company, for Cape Cod was a poor place. The soil was thin and the climate hard; a man who wanted to farm would do better inland. Only the sea offered the promise of adventure and perhaps fortune.

Benjamin Clark Dillingham, Frank's father, followed the sea for a living. He had married Lydia Howes of nearby Dennis, who was also from a seagoing family; Frank, their first child, was born some three years later. Lydia was about twenty-five at the time of Frank's birth, and the father probably not much older.

Surprisingly, three months after Frank was born the young couple picked up their baby and, turning their backs on the Dillingham and Howes families, moved in the middle of December to Southboro, a small town some 25 miles west of Boston. We have no real clue as to why they left Cape Cod, or why they chose Southboro. Perhaps this move, even then, formed part of a grand scheme in the father's mind. Following the sea was a hard life and a dangerous one, and many a sailor dreamed of putting into Snug Harbor before he got

Benjamin Clark Dillingham, father of Benjamin Franklin Dillingham. Dillingham *père* left the sea to become a farmer, and died of sunstroke while still a comparatively young man, leaving fifteen-year-old Frank the sole support of his mother. (Daguerrotype, Bishop Museum)

snugged into Davy Jones' locker. When Frank was twelve his father made the break; retiring from the sea, he went into partnership with a brother-in-law, Silas Howes, to buy and work a farm of 58 acres in Worcester Township.

Worcester, a little farther west than Southboro, is today an industrial city, and even in 1857 it was a town of considerable size. The Dillingham family evidently continued to live in Southboro, for Frank speaks of attending the "village school" in the winters of 1857 and 1858, while working on the farm during the summers. Frank's father still owned the Southboro property at the time of his death. He and his wife and Frank's sister are all buried in that town.

Frank had a brother, Charles, nine years younger than he, and a sister, Abbey, still a baby when he left home. Not much is known about Frank's boyhood. Sixty years later he remembered chopping wood one evening as a small boy; the sunset was glorious and he gazed at it wondering whether he would ever go west to the lands where the sun disappears.

His later life suggests that Frank enjoyed a happy childhood in a close-knit family. Evidently he made many visits to relatives, particularly in Chelsea, across the Charles River from Boston proper, for a letter which he wrote in 1908 to his cousin Isaac speaks of "those two homes [in Chelsea] with which I was so familiar in my childhood." Another letter written late in his life mentions a little band of sisters and cousins whom he remembered with great affection. In spite of the distance involved, he kept in touch in later life not only with his

The earliest known photograph of Benjamin Franklin Dillingham, with his mother, Lydia Howes Dillingham. (Daguerrotype, Bishop Museum)

sister and mother in Worcester but also with a bewildering number of cousins in the East.

It would also seem that his family practiced the New England virtues of hard work, piety, and respect for learning. Although Frank had little formal schooling, he worked all his life to educate himself, and in his maturity he handled the written word with force and clarity.

For his incredible drive, energy, and perseverance we have no explanation; they were a phenomenon of nature.

Frank was twelve when his father went shares with Silas Howes to buy the farm in Worcester. The inventory of farm property taken at the time of the father's death gives a homely glimpse of a hard, spare life: one heifer, one dark red cow, one white cow, one "loped horned cow," one "poor house cow," one "Yankee cow," two calves, one horse, one yoke of oxen, ox sled, sleigh, ox cart, "pleasure waggon," stone boat, harness, hay cutter, manure fork, cider barrels, twelve chickens (at 20 cents each), eleven "fowls," plows, harrow, cultivator, horse rake, scalding tub, churn, skimmer, cream pail, jugs, wheelbarrow, whetstones, 19 bushels of second-quality corn, 11½ tons of hay, oats, parsnips, small potatoes, turnips, apples, beets, and—evidently a cash crop—2½ tons of carrots at $12 a ton. The farm must have provided a few cash crops and food for the families, but no prospect of an abundant life.

Mr. Dillingham retired from the sea so that he could stay home, and also in order to remove his sons from the temptation to go to sea. Like many other such plans, his scheme failed completely.

Frank simply did not take to the farming life. He had heard so many tales of his seafaring relatives and read so many romantic accounts of life at sea that putting him on a farm was like hiding young Achilles among the maidens; when the sword dropped in front of him, he had to pick it up.

When Frank was fourteen his father and mother bowed to the inevitable, comforting themselves with the thought that Frank had had lung trouble and that life at sea would strengthen him. His father even helped him plan his first voyage.

# CHAPTER 3

*His [R. A. Howes'] father was First Officer of the ship* Southern Cross *in 1859. . . . He was a kindly, considerate man, and I have taken an interest in his youngest son, knowing that the father has passed over The Great Divide.*

B. F. Dillingham

FOR a brief period up to the Civil War, American ships and American sailors led the world. The famous Yankee clippers were the fastest merchant sailing ships the world has ever seen. Built with sharp bows, rather flat bottoms, and tapering sterns, these big ships could carry immense cargoes. Their most characteristic features—tall masts and wide yards—allowed a driving captain to crowd on a huge amount of sail, as witnessed by the *Lightning*'s incredible record of 436 nautical miles in twenty-four hours.

The 1850s were the great decade for the clippers. Sail reached its supreme development just at a time when an ominous smudge of smoke on the horizon warned of the coming age of steam that would drive the proud clippers from the seas.

The *Southern Cross,* in which Frank Dillingham sailed for almost four years, was rather small for a clipper and built more for reliability than extreme speed. Her passages from Boston to California averaged around 132 days of sailing time—respectable but not sensational. But she was one of the best known of the clippers because of her wonderful record of consistency. Beginning in 1851, she made nine consecutive round-the-world voyages in nine years, starting each time from Boston, then to San Francisco, and proceeding around the world via the Cape of Good Hope.

The *Southern Cross* was rated at 938 tons. She was 170 feet long on her deck, with a beam of 36 feet, and carried three masts, each with five yards. Her frame was seasoned white oak, and her planking and decking hard southern pine. She bore as her figurehead a gilded eagle on the wing. On her deck, between the fore and main masts, she carried a "house," 37 feet by 14 feet, containing the crew's quarters and galley. This deck house represented a great advance over jamming the crew into the fo'c'sle, and it meant that Frank did not literally go to sea "before the mast."

Skipper of the *Southern Cross* was Frank's maternal uncle, Benjamin Perkins Howes, himself only twenty-three years old and making his first voyage as captain. This Uncle Benjamin must have had a tremendous influence on the lad, for they sailed together for four years. Fortunately Captain Howes possessed not only professional competence but also a love of book learning unusual in a seafaring man.

Captain Howes was a bachelor at this time, but between his (and Frank's) first and second voyages he married Lucy Lord. Once they

A model, owned by the Dillingham Corporation, of the *Southern Cross.* Frank Dillingham went to sea in the *Southern Cross* at the age of 14, under his maternal uncle, Captain Benjamin Howes. Frank completed two voyages around the world in this ship; on his third voyage the *Southern Cross* was captured and burned by the Confederate raider *Florida.* (Courtesy of Dillingham Corporation)

were married, Captain Howes took his wife to sea with him as a matter of course, and she must have been the only woman Frank saw for months on end. She was only six years older than Frank and he evidently remembered her with pleasure, as he was corresponding with her near the very end of his life.

The first mate was also named Howes, "a kindly, considerate man" and another relative.

Frank sailed as a "boy," or apprentice seaman, at an articled wage of $1 a month. One of the duties of a boy was to handle the sails on the very lightest spars, which might not hold the weight of a full-grown man. Since these sails were naturally those farthest from the deck, the job must have had more than its share of excitement.

According to family tradition, Frank was not a particularly robust lad, and on his first voyage was homesick and seasick to boot. Moreover, his shipmates were evidently a pretty ragtag lot. The tremendous number of ships built in the early fifties had spread the old-time sailors pretty thin, and many of the best men had left the sea to go west. Ship captains had to find crews where they could. In later years Frank told his children that to close his mind to the rough talk around him, he would lie in his hammock and repeat verses of poetry that he had memorized.

This first voyage of Frank's remained vivid in his mind all his life. More than fifty years later he was corresponding with one of his shipmates, A. M. Pendleton, an older man whom he had seen once or twice in the meantime. Pendleton, then a retired minister living in New Hampshire, wrote that he was "old and sick and poverty-stricken." Dillingham wrote back a warm letter in which he spoke of Pendleton's many kindnesses to him when he was a lad and enclosed a substantial check. In thanking him, Pendleton replied that "it seems strange that the few little things I did for a forlorn boy so many years ago should now bear such rich fruit."

Undoubtedly, as soon as Frank got his sea legs under him, he set out to learn everything there was to know about being a sailor. To a lad with Frank's outlook on life, grasping the next rung of the ladder was a reflex action. He was a sailor, therefore he would become the best sailor in the Yankee fleet, which meant naturally in the world. Any other course would never have occurred to him.

Luckily for Frank, Captain Howes carried with him a library of several hundred books into which the lad plunged during the long voyages. Here he could not only teach himself navigation and seamanship, but he could explore new worlds of history and travel and lose himself in poetry and fiction. The results pay tribute not only to his self-discipline but also to a remarkable thirst for knowledge. Frank sailed as a lad of fourteen with a grade-school education; he left the sea six years later a man of considerable knowledge, who could write creditably and whose enthusiasm for learning never diminished.

At some time during his seafaring career, Frank had himself tattooed with a blue-green star on the back of one wrist and an anchor on the other. In later years, he became quite self-conscious about these marks of youthful indiscretion; his grandson Walter remembers him pulling his cuffs down to hide the tattoos. But it is pleasant to think of them as symbols of the great currents of his life: the star of ambition and adventure and the anchor of home and family.

For this raw lad carried in himself the seeds of greatness. Besides ambition, he had ability; besides ability, perseverance; besides perseverance, direction. And beneath his direction lay a firm commitment to decency and to raising a family which would be a credit to his name.

On Frank's first voyage, the *Southern Cross* left Boston on 10 June 1859 and reached San Francisco on 22 October after a normal passage of 134 days. Here Frank found letters sent via the Isthmus of Panama telling him that his father had died of sunstroke.

This shocking death of a man in the prime of life left Frank's mother with two children at home: Charles, who was just six, and Abbey, two. After the share of the farm was sold and some fractional interests in property on the Cape, she had a little money, but hardly enough to live on. Frank, at the age of fifteen, found himself not only the nominal head of a family but also its sole wage earner.

Luckily, Frank's uncle paid him off in San Francisco not at his articled amount of $1 a month, but at the princely rate of $8, this being the custom on American ships.* Better than that, he received a promotion to ordinary seaman at $20 a month.

At San Francisco the *Southern Cross* unloaded her cargo of general merchandise and loaded flour for Hong Kong. After less than a

*There is a story of one Cape Cod boy who learned of this custom only after being paid off by his uncle in Boston at the rate of $1. The lad walked from Cape Cod to Boston in the middle of winter to inquire whether uncle intended to pay him the difference. Uncle replied that he would think about it, and shut the door in his face.

month in San Francisco, she sailed, carrying also a load of Chinese returning to their homes, and made Hong Kong in the fast time of forty-four days. From Hong Kong she proceeded to Manila and thence around the Cape of Good Hope to Boston. A voyage around the world, with stops for discharging and loading cargo, customarily took a year or more.

Frank Dillingham between voyages as a young sailor. Photo marked in his own handwriting, "1860 or 1862." (Ambrotype, Bishop Museum)

For his second voyage Frank had made able seaman, another rung up the ladder. The *Southern Cross* left Boston on 6 July 1860 and made San Francisco in November, 131 days out. Frank recalled: "Off Cape Horn about 30 days, blown by gales and swept by currents repeatedly to latitude 60 south. We lay a month in San Francisco—taking flour and Chinese passengers to Hong Kong."

Many years later, when he was old and sick, Mr. Dillingham dictated to his beloved Emma a short memoir of his life up to the age of about forty, from which the above quotation is taken. This memoir skips entirely or touches only lightly many interesting topics, such as his father and mother and his Uncle Benjamin, but it does reveal his intense preoccupation with the mechanics of how things work. From Hong Kong the ship sailed for Saigon to pick up a load of rice, which necessitated working her 72 miles upstream from the mouth of the Saigon River to the port. Fifty years later Mr. Dillingham covered his early life in six lines but devoted well over a page of typescript to the ingenious method by which a sailing ship was brought up this extremely winding river.

"The French were having some trouble with the natives at that time," he added, "and we were not allowed to go ashore."

The load of rice was taken from Saigon to Macao, and the *Southern Cross* sailed in ballast for Bangkok, where she loaded a cargo of sugar, hides, and horns. *"Pilau nui loa"* ("big stink"), he commented.

From Bangkok she sailed for Falmouth, England, and then back home to Boston, arriving 20 January 1862.

In February Frank sailed again for San Francisco. This time he was seventeen years old and third mate of the *Southern Cross*—a big step upward in his career. The ship made San Francisco in 128 days and sailed a month later, 28 July 1862, again bound for Hong Kong. This time she anchored off Honolulu to take aboard freight for Hong Kong and fresh meat and fruit for the crew. "I shall never forget the good feast we all had on watermelons," wrote Mr. Dillingham in his memoir. "They were so sweet and delicious. I did not come on shore that time, nor did I dream I should ever become a resident of this beautiful country."

On this trip the *Southern Cross,* for the only time in her career, passed up the route around the Cape of Good Hope in favor of returning to San Francisco from Hong Kong, reaching the Golden

Gate on Christmas Eve 1862. Cargoes were scarce; in February she proceeded to Buena Vista in the Gulf of California to load logwood, which was used in making dyes. In March she sailed for New York, made a good passage around Cape Horn, and by 6 June 1863 had reached a point near the equator.

Shortly after noon on 6 June a tiny speck appeared on the horizon, a speck which turned out to have a profound effect on Frank Dillingham's future.

# CHAPTER 4

*The war of the "Rebellion" was at its height at that time. The rebel cruisers* Florida *and* Alabama *were out on the high seas, capturing and burning all the merchant ships they could find, owned in the North and flying the American flag.*

B. F. Dillingham

NAVAL action had a decisive effect on the outcome of the Civil War. The Union blockade of Southern ports cut the Confederacy off from the mills and foundries of Europe, leaving her unable to procure the locomotives, rails, machinery, and manufactured goods of all kinds which she needed to carry on the war, and she gradually strangled to death under the blockade.

The South in turn attempted to destroy the North's merchant fleet by sending out fast, well armed cruisers to seize any ship found flying the American flag. The most famous of these cruisers, the *Alabama* and the *Florida,* were built in England during the war—in violation of British law—and both were commissioned in August of 1862. Operating from neutral ports, without ever touching the Confederacy, these two ships between them destroyed 124 American vessels. The U.S.S. *Kearsarge* finally sank the *Alabama* in a famous duel off Cherbourg, France, in June of 1864. The U.S.S. *Wachusett*—in violation of international law—rammed and captured the *Florida* in the Brazilian port of Bahia in October 1864. The United States apologized to Brazil for the incident but because of an unfortunate accident was unable to return the *Florida* to Bahia, and she finished the war on the bottom of Hampton Roads.

Unfortunately for the Confederacy, however, the spectacular destruction of Northern shipping by the commerce raiders had little effect on the course of the war. The North was largely self-sufficient and could easily obtain what goods she needed through ships of neutral countries. The destruction, however, did deal a lasting blow to shipping in American bottoms, and the American merchant marine never regained its position of supremacy.

Like the *Alabama,* the *Florida* carried sails and also a coal-burning steam plant for propulsion. Thus equipped she could economize on coal when cruising and run down most merchantmen in a chase.

Mr. Dillingham's own memoir tells the story of the *Southern Cross'* encounter.

> On June 6th, 1863 we were near the Equator. The weather was squally, the wind at times blowing quite hard, with heavy rain and calms intervening. Between 12 noon and 1 o'clock p.m. I came on deck just as the look-out called out "Sail ho!" Away ahead just on the horizon could be seen a little speck, which soon increased in size as we moved forward with wind "dead after." By 1:30 p.m. we could see the whole hull of a long rakish looking craft which proved to be the steamer *Florida.* The rain squalls and clouds which frequently enveloped us prevented the people on the *Florida* from seeing us. That steamer was steering eastward and had got off two or three miles on our starboard beam before they sighted our vessel. As soon as we were sighted the *Florida* was headed straight for us, carrying the English flag at her "mizen."
>
> In the meantime, our wind all died away and we could do nothing but watch the pirate speeding towards us under a full head of steam. She soon passed close to our stern, hauled down the British ensign and raised the "Stars and Bars" and at the same time ordered our Captain to "heave to."
>
> A boat was lowered from the *Florida* filled with armed men. They came along and boarded the ship. The officer in charge stepped on to the quarter deck and told the captain that he, his officers and crew were prisoners of war.
>
> Before we had time to collect a few of our belongings, we were ordered to board their boat. As we passed over the gangway to the deck of the *Florida* we were "hand-cuffed" and kept on deck in the rain for a week. Our Captain Howes had his wife with him, and this brought the Southern chivalry of Captain Moffitt [Lieutenant John N. Maffitt, Confederate States Navy] to the surface, resulting in his giving up his commander's apartments to Captain Howes and his wife.
>
> The cabin stores were all brought from the *Cross* to the *Florida.* The burning torch was applied to the cabin, fore, main and mizzen hatches; yards were braced up sharp; helm lashed and the ship was then left

to be devoured by the flames. To those of us who had made our homes on the good ship *Southern Cross* for nearly four years, it was a painful sight to witness such ruthless destruction.

It was almost dark when the consuming fires were kindled. In less than an hour the flames were shooting up the rigging, the sails took fire, and about eight o'clock the masts, no longer held by shrouds, fell over the sides, prying up the burning decks and exposing the internal fire, which now burst forth with dazzling brightness, painting the heavens red for miles around.

Captain Moffitt, commander of the Rebel Steamer, *Florida,* possibly for the purpose of indicating his sympathy for the Captain and crew of the *Southern Cross* which he deemed it his duty to destroy, wrote the following on June 9th, in his log notes:

"Those who go down to the sea in great ships see the wonders of the Lord."

At the time of our transfer to the *Florida,* Captain Moffitt was so much under the influence of liquor that he was unable to walk the deck without losing his equilibrium. The usual discipline of naval ships was sadly wanting on board the *Florida.* The crew and officers consisted of 325 men. As soon as the *Southern Cross* was level with the water's edge, we steamed away for a short distance. Sails then took the place of steam, and the vessel resumed her search for other objects of prey.

Speaking of the discipline, I awoke one night and crawled from a cramped position from the hammock netting, where I had sought shelter from pouring rain; finding one of my hand cuffs loose and impressed by the absolute silence that reigned supreme, I ventured upon a tour of inspection—to discover what had become of the watch on deck. I walked forward on the port side of the ship, to the top gallant forecastle, where the form of a man supposed to be on the lookout was leaning over the capstan, apparently asleep. Passing around to the starboard side, I walked aft to the gangway amid ships, where I found an officer with arms folded upon it, his head resting on the arms—also apparently asleep. Proceeding toward the stern, the quartermaster at the wheel was the only one of the ship's company who seemed to be on deck and awake.

My captive mates were stowed about the after part of the deck. There arose in me a wild desire to capture the vessel and take her into some Northern port. The enthusiasm for this undertaking began to wane when the true conditions of the situation were duly weighed. My mates, though brave and daring, numbered but 13, and were all in irons, and though the whole ship's crew were below decks and might be secured with comparative ease, keeping them there would be a different proposition. Loath to relinquish this coveted prize, glancing upward for help—a rope hanging at the yard arm was too suggestive of the painful cost for a youthful mind longer to contemplate so daring a deed.

At the end of a week spent on board the *Florida* (June 6, 1862 2:30) a bark was sighted, which proved to be the *Fleur de Para.* Up went the English flag and the *Florida* started in pursuit. Being shortly overhauled, the captain of the *Fleur de Para* was informed that the *Florida* had a crew on board taken from a burning ship, which Captain Moffitt desired to transfer to his vessel. The captain of the bark refused to take more than 7 of the whole number, which consisted of the captain and wife, four officers and a boy.

Our party was at once transferred to the French bark, which was from Havre bound to Sierra, Brazil. We were 24 days in making what should have taken but a week. The vessel was built on the down east pattern—that is "produced by the mile and sawed off to suit purchasers!"

The French captain received our captain and wife into the cabin and the rest of the party bunked with the crew and were initiated into the mysteries of living on wormy bread and a muddy compound called coffee.

Sierra proved to be a very attractive little place. Here we were taken into the care of the representative of the American Consul who was an English merchant of that port. Rooms in a pleasant cottage were furnished us, with fancy colored hammocks to sleep in and we were invited to take our meals with the consul in his own house.

The custom had been, on the landing of captives in sufficient numbers, to charter vessels to return them to Northern ports, but the number of our party being so small, we were in a few days forwarded to Pernabuco on a Brazillian steamer.

Here the American Consul, Mr. Adamson, assumed the care of us and we were sent to a regular sailor's boarding house. The brig, *William Dodge* of 190 tons, plying between New York and Pernabuco was the only vessel in port bound to the United States. Our first officers were fortunate in securing positions immediately on this vessel, to work their passage home.

The second officer and myself, after several days of persistent effort, secured a similar privilege for ourselves and went on board at once to work for the same object. We were employed in rigging, tarring down, painting, repairing sails and stowing cargo for nearly a month and then sailed for New York, only to put back in 48 hours with the vessel leaking like a sieve.

In the absence of drydock facilities in this port, the vessel was hauled alongside of a store ship, into which the cargo and every moveable thing was transferred. The primitive method of throwing a vessel down upon her beam ends for the purpose of recaulking and coppering was followed.

All this, together with reloading and preparing for sea occupied another month and the voyage to New York was accomplished in thirty days. When I landed upon the wharf in New York my wardrobe consisted of the clothes in which I stood, namely canvas trousers heavily loaded with tar, red flannel shirt out at the elbows, and a man of war's man cap.

As we were captives, we were given a deck passage on a Fall River boat to Boston, which city we reached the latter part of 1863. Calling on the owners of the *Southern Cross* we were paid our wages up to the time of our capture.

# CHAPTER 5

*A brief sojourn in the city enabled me to realize that I had no training in any other vocation, save that of the sea, and learning that Capt. Paty of the bark* Whistler *plying between the coast and Honolulu was in need of officers, I applied and obtained the position of first mate without delay.*

B. F. Dillingham

BAKER and Morrill of Boston, owners of the *Southern Cross,* must have carried full insurance, for they set about immediately to replace her with a new ship, the *Oriola.* Possibly, the best shipwrights had gone into defense work by that time, because the *Oriola* had no sooner been launched than she sank beside the dock when a piece of spongy wood in her keel gave way. Frank, who had signed on as second mate, got an extra vacation while she was raised and repaired; he spent the winter and spring of 1864 at the Howes family homestead in Dennis—his longest time ashore in five years.

Benjamin Howes was supposed to command the *Oriola,* but a dispute developed between him and the owners. Because of the danger from Confederate raiders, the owners refused to let him take his wife with him on the ship, and rather than leave Lucy at home the young captain turned down the *Oriola* command and bought a one-third interest in the brig *Lubra* out of Boston. The decision proved a fatal one for him. On his first voyage in *Lubra* she was boarded by Chinese pirates near Hong Kong and after a prolonged ordeal Captain Howes was murdered. Lucy and her child somehow lived through it and made their way back to New England, where Lucy lived for another fifty years or so.

His uncle's decision also affected Frank in an unforeseen way. He stayed with *Oriola,* but when she finally sailed he found that her new captain and first mate were "of the type known as 'bullies'." All his life Frank disliked this sort of character, which was completely foreign to his own nature. Besides his antipathy to his shipmates on the *Oriola,* Frank's experiences at the hands of the *Florida* may have soured him on the sea, and his sojourn at Dennis may have made him realize the pleasures of life on shore. At any rate he decided to try life ashore in San Francisco; in his own words, "I left the ship as soon as she was moored to the wharf, and determined to seek a livelihood on land."

Frank at that point was just twenty. For more than five years he had been a sailor, and a good one, but as he quickly realized, he totally lacked skills that were saleable on land. His tramping of the streets of San Francisco yielded nothing in the way of a job.

He then heard that Captain John Paty of the bark *Whistler* needed officers, and on applying he was quickly hired as first mate. Again, this proved a fateful step for the young man, as the *Whistler* was

"The first evening I left the ship was spent at the Wednesday evening prayer meeting in the Bethel vestry." The Reverend Samuel C. Damon served as chaplain of the Bethel Union Church; when he took a sabbatical year in the United States in 1896, he left his house on nearby Chaplain Lane in the hands of Frank and Emma Dillingham, and they spent the first year of their married life there. (Photo by Ray Jerome Baker, Bishop Museum)

owned in Honolulu and spent her time running between there and San Francisco. Captain Paty made his home in Honolulu; he died a few years later, but his son John H. Paty was closely associated with B. F. Dillingham in later years.

As Dillingham later wrote,

> The *Whistler* was one of the regular passenger and freight packets plying between Honolulu and San Francisco. Captain John Paty had been associated with the trade carried on between the Islands and China, also the American coast for many years, and had commanded a number of vessels. When he had completed his one-hundredth trip between Honolulu and San Francisco, the citizens of Honolulu gave him the title of Commodore.
>
> At this time his trips numbered 140. On this, my first trip to the Islands, we had among the passengers some well-known residents—Mr. Afong, Mr. D. F. Vida, Mrs. J. H. Black, and the wife and daughter of the captain.
>
> We reached Honolulu early in January 1865. After my tempestuous experiences in rounding Cape Horn and the Cape of Good Hope the trip seemed to me like a pleasure excursion. I felt as if I had anchored in a home port; the cordiality experienced from all those whom I met removed at once the feeling of being in a foreign land though the streets were filled with several nationalities. The luxuriant foliage, the balmy breezes, the tropical fruits, all afforded such delights that I felt sure I should return.
>
> Among my earliest acquaintances may be numbered Henry MacFarlane, John Paty, I. B. Peterson, J. P. Cooke, Father Damon, Mother Crabbe, Mother Castle. One of the first calls I made was at the home of Rev. Lowell Smith. The first evening I left the ship was spent at the Wednesday evening prayer meeting in the Bethel vestry.
>
> The usual return freight from the Islands was sugar, and the work of discharging and loading occupied several weeks and early in February we left on our return trip. This voyage was succeeded by another complete voyage, and a third trip to the Islands was made early in July.

# CHAPTER 6

*The First Officer of the Bark* Whistler, *Mr. Dillingham, whose leg was broken last Friday night, by being thrown from a horse, in collision with a carriage on the valley road, is now in the American Marine Hospital where he receives every care and attention, and is in a favorable condition for recovery.*

*Pacific Commercial Advertiser*
29 July 1865

FRANK Dillingham's condition for recovery turned out to be not as favorable as the *Advertiser* supposed, for he had to remain in the hospital for forty-five days during a painful and trying convalescence before being allowed out for a few hours on crutches. A week later he was discharged. Mr. I. B. Peterson, then employed by C. Brewer and Company and later a partner in that firm, took him into his home until he could get on his feet. The story continues in Frank's own words.

At the Marine Hospital I was cared for at the expense of the United States Government. The small amount of money I had been able to save I invested in bananas and shipped to San Francisco on the return voyage of the *Whistler* following my accident.

Walking out one morning on crutches, through the business part of the town I sought Mother O'Neill's haberdashery, thinking to replenish a portion of my scanty wardrobe. My funds were truly at "ebb tide," but I had the temerity to ask the price of paper collars; these were at the time among the novelties in gentlemen's wearing apparel. "Fifteen cents apiece" said the good woman. "Fifteen cents" I exclaimed, "Then I can have no paper collar for I haven't money enough to buy one" and I walked off contenting myself with the expectation of the means for such "luxuries" when my ship should come in with returns from my small cargo of bananas.

> The vessel, alas, made an unusually long passage and my first commercial and mercantile venture proved a total loss. The fruit in a decayed condition was consigned to the sea before the ship arrived in port.
>
> A few weeks later, having substituted a cane for my crutches, I sauntered into "No. 10" on Fort St. where I met Henry Waterhouse and Edwin Dimond. These young men sympathized with me in my crippled condition, and our conversation drifted into the channels of occupation. My condition had given me cause for anxiety as to what my future should be. At this time I gave free ventilation as to my views, as to business honor and integrity in general and the method of its application in practical life. As a result of this conversation Edwin Dimond suggested to his father that they give young Dillingham a place in their store; he thought him just the man they needed.
>
> A few days later "Father" Dimond called upon me and offered me a position as clerk in his store, on a salary of $40 a month for a trial period of six months.
>
> Before six months had expired, an unexpected and very tempting offer was made me by the owners of the bark *Whistler* who desired to send the vessel to New Bedford from Honolulu, with a cargo of whale oil, and to place me in command. After carefully considering the matter, I decided not to allow even the coveted honor of "Captain at 21" to dissuade me from my purpose of abandoning the sea. I found the position I had taken in Mr. Dimond's employ to be entirely congenial, and my interest continued to grow with the business. At the end of six months my wages were advanced at the rate of $5 per month for a term of two years; then raised to $75, and a little later to $100.

The "Father" Dimond referred to was Mr. Henry Dimond, a lay missionary and a bookbinder by trade who had run the Mission Press and Bindery at Kawaiahao. In 1850 the board of commissioners in Boston released him from the mission, and he decided to remain in Honolulu and go into the hardware business. His son Edwin was two years younger than Frank Dillingham. An elder brother, William Henry Dimond, was undoubtedly the son referred to in the firm name, "H. Dimond and Son"; his decision to move to California in 1867, together with Father Dimond's wish to retire from business, opened the way for Frank's advancement in the firm.

The Honolulu of which Frank found himself a resident boasted about fourteen thousand inhabitants, or a little more than a fifth of the total population of the kingdom. Native Hawaiians still accounted for better than 90 percent of the population of the islands, but their numbers dropped every year. Foreign diseases, abetted it seems by a deep malaise of the spirit, kept up the terrible work of decimating the Hawaiian race, and it would be another ten or twelve years before the immigration of foreigners began to over-balance the dying-off of Hawaiians. In 1865 the foreigners in the kingdom—Americans, Britishers, a few French and Germans, and a small but growing number of Chinese—tended to cluster in Honolulu.

Honolulu in 1865 was still a small town, lacking sewers and paved roads and constantly short of water, but it had one incomparable advantage that lifted it above all other towns in the islands: the only safe, natural harbor that could be entered by deep-draft sailing ships. Year after year, as the tall ships glided in from America and Europe, the relative importance of Honolulu grew. In the time of Captain Cook, Hawaii and Maui outranked Oahu, but by February of 1845, some five months after Frank Dillingham's birth, the importance of Honolulu in the kingdom had become so obvious that Kamehameha III moved his court there from Lahaina, Maui. By that time the whaling era was in full swing, and Honolulu had clearly outdistanced Lahaina as the leading whaling port in the Pacific. By the time Frank Dillingham reached the islands twenty years later, whaling had

A view of Honolulu Harbor in the 1860s. (Bishop Museum photo)

Honolulu from Punchbowl, taken about the time Frank Dillingham settled in Honolulu. The watery areas on the middle right are Kawa Pond and Kuwili Pond, portions of which were later filled in for the Oahu Railway terminal. (Photo by Ray Jerome Baker, Bishop Museum)

Honolulu in the 1860s as seen from the harbor entrance, with Pacific Heights and Punchbowl in the background. (Photo by Ray Jerome Baker, Bishop Museum)

passed its peak, but although the population of the islands was steadily shrinking, Honolulu at least was holding its own.

In 1865 Honolulu faced, even more acutely than at most times in its history, the problem of how to make a living. In the country districts life still went on pretty much at a subsistence level, except where a few small sugar plantations struggled along, but in town the demand for cloth, flour, whiskey, hardware, and all the paraphernalia of civilization could only be met by exporting Hawaiian products or through services paid for in foreign dollars. Sugar, coffee, rice, hides, and other farm products were exported, but the quantities and the profits were small. Supplying the whaling fleet with everything from fresh food to women provided the mainstay of commerce but an erratic and undependable one and plainly on the decline. The best brains and energies of the town sought an alternate source of income.

Meanwhile, life was pleasant enough. The unpaved streets were dusty in summer and muddy in winter, but shade trees gave their shelter from the sun and trade winds blew away the town's odors. The night air was soft and gentle, and the stars close and bright overhead. Young Frank Dillingham slipped into the town like a fish into water.

Wherever he was, Frank never sat still. In Honolulu he rowed in the harbor, joined the volunteer Fire Department and the Home Guards, and became one of the first members of the Honolulu Olympic Club, founded to provide a gymnasium and reading room. Probably during his bachelor years he studied bookkeeping and read whatever he could find about business in general. When his chance came, he was ready for it.

# Part II
# THE HONOLULU STOREKEEPER

# CHAPTER 7

*Love of children is the strongest passion of my nature and teaching is my natural condition.*

Abigail W. Smith

THE Protestant missionaries, most of them Congregationalists from New England, who came to Hawaii between 1820 and 1850, wrote one of the most controversial chapters in the history of the islands.

Most of the missionaries were intelligent, educated, altruistic, and dedicated to their work of teaching, healing, and ministering to the native Hawaiians. They worked with incredible energy and zeal in the face of physical hardships and constant discouragements in a country completely foreign to the world they knew. They gained converts to their faith, reduced the Hawaiian language to writing, translated the Bible into Hawaiian, began the first schools of Western knowledge in the islands, and helped to lay the foundations of Western medicine in Hawaii.

On the other hand they were religious zealots of such overbearing conviction that they offended many of the people they sought to save. Theologically they followed John Calvin's thorny doctrine of predestination. They believed in a total control of life by religious doctrine, they had, at least in theory, no tolerance for other points of view, and they emphasized a long list of "thou shalt nots" until their religion sometimes seemed more negative than positive.

Perhaps worst of all, they believed in themselves as a chosen elite to a point where they often prohibited their own children from mingling with Hawaiian youngsters, whom they regarded as depraved and promiscuous. As a whole they had no interest in Hawaiian civilization, learning the language merely as a means to convert the natives.

The missionaries, however, seem innocent of the charge of enriching themselves at the expense of the Hawaiians. Most of the missionaries remained poor as church mice. A very few of them, notably S. N. Castle and A. S. Cooke, eventually became wealthy through business endeavors, long after the governing body of the missionaries had cut them off the payroll as an economy measure. Neither of these men were ministers; Mr. Castle came as a business agent of the mission and Mr. Cooke as a teacher.

Organizationally, the missionaries with a few exceptions were sent and controlled by the American Board of Commissioners for Foreign Missions (A.B.C.F.M.) in Boston. The board monitored their activities in minute detail, but gave them something less than they needed in material support.

One aspect of the missionary life seems largely to have escaped comment: the missionaries knew the islands as a whole probably better than any other foreigners and most natives of the time. Of necessity they spoke Hawaiian fluently. They sought contact with Hawaiians of all classes, and in spite of the difficulties of transportation traveled incessantly within the web of mission stations that covered Kauai, Oahu, Molokai, Maui, and Hawaii. Their knowledge passed in large measure to their children, so that when Frank Dillingham allied himself with one of the missionary families, he found himself an apprentice member of a club which knew and loved Hawaii.

Like other people, the missionaries came in various shapes, sizes, and personalities. In temperament they ranged from the domineering Hiram Bingham to the poetical and emotional Lorenzo Lyons and the shrewd, reserved Samuel Castle. The Reverend Lowell Smith probably came as close as any to the ideal of selflessness in bringing the word of God and the blessings of civilization to the Hawaiian people.

Lowell taught no watered-down religion. He preached hellfire and eternal damnation, and he fought manfully against the devil and all his works. Among the latter he particularly included rum, popery, topless clothing, and *puhi paka* ("tobacco smoking"), not necessarily in that order. The wearing of leis in church, though severely to be censured, ranked as less serious.

In his photographs, Lowell's great, burning eyes stare out of deep sockets in a strong, sensuous face, giving an impression of fires within held in check by iron will. And iron will he had in plenty. At the age of twenty, apprenticed to a farmer in Massachusetts, he heard the call to preach the gospel, and asked to be released from his contract. Refused, he served his time until he reached twenty-one, then went

The Reverend Lowell Smith, father of Emma Dillingham, was pastor of Kaumakapili Church for more than thirty years.

back to school for two years to prepare for college. For four years he studied at Williams College, then a hotbed of evangelical fervor, and finally attended Auburn Seminary for three years, graduating at the age of thirty and receiving ordination and a license from the American Board of Commissioners for Foreign Missions.

Shortly after his ordination he married Miss Abigail ("Abba") Willis Tenney, who had lived for a time in his parents' home at Heath, Massachusetts, while teaching school. Less than two months later Lowell and Abba sailed from New London on the ship *Mentor* as part of the Sixth Company of Missionaries to the Sandwich Islands.

Lowell served first on Molokai, where with his own hands he helped to build a stone house, the first Western-style building on the island, using rocks from an abandoned *heiau*. "We thought it would be no sacrilege," noted Abba, "to appropriate to our own use what was once impiously devoted to one of those abominable things which God hates."

Abigail's health suffered on Molokai, and in 1834 the general meeting of the missionary brethren transferred the Smiths to Ewa

Station on Oahu, just past the present town of Pearl City. (The present town of Ewa, some distance away, takes both its name and its existence from the founding of Ewa Plantation in the early 1890s. There was no Hawaiian town of Ewa, only a large district of that name.) To the Smiths' disappointment, the stay at Ewa lasted only two years, as the 1836 general meeting voted to send Lowell to teach school at Kawaiahao in Honolulu. In the following year, Amos Starr Cooke, a teacher, arrived with the Seventh Company of Missionaries, freeing Lowell Smith to return to his work as a minister.

At that time Kawaiahao Church served the whole town of Honolulu. Reinforced by the Seventh Company, the missionary brethren decided to start another church on the far side of town, with Lowell Smith as its pastor. The section of town, Kaumakapili, gave the new church its name. High Chief Paki summarily displaced a few native families from what is now the corner of Beretania and Smith Streets, to make room for a large adobe church and a house for the Smiths.

Kawaiahao Church already enjoyed the patronage of the king and his court and of the other great chiefs. Kaumakapili, or "Smith's Church," became known as the church of the common people. Here Lowell Smith carried on the great ministry of his life for more than thirty years. Here the Smith children were born, and here four of them were buried as infants.

The original Kaumakapili Church, where Lowell Smith served as the first pastor. "Smith's Church," as it was called, stood at the head of Smith Street, on Beretania. It was later replaced by the twin-towered structure which burned in the great Chinatown fire of 1900. (Hawaii State Archives photo)

Lowell Smith at the age of thirty-eight declared, "I am fast approaching the hour of my dissolution," and at fifty-four complained of "unmistakable symptoms of decay." Somewhere in his seventies he caught his second wind, and he died peacefully at eighty-eight, serene in his faith and beloved by all who knew him.

Abba, in spite of the best medical attention in the islands, remained an invalid of sorts for a good part of her life. She was, however, a very special kind of invalid. While still at Kawaiahao, she tutored young Alexander Liholiho, later King Kamehameha IV; at Kaumakapili she taught Hawaiian women of the church to raise money by making the first sugar bags for Koloa Plantation; she founded in her home the first school to teach ordinary native children the English language. Later she started another school for foreign children, in which the last and youngest pupil was her grandson Walter. In her spare time, of course, she ran the household, cooked, baked, sewed, and wrote voluminous letters to her relatives and friends in the East.

When Emma Louisa arrived in 1844, Abba had already had four children: two stillborn and two who died in infancy. After Emma there came another daughter who died young, and finally Lowell Augustus ("Gussie"), seven years Emma's junior, who lived to be forty. Over the years Abba had many miscarriages. Emma was a strong, healthy girl, but it is hardly surprising that her mother refused to believe it.

In 1843, the year before Emma was born, Lowell and Abba sought relief from the city heat by building a summer cottage in Nuuanu

Nuuanu Cottage was the Lowell Smith residence at the top of Judd Hill. Frank and Emma Dillingham stayed there with her parents for six years, beginning in 1870.

Valley. "Nuuanu Cottage," as they called it, stood at the top of Judd Hill, just above the Nuuanu Cemetery, on what is now Robinson Lane, not far from the spot where Frank Dillingham later had his fateful collision with a carriage. So pleasant did they find the location that eventually they lived there altogether, and the original two rooms turned into a good-sized home.

Emma grew into an intelligent and loving girl, close to both her parents. Like Abba, she had the urge to teach. At the age of six she wrote in her diary: "Tomorrow Sammy Damon is coming. . . . I mean to teach Sammy some little sums in Addition." This was Samuel Mills Damon, one year her junior, later the owner of the bank of

Emma Smith Dillingham at the age of six, with her mother. At this age Emma confided to her diary, "I mean to teach Sammy (Damon) some little sums in Addition."

Bishop and Company, of whom we shall hear more later. Evidently he learned his sums well.

When Emma was twelve, her mother wrote that "she can put a horse in to a carriage—better than the Irishman did—wash dishes, darn stockings, play the piano and some other things about equally well."

At Punahou, where she went as a matter of course, her father having been one of the founders, she excelled particularly in music, which remained one of her great joys and resources throughout her life. Emma was blessed with both a happy nature and great inner strength; her mother called her on one occasion "the light and joy of her father's house," and it is easy to believe that Abba's maternal pride did not deceive her.

Emma graduated from Punahou in 1863 "with much credit to herself, and much comfort to her parents." For a year she stayed at home and helped her mother teach school. Early in 1865, Lowell's doctor having urged on him the importance of a long vacation, the whole Smith family left for a prolonged visit to the eastern United States. For Lowell and Abba, this trip meant the long-awaited renewal of old friendships and a return to the beloved scenes of their youth. To Emma it was the great adventure of her young life.

# CHAPTER 8

*Emma . . . being at home makes a golden period in our life's calendar. She lightens so many burdens and smooths away so many rough places and keeps perpetual sunshine about us.*

Letter of Abigail W. Smith
20 September 1867

THERE is a romantic story, which really ought to be true, to the effect that when Frank Dillingham broke his leg he was carried into the Smith house and nursed back to health by Emma. Unfortunately, at the time of the accident Emma and her parents were "back home" in New England some five thousand miles away.

Long before then, however, Frank had met Emma and found her attractive. He tells us that on the first evening he spent in Honolulu he attended the prayer meeting at the Bethel chapel, where Emma led the choir, and adds that the first social call he made in Honolulu was at the home of the Reverend Lowell Smith.

At the Smith house, however, he must have learned what would have discouraged a less determined man: Emma was already engaged.

Emma's fiancé, young James Alexander, had her mother's blessing; in fact, as Abba admitted later, she had pushed the match. Alexander in her eyes was suitable in every way. He was the son of the Reverend William P. Alexander of Maui, one of the most admired and loved of all the missionaries, and the brother of William D. Alexander, the brilliant young head of Punahou (Oahu College at that time). Weighed against such credentials, the fact that Emma really didn't love him seemed a detail which time would doubtless correct.

The engagement began about the time Emma graduated from Punahou in 1863, long before Frank Dillingham hove on the horizon, and lasted for three years. Young Alexander during this time

An early picture of Emma Louise Smith Dillingham. Emma taught in her mother's school and at Punahou, and after marriage gave piano lessons to help out with the household finances. (Bishop Museum photo)

moved to California, and it was not until the homeward leg of the Smith family's trip to Massachusetts that the question of marriage really came to a head. James pressed for an immediate wedding, but Emma demurred on the grounds that she had not yet learned to love him. James was unwilling to wait longer, and by mutual consent the engagement was called off, with a minimum of hard feelings. Abba, of course, had to have the last word; she wrote the young man an extremely tart letter and undoubtedly felt better afterwards. "I am determined," she wrote, "that she [Emma] shall not receive proposals again until *she desires it very much.*"

James Alexander subsequently returned to Maui, where he operated a small sugar plantation near Paia known as "Seaside Farm" and had a one-tenth interest in the Hamakua Ditch Company. His son, Frank A. Alexander, much later became the manager of McBryde Sugar Company, one of the sugar plantations put together by Frank Dillingham.

The Smiths arrived back in Honolulu from their trip to the States just in time for the 1866 Punahou graduation. Frank Dillingham,

Another early picture of Frank Dillingham, wearing an anchor tie-pin reflecting his nautical background. (Bishop Museum photo)

meanwhile, had been clerking at Dimond's store for eight months or so.

In spite of her broken engagement to his brother, President Alexander of Punahou particularly sought Emma's services as a teacher, and she accepted an appointment in music and drawing at a salary of $400 for nine months, starting in September of 1866. She boarded at school during the week and was able to go home for weekends.

Just when Frank began to court her is not clear. In contrast to his usual impetuosity, he made a low-key approach: one suspects that Abba may have had a little talk with him to the effect that Emma was not to be bothered with romantic nonsense. In January of 1867 he wrote Emma that

> I have just returned from the *Good Union Prayer Meeting*. . . . after glancing carefully over the whole assembly I was quite disappointed not being able to see her whose *kindness, sympathy* and *true friendship* has won upon my heart and permits the enjoyment of such feelings of *Love* as I think I should cherish for a *Sister!* . . . I proposed to Mr. Nott to call on you next Thursday. . . . remember me as truly and sincerely your friend & Bro' in Christ. B.F.D.

"Mr. Nott" was undoubtedly Frank's friend Sam Nott, who, as it turned out, went calling with Frank once too often. In October of the same year he rode up to the Smith's with Frank while Frank delivered a parcel; a letter of Lowell Smith's tells the story:

> Mr. Nott waited outside. His horse becoming restless, he reined him in, whereupon the horse reared up and stepped backward into a ditch and fell over backward upon his rider and broke the two bones of his left leg between the knee and ankle. . . . we brought him in and laid him on Gussie's bed. . . . He is now convalescent. . . . Emma is cheerful and lively as ever and does much in providing meals and otherwise entertain Mr. Nott. . . . The young men down town think Mr. Nott was very fortunate in breaking his leg so near our door. Mr. Dillingham broke his leg while we were home on our visit and was carried to the hospital, but he thinks that sailors and others in the hospital have pretty rough treatment compared with Mr. Nott's little private hospital.

On 17 June, Frank sent Emma a note: "There will be a riding party this eve 'got up' by the 'Home Gards'. I should be very happy to have your company—and if agreeable I will call for you at about 6:30 P.M."

This may have been the last time Frank saw her for several months, as she spent most of the summer of 1867 visiting mission families on Hawaii and writing kittenish letters to young "Willie" Bond, another missionary offspring, who was seven years her junior and one of her students at Punahou. Willie had come down with a bad case of puppy love, and Emma as the object of it was far from displeased.

By September Emma was back at Nuuanu Cottage, making shirts, coats, and pants for Gussie to wear to school. In October came Sam Nott's accident, and in November Gussie celebrated his sixteenth birthday and reported that he "got a very fine bridle from Mr. Dillingham and a whip to match." In December Frank wrote "Friend Emma" that he had taken Gussie to the tailor under a pretext and had got him measured for a vest. He remained "Respectfully your friend." By October of 1868 he was sending her a handwritten poem.

On 6 February 1869, Abba wrote to Henry M. Whitney, son of the missionary Samuel Whitney, who was traveling abroad, to thank him for some presents. Her letter tells the story of the engagement.

Emma was engaged matrimonially last week to Mr. Dillingham. I can write this with composure and satisfaction even, now that I witness their great happiness. It was not in a mother's nature to hold out longer against that patient, uncomplaining, enduring, waiting.

So I dug a deep grave, away down in my heart, and buried deep all the pride and ambitious dreams I had indulged for this most precious, perfect daughter, and I feel a great deal better. Mr. D. is a man of great refinement and delicacy and tenderness of heart and character generally. He is smart, energetic and industrious, pure in all his habits, ambitious to excel in his business, and with a thirst for knowledge and a love for good and improving books, that promises well for his growth in all that makes true manhood, and best of all, he is a good working Christian. All that he has, and is, and hopes to be, next to his God, is devoted to Emma, and I can now say that I am glad she has so much to give in return of all those graces and accomplishments which render a woman attractive to a man. They have held fast in patient waiting during nearly a year of opposition from me instead of asserting their independence and taking matters into their own hands as some might have done, and I feel sure that this is God's way if it was not mine and I know that I wish above all things to have God's will be done in the matter, so as I said, I submit, thankful that my precious daughter has so fair a prospect for happiness after all the trials her young life has known.

You would be amused to see how fast Mr. D. is doing up matters now that he may. Already there is a house engaged and all the pleasant little arrangements and consultations in active progress. I always did love to watch young birds build their nests, and this reminds me of it.

I must tell you to the honour of my precious daughter that during the three years that I insisted upon her keeping her engagement with a man she did not love and also during the time that I have opposed her engagement to the man she could love, she has never spoken to me one rebellious or disrespectful word, but has been through all a most tender devoted and ever self-sacrificing daughter. I know you will join me in my prayer for God's blessing upon them in this life and in that which is to come.

Emma's father married them on 26 April in Kaumakapili Church, at eight o'clock in the evening. Emma made her own wedding gown of white tarlatan—a sort of thin muslin—at a cost of four dollars. Her six bridesmaids—Ida Sloane, Hattie Baldwin, Sarah Brown, Mary Cooke, Helen Whitney, and Anna Hobron—wore tarlatan gowns also: two pink, two blue, and two green. Frank had Sanford Dole,

Alfred Castle, Sam Damon, Henry Macfarlane, and two Weedon brothers as his groomsmen. Sanford Dole reported to his brother George that "the groomsmen are to wear black suits throughout and white neckties and gloves; the bridegroom will [be] distinguished by wearing a white vest."

Along with a simple notice of the wedding, the *Advertiser* carried the following announcement: "The printers acknowledge a generous slice of wedding cake, which was duly distributed to the compositors with an injunction to put it under their pillows to dream on. They wish all the blessings to the newly married couple."

Frank Dillingham always knew how to get along with the press.

In Emma, Frank Dillingham gained a wife of absolute integrity, overflowing love, great good humor, and astonishing flexibility. She was magnificent in a crisis, of which many lay unknown in the years ahead. She gave him splendid children and raised them with great common sense. Without her the career of Frank Dillingham might have remained an impossibility.

# CHAPTER 9

*Your treatment of me has* always *been most considerate in the* extreme, *you have been more like a* father *to me, than a business acquaintance or friend.*

B. F. Dillingham to S. N. Castle
9 April 1889

FRANK started with H. Dimond and Son in 1865. In 1867 both Mr. Dimond and his older son withdrew from active management of the firm. In 1868 the son, William Henry Dimond, returned from San Francisco to take over the business, but after two months he went back. Apparently, Frank Dillingham ran the daily affairs of the store.

Early in 1869 Mr. Dimond determined to sell out entirely, and offered Frank a chance to buy the store for $28,000, the value of the inventory. Frank jumped at the opportunity. The fact that he had no money to invest deterred him not at all, then or later.

Of course, $28,000 was a very substantial sum of money. When thinking of it in terms of today's currency, we have to remember not only the terrible debasement of the dollar since then, but also that business in Honolulu at the time had a weak and shaky foundation and that the islands suffered from a severe and perennial shortage of capital. As a totally unscientific guess, we might venture that $28,000 in the mind of a Honolulu businessman in 1869 would equate with something like $300,000 or $400,000 in 1981.

Frank not only had no money, he had no credit. Charles R. Bishop ran the only bank in town, and he was constantly running out of money to take care of even his best customers. As usual, Frank improvised and made his own luck.

Just at this time Charles Alfred Castle returned from studies in America to become the registrar of public accounts for the kingdom. Alfred, who was exactly the same age as Frank, had no more money

The Dillingham store on King Street, a photo taken presumably between 1869, when Frank took the business over from Henry Dimond, and 1872, when he moved to larger quarters on Fort Street. The third figure from the right has been identified as Frank Dillingham. (Photo by Ray Jerome Baker, Bishop Museum)

than Frank did, but he had one priceless asset—his father, Samuel Northrup Castle.

Mr. Castle had come to Hawaii in 1837 as a member of the Eighth Company of missionaries. Because of his business background he was assigned to assist Levi Chamberlain, the superintendent of secular affairs, that is, business manager of the mission. Mr. Chamberlain eventually had to retire because of illness, and Mr. Castle succeeded him. In 1849 Amos Starr Cooke became assistant superintendent. At about the same time the Board of Commissioners in Boston decreed that the missionaries in Hawaii must become self-supporting, and in accordance with this policy released Mr. Castle and Mr. Cooke from the mission in 1851 to enter private business. They founded the celebrated firm which still bears their names, starting out in a small way by running the Mission Depository (warehouse) under contract and gradually expanding into a general mercantile business with increasing emphasis on hardware and plantation supplies. By 1869 the firm had become solidly established as one of a handful of responsible houses in the city; it supplemented its merchandising activities by factoring sugar plantations, that is, by acting as purchasing and sales agents and advancing funds against unsold sugar. Mr. Castle's standing as a sound man of business was second to none in the islands.

Frank sought out Alfred Castle, whom he had apparently not known before, and laid Mr. Dimond's offer before him. Alfred liked the idea and went to his father for help. Mr. Castle's endorsement enabled the young men to borrow $14,000 from the bank of Bishop and Company at 10 percent interest. This $14,000 went to Mr. Dimond as part payment, and for the remaining $14,000 he accepted five notes of $2,800 each at 8 percent interest, one note being payable each year for the next five years. The new firm thus came into being without a cent of capital, with interest expense of more than $200 a month, with principal payments due to Mr. Dimond at the rate of $2,800 a year, and with a large bank borrowing supported solely by the endorsement of an aging gentleman not a member of the firm.

Frank and Alfred were equal partners in the new firm, but Frank assumed the management and the business took the name of Dillingham and Company. Probably it was thought unsuitable to include Alfred's name in the firm while he held public office. As a matter of economy, he kept the books of the company until it got well started.

The new business began on 1 April 1869, less than a month before Frank and Emma's wedding. The opening advertisement offered hardware, cutlery, paints, oils, varnishes, dry goods, and general merchandise, all dispensed from the store at 95 King Street. For the Christmas trade in the same year, the firm advertised prints, ladies' white cotton hose, quilts, huckaback towels, flannels, damask napkins, handkerchiefs, threads, corsets, files, saws, knives, cutlery, and razors.

This sudden jump from employee to partner was one of the great turning points of Frank's life. From then on he always functioned as the planner, the organizer, the leader, the inspiration for those who followed. With his drive and energy he could no more have remained a clerk than he could have stayed as a "boy" on the *Southern Cross.*

Although Frank could not have known it at the time, the debut of Dillingham and Company also marked the beginning of twenty-five years of close and sometimes painful association with Samuel N. Castle. Of all the men with whom Frank did business during his long life, probably none affected him as deeply as Mr. Castle. Frank was not an easy man to affect, but the hard rock of Mr. Castle's stubbornness became the anvil on which Frank's determination was beaten into useful shape.

In many respects the two men could not have presented more of a contrast. Frank was rash and impetuous; Mr. Castle, cool and cautious. Frank was an incurable optimist; Mr. Castle always saw the hole in the doughnut. Frank loved to live well and to spend money freely; Mr. Castle was distinguished for frugality of truly awesome proportions. Yet, they had in common a love of hard work and tremendous force of will.

The question might well be raised why Mr. Castle chose to back the young men's shoestring venture, in which he had much to lose and little to gain. Alfred was his oldest living son and his favorite, and he doubtless wanted to see him prosper. Then too, Mr. Dimond's business was competitive to his own, and he probably liked to see it kept in friendly hands. Also, Frank Dillingham was an extremely persuasive talker. But Frank's persuasion might have fallen on deaf ears, except for the surprising fact that Mr. Castle, in spite of all his caution and conservatism, was a gambler himself: a very careful gambler, who checked every detail before he put his money down, but still a living illustration of the old adage that those who got rich in Hawaii didn't make it on 6 percent bonds. In a day when sugar plantations were dropping right and left, Mr. Castle made money by backing a few small, struggling plantations in whose managers he had confidence.

And so, at the age of twenty-four, through a succession of unpredictable and apparently fortuitous circumstances, Frank Dillingham found himself the head of a respectable though bare-boned enterprise, with all the world ahead of him and his beloved Emma to cheer him on.

# CHAPTER 10

*Father's hair was dark, shiny and curly, his green-blue eyes smiled at the corners. He had a dimple in his shaven chin between his curly side-burns, and a sweet-breathed mouth. (He used no tobacco until he was a grandfather.)*

May Dillingham Frear

FRANK and his bride began married life near the heart of Honolulu. The Reverend Samuel C. Damon, chaplain of the Bethel Union Church and father of Samuel M. Damon the banker, took a sabbatical year in the United States and Europe, leaving his house on Chaplain Lane in the hands of the newly married couple. When the Damon family returned in 1870, Frank and Emma moved a couple of blocks up Beretania Street to the house of J. G. Dickson, who was also traveling abroad.

In June of 1870, while they were still living in the Dickson house, Emma gave birth to Mary Emma Dillingham, known throughout her life as May. May proved to be a strong, healthy, precocious child who gave great joy to her parents and even more to her grandmother Abba.

That fall, when the Dicksons returned, Frank and Emma and May moved into Nuuanu Cottage with the Smiths. Gussie was living in Hilo, where he managed a branch of Dillingham and Company, so that there was plenty of room in the house. The Board of Commissioners in Boston had pressured Lowell into retiring from his beloved Kaumakapili the year before, to his great indignation, and while he kept himself busy, he was doubtless glad to have the young people around. As for Abba, to have a baby in the house was her idea of heaven. So well did the move work out, in fact, that Frank and Emma stayed for six years, until the increasing size of their household made it impossible.

The Reverend Samuel C. Damon, pastor of the Bethel Union Church, in whose home Frank and Emma Dillingham began their married life. Damon was the father of Samuel Mills Damon, banker and owner of Moanalua. (Photo by Bradley & Rulofso, Bishop Museum)

Life settled into a pleasant routine. The economy of living with the Smiths permitted certain luxuries: a nursemaid for May, a big carriage and a good horse, a rented summer cottage at Waikiki, where Emma's friends would come down to spend the day and swim. Frank and Emma bought two acres on the south side of Beretania Street between the present Ward Avenue and Alapai, next to the Alfred Castles, and improved it with shade and fruit trees and a vegetable garden, keeping a man on the place to take care of it. For Christmas of 1871, Frank sent to China for a set of crystal bracelets, earrings, and necklace for Emma, and the following year he had them all set in gold.

In July of 1872 Abba wrote that Frank had given up the idea of rowing in the boat race on the Fourth of July because he had so much to do with the lunch, having undertaken to supply 16 gallons of ice cream. In December of the same year she reported to Gussie, still in Hilo, that "on the King's birthday Frank did not open the store at all (we hope you did not). He and Emma and little May and Mary and all the Atherton family went up to the 'Pelly Place' and spent the day. On the way they overtook Mr. Frear and all his family, going aimlessly somewhere. So they took them along and they all had a grand time rambling in the woods and gathering ferns." We assume that May's future husband, nine-year-old Walter Frear, was among the company.

Another of Abba's letters from 1872 sheds a happy light on the young couple: "Emma had a nice letter from Sarah [Albion] the other day. She seems to get along quite comfortably in her married life, but I judge there is not much romance about it. Writing of her brother Willie and his wife of three months, she said 'They have settled down into old married people, although Willie *did* seem a little affectionate today when I was there, and he wanted his pants mended, but you know this will not last long.' Emma with her *lover husband* was confounded."

In December of 1872 came the event to make their happiness complete: Emma bore a beautiful, huge baby boy, who was named Charles Augustus in honor of his two uncles. Abba wrote to Gussie to apologize for the order of the names; in her opinion it should have been Augustus Charles.

By any name, he was a much loved baby. When he was almost one and teething, Abba wrote: "Our little man has a way of getting up very early, sometimes by half past four in the morning and this too after he has disturbed his poor mamma near a dozen times during the night. Then his good papa takes him into another room and cares for him, while the tired mamma gets a nice morning nap. . . . [in the evenings] Frank and Emma read in their rooms subject to interruptions from the baby!"

Business, meanwhile, was less idyllic than was the home life. For the first year all went well within Dillingham and Company. The firm reported a profit of $6,000 and met its obligations promptly. But in 1871, thirty-three ships from the American whaling fleet were caught in the Arctic ice and destroyed, dealing a terrible blow to the Hawaiian businesses that supplied the fleet. Sugar prices fell so low because of the American tariff that in 1872–1873 Hawaiian sugar

B. F. DILLINGHAM. C. A. CASTLE.

# DILLINGHAM & CO.,

IMPORTERS AND WHOLESALE AND RETAIL DEALERS

—IN ALL KINDS OF—

## HARDWARE AND AGRICULTURAL IMPLEMENTS!

Sauce Pans, Fry Pans, Tea Kettles, Iron Pots, Furnace Boilers,

GALVANIZED IRON AND WOODEN PAILS AND TUBS,
HEAVY BLOCK TIN PAILS AND PANS,
THE BEST HICKORY CARRIAGE MATERIAL,

Table and Pocket Cutlery, Scissors and Razors

BUTCHER KNIVES AND STEELS,

*GUNS, PISTOLS, CAPS AND CARTRIDGES,*

BEST SPORTING AND GIANT POWDER,

**SEINE AND WRAPPING TWINE**

*Fish Hooks and Lines, Byam's Celebrated Card Matches,*
*Kerosene Lamps, Chandeliers, Lanterns and Oil,*
*Hubbuck's Best White Lead, Zinc and Linseed Oil,*

FINE COLORED PAINTS, IN OIL AND DRY,

THE REAL MANILA CORDAGE, SIZE FROM 1-2 TO 1 1-2 INCH,

**Horse Cart and Plow Harnesses,**
**Mule and Horse Collars and Hames,**
**Carriage Whips, Horse Bits, Bridles and Spurs,**

**BAR STEEL AND IRON, LOG AND TRACE CHAINS, TOPSAIL CHAINS.**

☞ All the above will be sold at the LOWEST MARKET PRICES, and on the most Liberal Terms. A good discount will always be made for Cash. Orders will receive prompt and careful attention.

**Nos. 95 and 97 Concrete Block,**

King Street, - - - - - - - - - - - HONOLULU.

B. F. Dillingham advertised with enthusiasm. This ad appeared in an edition of Jarves' *History of the Hawaiian Islands* published in Honolulu in 1872, three years after Dillingham and Company was founded. Charles Alfred Castle was still a partner. (Hawaii State Archives photo)

began to be shipped all the way to Australia and New Zealand. The population of Hawaii kept dropping lower and lower. Trade was stagnant, and Frank's business suffered along with the others.

Dillingham and Company was not a ship chandlery, but it did handle ropes and other ship stores and salt salmon and other provisions. It sold plows, hoes, and so forth to plantations. No doubt even its hardware sales to householders suffered in this period.

To make matters much worse, the firm's mainland suppliers cut it off. In the words of Mr. Dillingham:

> Through the representation of William Henry Dimond, eldest son of the former owner of the business, a large credit of $40,000 had been secured from the San Francisco branch of the Russell & Erwin Mfg. Co. of New York, and subsequently a similar credit was granted to our firm by their San Francisco successor, Messrs. Huntington Hopkins & Co. Both of these firms in turn gave up their business in the islands, cutting off all further credit from the date of their notices which were given without any previous intimation, causing considerable embarrassment among some of the older houses. As for the firm of Dilling-

The second Dillingham and Company store, on Fort Street—"more like San Francisco than anything else in town," according to Frank's mother-in-law. (Photo by Ray Jerome Baker, Bishop Museum)

> ham & Company we were placed under heavy financial strain for a period of two and one-half years, from 1872 to 1874. Besides keeping up the stock so as to hold our trade, I was obliged to hold off a debt of $24,000 to Huntington Hopkins & Co. at the rate of $1000 per month, and at the same time keep up remittances of $500 to $1000 per month to the Russell & Erwin Mfg. Co.
>
> By dint of hard work and close application, the monthly payments were kept up until the last dollar was paid—very much to the astonishment of Huntington Hopkins & Co. who told me when the last payment was made that they never expected to collect 40% of the account.

In 1872, shortly before the blow from Huntington Hopkins, Frank decided he needed a better store in Honolulu. The original location on King Street was somewhat ramshackle; Frank and his partner together planned a new store on Fort Street which was, according to Abba, more like San Francisco than anything else in town. Mr. Dimond apparently built it to their specifications, but Mr. Castle had to guarantee the rental payments. About the end of the same year Frank decided to close the Hilo branch.

The year 1873 was a particularly bad one for Hawaiian sugar. Kamehameha V, the last of the Kamehameha dynasty, had died at the end of the previous year, and the popular but ineffective Lunalilo succeeded him. By that time the merchants of Honolulu had concluded that their only hope for salvation lay in a Reciprocity Treaty, by which they meant a treaty between Hawaii and the United States under which the United States would admit sugar and other Hawaiian products duty free in return for Hawaii's waiving its tariff on American manufactured goods. Frank took a leading part in getting signatures on a petition for Reciprocity, but the short reign of Lunalilo accomplished nothing in that direction.

Early in 1874 Kalakaua succeeded Lunalilo as king, amid high hopes for his reign. He was handsome, popular, and well trained for his duties; his early actions gave no hint of his later involvement with Caesar Moreno, Claus Spreckels, and Walter Murray Gibson, and the sordid scandal of the opium license.

Kalakaua realized the necessity of revitalizing his country's economy and made Reciprocity a prime objective of his reign. His own visit to the United States at the end of 1874 played a key role in the ultimate success of his policy, but the actual attainment of that objective lay several years in the future. Meanwhile, running a business in Honolulu continued to be a struggle.

King Kalakaua in Court dress. Kalakaua's visit to the United States in 1874 helped to pave the way for Reciprocity and hence for the commercial development of Hawaii. (Photo by Ray Jerome Baker, Bishop Museum)

# CHAPTER 11

*The sorrow has had a beautifying effect upon the character of Emma.*

From a letter of Abigail W. Smith
December 1874

MEANWHILE, five years had slipped by since Frank and Alfred Castle had joined in the partnership of Dillingham and Company. Technically, the agreement expired on 1 April 1874, its fifth anniversary. The two partners had agreed verbally on some form of buy-out by Frank, but had put nothing in writing. Alfred's health was bad; he had overworked, and he suffered from a flare-up of a chronic bone infection dating back to a childhood injury.

In April Alfred's wife Ellie and their two children were visiting in California, and Mr. Castle was also in San Francisco on business. On returning to Honolulu Mr. Castle found that his favorite son, Alfred, had died during his absence. It was said that he never entirely recovered from the blow.

Frank wrote to Ellie to express his condolences, and in a rare lapse from common sense used the same letter to propose that he buy out Alfred's share of the partnership on the basis of the verbal agreement between the two of them. Probably he was seeking to reassure Ellie as to her financial future, but he apparently alarmed or confused her instead. At any rate he found himself dealing not with the young widow but with Mr. Castle himself, who was shortly appointed trustee not only for his two granddaughters but also for Ellie. Since the partnership was practically their only source of income, Mr. Castle determined that they should get everything that was coming to them.

Undoubtedly Frank was genuinely distressed at the death of Alfred, who had proved a good friend as well as a compatible business partner. But this blow to Frank was as nothing compared with the tragedy that was about to strike Frank's family. In June Abba wrote:

> We are in deep waters as you see. I cannot summon strength to say more than our precious, peerless, Charles died of cholera infantum

after eight days of suffering. The disease had been conquered and for more than 24 hours everything seemed favorable for his recovery—tho so weak—our poor hearts were hoping strongly that with the tenderest care our treasure would be continued to us. While lying in his tender mother's arms, the place he loved best, his head resting on his little pillow, he suddenly raised his sweet eyes upward, when a look of glad surprise irradiated and glorified his little face and in a few brief moments he had spanned the river not dark to him and was safe in the arms of the Savior of little children.

Frank was devoted to the boy; some forty years later he wrote that he had "brightened our lives for seventeen months, and then with little fearless feet, passed through the 'little gate' into the celestial fields, where there was naught to weary or affright him." Frank lived in an age when sentiment was as much the style as the wisecrack and the put-down are today, but there is no mistaking the sincerity of his grief.

If Frank was devastated by the death of his son, Emma was doubtless more so, while Abba lived again the loss of her own dead infants. Mother and daughter were sustained by their faith and by the bright, happy presence of young May.

Frank, of course, had his business to occupy his mind. In the fall of 1874 he went to San Francisco on business, his first trip away from the islands of which we have any record. He was thirty at the time, and obviously still in a hurry. Abba wrote of meeting the steamer on his return: "Long before she came to her moorings, Frank had stepped into a little boat that had come alongside, and was in the carriage and well on his way home before the anchor was dropped."

His daughter May has left some recollections of the family life at about this time.

Father wore white linen clothes that Mother achieved by good patterns and superintendence of sewing machine work done on the hard running machines of that day by some strong Hawaiian woman. Father approved of Mother's economies for she helped him financially in wiser ways than machine mending. Not being robust, she had paid for a cook in her first housekeeping days by giving piano lessons. Later, in her own bedroom in the home of her parents where she and her husband spent six years, even while nursing whichever child was the baby, she taught "the higher arithmetic" to her mother's scholars in the Nuuanu home school.

One thing Father did not appreciate was "the missionary horse." He

Frank Dillingham, probably in 1876 when he was thirty-two; photo taken in San Francisco. Frank was a bit of a dandy; he liked to dress well, and as a young man frequently changed the style of his sideburns, moustache, and (sometimes) beard. (Bishop Museum photo)

took pleasure and pride in his own swift-stepping horse and a "close communion" buggy.

He attributed his own safe and clean life to a natural abhorrence of filth and disease. And all of his life all his children remember how unpleasant sights, odors, or subjects of conversation gave him sufferings of physical nausea.

On Sundays we went to the old Bethel Church near the wharves, its coral walls topped by wooden clapboarding and shingled roof with a tower and mast flying the blue and white Bethel flag as welcome to seamen half a world away from home. It was in this church that father first met mother. Now they both sang in the quaint choir gallery at the rear of the building. It is a grateful memory that when the long sermon began Father would roll the end of a pew cushion for a pillow and lift the long hair from my little neck, lay me down and sit beside me with a large palm leaf fan wafting me into cool slumber.

These were years when the whaling days were about over and the Bethel in its simplicity born of little means attracted the less well to do residents to its congregation. Church workers were few and among them were our parents. Mother transferred her activities from Kaumakapili after her father's pastorate there had ceased. Father was often superintendent of the Sunday school and mother a teacher. . . . How Father enjoyed Sunday school picnics when his store wagon was available for transporting children to some not too far valley or some grassy pastureland.

# CHAPTER 12

*Little May is growing in stature and knowledge, reads well and is a bright little girl. Her brother Walter will be 10 months old tomorrow Feb. 5th. He is well, lively, active, zealous, almost goes alone, and is a great pet in the family.*

The Reverend Lowell Smith to his son Gussie
4 February 1876

KALAKAUA'S personal magnetism and the glamor of seeing a real crowned head in Washington gave a tremendous shove forward to Hawaii's hopes for Reciprocity. As the year 1875 dawned, it became more and more evident that sooner or later such a treaty would prevail, and the pessimistic mood of business in Hawaii began to change.

The Dillinghams had their personal reason for rejoicing. In April, less than a year after Charlie's death, Emma gave birth to another baby boy, Walter Francis Dillingham.

> At precisely one o'clock, on Monday morning, April 5th, [Abba reported], another precious little boy announced his advent among us in clarion tones, not to be mistaken. They were the sweetest sounds heard in this home since our precious Charlie's little voice grew mute in death. . . . He weighs ten pounds, of course, that being Emma's pattern in babies. He is very tall, with long tapering fingers, has a double chin with a deep dimple, a big nose . . . and large eyes. . . . He is perfect in all respects and very vigorous, and our gratitude none can imagine save those who have been similarly bereaved and alike blest. Praise God from whom all blessings flow.

In another letter she added, "He looks just like my babies, so I call him my baby and he takes to his grandmamma."

His parents could not, of course, know it then, but without Walter Dillingham their lives might have had a very different ending. Years later, when Frank finally faltered after years of trouble and disappointment, Walter's young strength picked up the burden and helped to bring his father's projects at last into safe waters.

Two days after Walter's birth, Honolulu unexpectedly received news that the United States Senate had voted to approve the proposed Treaty of Reciprocity. In approving the treaty the Senate included a peculiar clause by which the treaty would not actually go into effect until passage of an enabling act by both houses of Congress, and Congress' schedule made it impossible to pass such an act before the end of the year. Nevertheless the news set off a huge celebration in Honolulu, where it was hailed as portending the certain attainment of the long-awaited treaty.

Business evidently improved at Dillingham and Company. In August Frank brought in a typewriting machine, the first ever seen in Hawaii. By the end of 1875 the net worth of the concern had risen to more than $24,000, from exactly zero at its inception. Legally, the partnership was in limbo, for the agreement had expired even before Alfred Castle died, but as a practical matter Frank and Mr. Castle as trustee carried on the business under the terms of the previous agreement.

During this time Frank was trying to buy out the Castle interests, but he and Mr. Castle proved equally stubborn in maintaining their own positions. The deal fell apart over the question of valuing the inventory. Called in to arbitrate, Mr. Dickson and Mr. J. B. Atherton, who was a partner in Castle and Cooke, proposed to discount the inventory valuation by 15 percent to allow for slow-moving merchandise, but Frank held out for 25 percent, which Mr. Castle would not grant.

Apparently the two men remained on cordial terms, however, for during the same period they together invested more than $7,000—partly borrowed from Bishop and Company on Mr. Castle's signature—in a venture to perfect a machine for processing ramie, a fibrous plant used in making cordage and rough textiles. Possibly they envisioned its use in making sugar bags. At any event, nothing productive came of the project.

When negotiations for Frank's proposed purchase of the Castle interest in Dillingham and Company fell through, it became necessary to regularize the situation by adopting a new partnership agreement.

Predictably, there resulted another massive clash of wills between Frank and Mr. Castle.

Frank as always needed more money. He lived well and spent freely. He and Emma had agreed that in 1876 they would build on their Beretania Street lot and set up housekeeping for themselves, which would mean a large outlay for furnishings on top of the cost of the house itself. He demanded that his salary be increased to a figure—extravagant in Mr. Castle's eyes—of $250 a month.

Mr. Castle on the other hand, whose endorsement had kept the business afloat from the day of its launching, demanded that he be paid a consideration for continuing to guarantee the firm's obligations at Mr. Bishop's bank. Frank denied that he was entitled to any such consideration, arguing that since Mr. Castle held a mortgage on the assets of the company and an insurance policy of $10,000 on Frank's life, he had no risk of loss on his endorsement.

Eventually they compromised. As usual in such cases, each partner got what he wanted most, at the expense of the business itself. Frank got his $250 a month, Mr. Castle got $240 a year for his endorsement, and Ellie Castle and her daughters got a promise of 10 percent interest on close to $8,000—presumably representing undivided profits—which they lent to the firm. The figures seem paltry, but taken together they represented a heavy burden on a small, struggling, and badly undercapitalized concern.

The partners agreed that 50 percent of each year's profits might be drawn out of the business, with the rest being added to capital. Obviously at the insistence of Mr. Castle, Frank agreed to devote his full time to the concern and not to engage in outside business or speculation. This commitment turned out to be one which Frank simply could not live with, and it sowed the seeds of discord.

Although the new partnership agreement was written to be effective 1 January 1876, the partners did not reach agreement and sign the papers until the end of March. Immediately thereafter Frank embarked on a project obviously close to his heart; his first trip back east in the twelve years since he had sailed out of Boston on the *Oriola.*

On this trip Frank visited many friends and relatives, and in anticipation of setting up housekeeping bought a houseful of furniture in the latest style: heavily carved black wood, with white marble tops for the dressers. Encouraged by the almost certain prospect of Reciprocity, he also bought heavily for Dillingham and Company, anticipating a great surge of business when the treaty became final.

On this trip he visited the great Centennial Exhibition in Philadelphia. There he undoubtedly sought out the Hawaiian exhibit, which featured among other things a prize-winning sample of sugar produced by the partnership of Campbell and Turton at Lahaina, Maui. Within the next year, Mr. James Campbell was to buy great ranch properties on Oahu and set in motion a train of events which would profoundly alter the life of Frank Dillingham.

Frank's mother, Lydia Howes Dillingham, "a quiet and gentle lady in delicate health." (Ambrotype, Bishop Museum)

Emma Louise Dillingham in 1876 at the age of thirty-three. When this picture was taken Emma had immediately ahead of her the terrible ordeal of Frank's illness.

Returning to San Francisco in August, Frank brought with him his widowed mother, "a quiet and gentle lady in delicate health," according to Abba's description. Emma was waiting for him in San Francisco, and the three returned together to Honolulu, where Mrs. Dillingham proposed to make her home with Frank and Emma. Frank's younger brother Charles, whom Frank had persuaded to move to Honolulu also, followed shortly after, bringing his wife with him.

Frank's party returned to Honolulu on the *City of San Francisco,* which brought news of the final approval of the Treaty of Reciprocity. The steamer also brought Claus Spreckels, a wealthy California sugar refiner, hot-footing it down to take advantage of opportunities opened up by the treaty. Dillingham strongly disapproved of Spreckels' later activities in the islands.

Frank and Emma's plans for building had not materialized, and their family had outgrown the Smith household. Frank rented a house farther down on Nuuanu Avenue, next to Dr. Hillebrand's botanical gardens (now Foster Gardens). A cottage on the same premises accommodated Charles and his wife.

And then, within a few weeks of his return from America, Frank suddenly and with little warning fell prey to a severe mental illness which made his life miserable for more than a year, threatened to end his career before it was well started, and plunged Emma into a time of suffering almost worse than his own.

# CHAPTER 13

*O, how we long to see our old, bright, hopeful Frank once more.*

Abigail W. Smith
27 December 1876

FRANK'S illness took the form of a terrible and unreasonable depression. He could not sleep at night, suffered burning pains in his head and chest, and refused to see a doctor. Abba wrote that

> his buoyant hopeful nature came under the cloud and a settled sadness supervened. In the meantime his business was prosperous, but he could not see it. . . . He goes daily to his business, with his sad face and weakened body, which has lost about 30 pounds of flesh! At home, he clings to Emma like a sick child, and she has risen to the occasion! She holds fast to the everlasting arms and is wonderfully kept up, is earnest and hopeful and strengthening in all her care of her husband. . . . Dear, dear child, I never admired and honored her as I do now.

On his trip to America, Frank had bought heavily against the prospect of Reciprocity. In August of 1876 Congress had passed and President Grant had signed the act to ratify the treaty, to take effect on 9 September, shortly after Frank returned to Hawaii. The treaty did result in an immediate stimulation of trade in Honolulu. Frank, however, had misjudged his firm's capacity, and it became apparent that the company could not pay for the goods on the terms which he had accepted. Quite possibly his mind was not working clearly during this trip, because he bought large quantities of goods of types which the firm did not ordinarily carry: stuffed birds from Cleveland, beef steak broilers, "croket sets," sham jewelry, $500 worth of sponges, and so on.

When the bills began to pile up, Frank asked Mr. Castle to take over the firm and employ him as a clerk. Instead, Mr. Castle obtained

Samuel Northrup Castle, cofounder of the firm of Castle and Cooke, spent years trying to collect money which Frank Dillingham owed to the heirs of Charles Alfred Castle, but in spite of the headaches involved he backed Frank Dillingham in his railroad scheme. ''You have been more like a father to me than a business acquaintance or friend,'' wrote Frank. (Hawaii State Archives photo)

a loan for the partnership from Bishop and Company, again with his endorsement. On 7 December 1876 he wrote to Frank urging him to make what sales and collections he could, to exercise care in extending credit, and not to make any orders or do any other important business without consulting Mr. Atherton or himself. It was not in the creditors' interest, he pointed out, to put Dillingham and Company into bankruptcy. ''Be courageous,'' he added, ''and I think all will come right.''

But Frank's spirits sank lower and lower. One of his purchases in America had consisted of a shipment of toys, which he had wholesaled to the firm of Thrum and Oat. Thrum and Oat could not pay their bill when it came due, and Frank took instead an interest-bearing note, which he proceeded to discount. Shortly afterwards he discovered to his horror that he had already pledged the original invoice as part of the security for a loan, thus placing himself in the position of having sold the same obligation twice. The incident involved less than $800 and would undoubtedly have been accepted as an honest mistake, but in his tortured mind he believed that he had committed a serious criminal act. He expected momentarily to be arrested and sent to prison. He took to carrying a loaded revolver with the idea of killing himself. Three times Emma took his gun away from him, but in the end only his belief that suicide would be a stain upon his character saved him.

Aside from the business, Frank presumably had money problems of his own arising from his mainland trip, his purchase of furniture, and the necessity of renting a house. In February of 1877 he and Emma sold their two acres on Beretania Street for $2,300, a transaction evidently arranged by Mr. Castle. At the end of March, by agreement with Mr. Castle, his salary was reduced to $150 a month.

On 5 March Mr. Castle wrote to his children Edward and Mary:

> Mr. Dillingham and his wife go up to Makawao [Maui] today to try the effect of separation from his cares or his imaginary cares on him, for he really has rendered no efficient help for four months. I have had the chief anxiety and burden of providing and directing on me. . . .
>
> If Mr. Dillingham was himself, and could take hold, and think and work as he used to do, everything would be right, but now it is darker, though not pitch dark. The business is good, better than ever before and I hope it will all be well, but I fear he never will. *He is not insane, as some think* but in danger from his long continued, and *unreasonable,* depression of spirits.

Three weeks later he wrote to his children James and Carrie: "Mr. Dillingham . . . started with his wife for Makawao by the Steamer of the 12th, which after being out 40 hours in the heavy gale, came back (a bad sentence) was very sick and is decidedly better. a/c of stock is being taken and I hope all will be found right and safe and I shall after a while be relieved at least partially, and after a while wholly."

At this juncture Frank's mother, who had taken a dislike to Honolulu, decided to return to Worcester to live. Frank took her up on the steamer to San Francisco and came back on the return trip "in no way improved in health" [he wrote] "save that I was able to sleep a little better."

Among the creditors of Dillingham and Company was Henry J.

Agnew, who had worked there as a clerk for some six years and who had lent the firm money at interest. In Frank's distraught state of mind, Agnew was able to persuade him to sell one half of his interest in the firm for $1,500 and to accept payment for it by cancelling that much of the company's indebtedness to Agnew. The papers were signed in May, soon after Frank's return from San Francisco.

The summer dragged on without improvement. In October came another dreadful trial of Emma's fortitude, a test which she surmounted triumphantly. Years later her daughter May told the story.

> Lying awake one night beside a restless baby, Mother suddenly saw in a mirror opposite her bed a burst of light which she knew must be in the end of the adjoining hall. Rousing Father with a cry of "fire" she leaped to the door only to see a sheet of flame from floor to ceiling. Father, dazed from sleep, thinking the other rooms inaccessible, seized sleeping Walter and rushed down the stairs. My mother's keen intuition knew it was something incendiary thrown into the hall window from a lower roof. Seizing a full water pitcher she rushed towards the blaze and with three dashes of water saw the flames descend. She then leaped over a burning mass into my room for more water and the danger was over. A sack filled with excelsior and soaked with kerosene lay smouldering, sullen but conquered, at her feet. Its position cut off the only doors into the maid's room and mine. The other apertures in those rooms were square windows in the steeply sloping roof. A rejected suit on the part of the oriental cook toward the Hawaiian maid was the surmised cause of the affair. That was our last night in the John Wood house.

"In the absence of direct proof," wrote Abba "[the cook] was allowed to leave the country."

After this near tragedy the family crowded back into Nuuanu Cottage, and here a seeming miracle took place. A new doctor, by the name of T. P. Tisdale, arrived in town; Frank fancied to consult him and began to improve. "Suddenly one morning the burning in his head ceased and he began to mend rapidly," wrote Emma.

Before Christmas Frank was well again, and at the end of the year Abba was able to write that

> Frank has come forth from the mists and thick darkness that have enveloped him a new man in Christ Jesus. Since his emancipation from the bondage in which he has been held so long . . . he has nearly re-

> covered his former health, his old energy and business tact have all come back and we have our beloved one among us again, almost like one risen from the dead, and such a sweet Christian spirit, so meek and so earnest. And so beloved we close the year with a psalm of thanksgiving upon our lips and in our hearts.

Frank and Emma had no sooner moved into another rented house, this one at the corner of Nuuanu and School streets, than they gave thanks in their own way. Frank's memoir tells this story:

> Early in January 1878 we received into our home a young stranger from San Francisco, who had come to the Islands in search of health but who had become desperately ill with dropsy. His case was considered hopeless from the first, but believing that "while there is life there is hope" with constant personal care and the devotion of a skillful physician (Dr. Tisdale) we fought the grim waiting messenger and at the end of ten weeks, had the happiness of seeing him on a steamer bound for home, with the dropsy eliminated from his system though in an extremely reduced condition of body.

And so Frank's bondage, as Abba called it, passed almost as rapidly and mysteriously as it came. Our knowledge of his illness, though we have several full and consistent accounts of it, leaves many unanswered questions. Quite probably, modern medical knowledge would have drastically reduced his time of suffering, but after the lapse of a century it would seem impertinent to attempt a medical diagnosis, and it might add nothing to our understanding. It is more tempting to speculate that in terms of his total character the sickness represented the dark side of the moon, the part unseen by human eyes. We know that Frank was young (thirty-two) and very much an idealist and that he had a strong urge to impose his own system of order on the chaotic world around him. We know that he had lost a business partner and a beloved son, that he was under heavy business pressure, and that there was friction between his wife and mother. Perhaps through his illness he was creating a period of withdrawal in which his subconscious mind could reconcile his ideals with reality.

At any rate, the remarkable fact is not his illness but his recovery. He emerged from his terrible experience stronger and abler than before.

# CHAPTER 14

*I think we are all more or less insane.*

Testimony of W. H. Dimond
at the trial of *Agnew v. Dillingham*

ONCE the euphoria of regained health had receded, Frank addressed himself to the problems which had piled up during his fifteen months of incapacity. Dillingham and Company, which like any small business depended heavily on the personal attention of its manager, had gone downhill. Sales had fallen off, collections lagged, parts of the inventory had become stagnant. In tackling these problems, Frank quickly found himself on a collision course with Henry J. Agnew.

The position of these two men toward each other was, to say the least, uncomfortable. In Dillingham's view—and it is pretty hard to disagree with it—Agnew had taken base advantage of his employer's illness to make himself an equal partner at a ridiculously low price. In Agnew's mind, on the other hand, Dillingham would have smashed the whole business without Agnew's intervention.

Frank was accustomed to giving orders, and Agnew had got out of the habit of taking them. The partners exchanged harsh words, some of them in the presence of clerks of the firm. Frank told Agnew their agreement was null and void and demanded he turn over the property of the firm. Agnew refused. Frank sought to settle out of court and Agnew named $10,000 as his price for withdrawing. Frank sought counsel with Mr. Castle.

Mr. Castle, who had stayed completely out of Frank's dealings with Agnew, retained a lawyer—his son, William R. ("Will") Castle—and together he and Frank brought suit in March of 1878 to dislodge Agnew from the firm, charging that Agnew had induced Frank by threats and improper advantages to admit him as a partner while Frank was in a depressed state of mind. Agnew denied the allegations and filed a cross bill praying for the dissolution of the firm and the appointment of a receiver. The same Chief Justice C. C. Harris, into

William R. ("Will") Castle acted as lawyer for his father, S. N. Castle, and for Frank Dillingham in the suit which they brought against Henry J. Agnew in 1878. Later, as a noble in the Legislature of 1888, he introduced the bill which gave Frank Dillingham his franchise to build a railroad to connect Honolulu and Pearl River Lagoon. Later still he was a prime mover in establishing Ewa Plantation. Despite intermittent bickering over business, he and Frank Dillingham remained life-long friends. (Photo by A. C. Platt, Bishop Museum)

whose home Frank had been carried with a broken leg twelve years before, tried the case based on Agnew's cross bill rather than the original suit.

Unless Agnew was acting entirely out of spite, his attempt to dissolve the firm amounted to blackmail, for in a forced dissolution the firm probably could not have paid its creditors in full, let alone the partners. As longtime bookkeeper for the firm, Agnew well knew the extent of Mr. Castle's endorsements of its obligations and counted on his having to keep it in operation at all costs.

Mr. Castle's caution and experience served him well; he showed clearly enough that he had had no part in admitting Agnew to the firm and had made no agreement with him whatever, in spite of Frank's publishing notices of Agnew's partnership under the firm name. Frank on the other hand sought to overthrow his entire agreement with Agnew by calling the agreement unconscionable, unfair, and obtained from him while in an unsound condition of mind by one exercising undue influence. Frank testified that Agnew had worked upon his depressed state of mind to make him regard his business affairs as even more hopeless, and had required him to keep the terms of their agreement secret, particularly from Mr. Castle, knowing that the partnership interest was worth several times what he was paying.

Excruciating though it must have been both for her and Frank, Emma took the stand and testified to taking a loaded pistol away from Frank on three occasions, and even to fearing for the safety of one of her children when Frank became overwrought. Sam Nott described Frank's clearly irrational behavior when they visited Hilo and the volcano together.

Justice Harris rendered his verdict promptly. He sustained Mr. Castle's contention that Agnew had never been a full partner in the firm but only a subpartner of Frank's, ruled that Agnew had no power to force a dissolution, ignored the contention of Frank's incapacity, and appointed his law clerk to act as master in chancery to determine how much Frank should pay Agnew to buy back his interest in the partnership.

At this point the trial took an ironic twist. Up to this time Frank had been claiming a high value for the partnership to support his contention that the agreement was unconscionable, and Agnew had been deprecating its value severely. Now Frank had to prove the worthlessness of what Agnew had bought, and Agnew had to demonstrate a high value.

The appraisal of a small, going business is at best difficult and hypothetical. A business is worth in the final analysis what someone will pay for it, but it is obviously impossible to effect a sale just to establish the value. Today an appraiser would probably rely rather heavily on a comparison of earnings with those of similar businesses, but in the 1870s such a technique had not been developed. In the case of Dillingham and Company, the appraisal came down to a matter of estimating the assets and subtracting the liabilities.

In attempting this analysis, the master in chancery ran smack into a roadblock which enormously complicated his problem: Frank had neglected to take inventory anywhere near the date of 20 March, which the court had set as the date for establishing the value. In fact, the latest inventory count was almost a year earlier. Frank's estimate of the inventory and Agnew's came out some twelve thousand dollars apart. Frank supported his figure with elaborate calculations which indicated a net loss for the past year of $673.15, while Agnew claimed a profit of $12,859.15. The master in chancery appears to have lacked a high degree of sophistication in accountancy, but one has to sympathize with his statement that "much of Mr. Dillingham's account seems to me calculated rather to mistify than to explain."

In fact, Frank and his legal counsel appeared to poor advantage throughout the trial, no doubt because of the extremely painful nature of the testimony. Frank's case rested largely on the "unconscionable" nature of his agreement with Agnew, but he shied away from directly asking the court to set aside the agreement on grounds of mental incompetence, even though a large part of the defense testimony pointed in that direction. Once the court had ignored his claims of improper advantages and undue influence, he floundered around rather aimlessly in his attempt to secure a low settlement.

In truth, the case had no winner. Agnew secured a settlement, confirmed by the supreme court in December, of close to six thousand dollars, much nearer to his figure than to Frank's. But he stood before the world as a man who had taken mean advantage of his friend's misfortune.

Frank for his part had put Emma through a terrible ordeal and had had the sordid details of his illness exposed in public, all to no purpose. When the trial ended, he was badly in debt and his business reputation was clouded.

Mr. Castle appeared to come off the best, and yet the damage to Frank hurt him also, by weakening Frank's ability to support Ellie and the grandchildren out of the partnership profits. Dillingham and Company was to give Mr. Castle many a worry in the years ahead.

*Agnew v. Dillingham* had years later an odd and rather touching sequel. Frank had a quick temper but no capacity for staying mad at anybody. In due time he and Agnew made up and had a few minor dealings together. In the 1890s Frank helped him subscribe to a few shares of Oahu Sugar Company, which proved a good investment. Agnew later moved to California and started a stock farm in Hillsdale, Santa Clara County. He was hard hit by drought and in desperation shipped some mares to William H. Rice of Kauai to breed on shares, without any written understanding. Later he wrote "Friend Dillingham" to ask him to straighten out the matter. Frank got him a clear agreement with Rice, induced Rice to take some more horses, paid the interest on a debt of Agnew's, paid off an assessment due on his Oahu Sugar stock, and helped him get a new mortgage on his ranch. "The only debt I have outstanding," Agnew wrote to Frank, "is to your dear self."

Within a matter of weeks, Mrs. Agnew, whom Frank had not met, wrote to say that her husband had died suddenly and to ask Frank to sell the Oahu Sugar stock for her. There is no record that Frank ever asked for payment of what Agnew owed him.

# CHAPTER 15

*Emma holds on to her 10 to 12 music pupils. They are the children of her friends and all come to her house for their lessons. She has good servants, and can do this pleasant work and insists upon it for the present.*

Abigail W. Smith
15 April 1878

NOTHING could keep Frank down for very long. By the summer of 1878, he was superintending the construction of a new store at 37 Fort Street, which he would lease from Thomas Cummins —again with Mr. Castle guaranteeing the lease. Emma meanwhile had suffered a reaction from the past two years, as well she might, and had gone to California, taking with her the children and Abba, who also had a touch of nerves.

"Emma gained in many ways," reported Abba. "I had no idea how much she needed the change until I came to be with her constantly. To the dear children the time passed in California was one long jubilee. . . . our homecoming was a very gladsome one."

Frank's memoir picks up the story:

> In October the two children had the whooping cough, from which they were not wholly recovered until January 1879. During this same month little May became ill of a fever and great was our surprise after a few days to have it diagnosed as typhoid, for this fever was almost unknown upon the Islands. We soon learned that there were eight or ten cases in town at the same time though they were widely separated from each other. The Government had been bridging a stream in our immediate neighborhood and making a new road of it. By some it was thought that the overturning of the soil was the cause of the fever in our family.
>
> The little girl was sick for five weeks before she could be lifted to a

chair for a few moments change of position. It was before the days of trained nurses and my wife took the entire care of her day and night during these weeks. At the end of this time she was ill herself with the same fever. A kind friend [Mrs. J. G. Dickson, in whose house she had been born] took May to her home; Walter went to his grandmother's and friends volunteered their kind services in my wife's behalf. She became very ill indeed—her life was despaired of. I was with her as much as possible myself with the result that before the crisis of her disease was reached, I also was helpless with the same fever. Then we were truly at the mercy of our friends, who took us in loving charge. Watchers by day and night were furnished for weeks. Our household was run by neighbors, food and delicacies for the sick and the assistants were superintended and furnished as well.

Our physician, Dr. Tisdale, was unwearying in his care and attention, often preparing with his own hands diet for the sick that it might be "just right."

In about six weeks we emerged from the shadow of death under which we had lain so long, and began to take some interest in life. Our physician ordered a diet of milk largely for us both, but alas, accommodating as was our Portuguese milkman and freely as he watered the milk to furnish the amount required, the article itself was quite lacking in the nourishing qualities desired. The stock of dairy cows upon the Island was of inferior breed at best. In this exigency a friend who was the owner of a pure Jersey cow offered to let us have one quart of milk a day. Our palates for the first time tasted pure rich milk. It was a revelation to us.

Just at this time a man had arrived from California with 30 head of Jersey cows for sale. The first time I was able to drive so far I visited his stock yard and there purchased a beautiful little Jersey, which I hitched to the back of the buggy and led home in triumph. The benefit derived by the entire family from the rich milk furnished by our pet "Daisy" was evident from the very first. The gentle creature was immediately installed as a member of the family.

Evidently the illness had interrupted some important family business. The time had come to move again, for the rented quarters at Nuuanu and School streets were in bad shape and the landlord refused to repair them. On 8 February 1879, the Smiths' old friend Henry M. Whitney signed a deed to Emma for 14½ acres at the corner of Beretania and Punahou streets, running up to the lower pasture of Punahou School. For this considerable area, which included the present site of Central Union Church, Frank paid $6,000, or a little less than a penny a square foot. The area was a dusty tangle of weeds and underbrush, but Frank could see its possibilities.

Frank went to work with customary vigor, building on his new property "a cottage, which had high airy rooms and spreading verandas." Over the years the cottage was to grow into a good-sized house as rooms were added for the still growing family. Frank and Emma demonstrated their faith by naming the new home "Woodlawn," in spite of the total lack of anything resembling a lawn. On 15 September they moved into what would remain their home for almost forty years.

As it turned out, they acquired not only a new home but a new way of life. Evidently Frank had got over the dislike for farming which he felt as a young boy, because the whole family pitched in to turn their property into a small farm. His memoir continues the story:

> Having now more than enough room for our one Jersey, I improved an opportunity that soon offered, and bought 14 head of Island bred cows and proceeded to complete the conditions necessary to conduct a small dairy. Part of the land was planted with corn, sorghum, and later with alfalfa.
>
> I rented an adjoining tract of 30 acres for pasturage; shed, rooms for the workmen, delivery wagon, horses, and farming materials, as well as an overseer of the work were soon a part of the outfit. To complete the farm life, we added several brood mares, a number of Essex and Berkshire pigs and a large poultry yard.
>
> The effect of this change of residence upon the health of the family and the interest that each member manifested in the various departments of our little farm was most gratifying.
>
> The Government completed a reservoir in Makiki Valley shortly before we occupied the place, so we had an abundance of water to use and the surface well was discarded.
>
> Customers of the dairy multiplied and as the stock of cows was not of the largest milking order, additions were made to it from time to time. There was a see-saw effect; too little milk for the customers, then too much for the same number; as these increased, too little milk again. There were many drawbacks in the way of dishonest drivers, drunken milkers and inexperienced farm hands; but though often desirous of abandoning the business, there never was an opportunity to do so without sustaining a heavy loss, so the burden was carried, waiting for the right time to arrive.
>
> The grounds immediately about the house were laid out in drives

> and spaces reserved for lawns and ornamental purposes. In time the lawns were freed from weeds and everything in the shape of flowers and shrubs grew with wonderful rapidity. Fruit trees entered largely into our plans for the improvement of the place. Walter was entrusted with the work of raising orange trees from seed in boxes, which in time were set out about the place.
>
> Life moved on apace; the various activities with their trials and drawbacks filled every day and evening, for upon my return from my business in town there were many things to demand my attention about the place, often till far into the night. The health of the family was excellent. Life in the open air was largely indulged in, and there were many pet colts and calves as well as chickens that were constant companions at such times.

A letter of Emma's in 1881 mentions that they were then milking eighty cows and delivering milk twice a day. Their livestock included "lots of very fine hogs," about two hundred poultry, and thirty little ducks. They were raising corn, sorghum, squashes, and bananas, and had set out fruit trees, one hundred grape vines, figs, pineapples, mangoes, guavas, oranges, alligator pears, Spanish plums, and pomegranates. They had had an artesian well dug, which came in at 280 feet. Frank never did things in a small way.

A view of Woodlawn with a horse and buggy in front. Frank Dillingham loved a fast horse and was always ready for an impromptu "drag race" with one of his friends. At other times he would become so engrossed in a business problem while driving his buggy that his horse would be left to go where it wished. (Courtesy of the Dillingham family)

Two months after Frank and family moved into Woodlawn, his brother Charles and his family moved into a cottage on three-quarters of an acre which Frank had sold him on the northwest corner of the property. Charles had come to Honolulu originally to work for Dillingham and Company, had moved to Castle and Cooke as bookkeeper, then back to Dillingham temporarily to straighten up things after Agnew left, then back to Castle and Cooke again. Mr. Castle thought highly of him and his future seemed bright. By that time he had two young children, Frank and Lizzie. In spite of the nine-year gap in their ages, the two brothers had a close rapport.

Beyond the confines of the little farm, events were moving forward that would change the islands drastically. James Campbell was busy fencing his great new ranch of Honouliuli and improving the cattle. In 1879 he brought from San Jose a well-digger named James Ashley. On 22 September, just a week after the Dillinghams moved into Woodlawn, Ashley brought in behind Campbell's ranch house an abundant flow of artesian water. This, the first artesian well in the islands, opened up undreamed of possibilities for using lands which up to then had been arid.

Reciprocity was doing its work. Exports of sugar rose from some 24 million pounds in 1874 to 49 million pounds in 1879, and in three more years would hit 114 million pounds. The population had passed its low point and was slowly starting to grow. Chinese immigration was up, Portuguese immigration just starting.

Transportation was recognized as a bottleneck. In 1878 Kalakaua signed "An Act to Promote the Construction of Railways," which permitted the chartering of public railroads with the right to condemn private property for their own use, providing "that the aid by this Act contemplated, shall be only extended to railroads of public utility, and not to railroads of mere private or limited convenience." Two years later the act was amended to provide for a subsidy of not more than $2,500 a mile for trackage actually completed.

In July of 1879 the first public railroad train in Hawaii ran on Maui's Kahului and Wailuku Railroad. In the same year Waiakea Mill near Hilo became the first to haul sugar cane with a steam locomotive; by 1889 the *Planter's Monthly* listed eight plantations that were using steam locomotives.

Back at Woodlawn, Frank must have followed these developments with interest, but for the moment his family, his business, and his new farm occupied his attention. With all the family in good health and with a wonderful new home to develop, this may well have been the happiest time of his life and of Emma's.

There was only one cloud on the horizon, but Frank was too good an accountant not to recognize it; they were spending more than they were taking in. Their ordinary living expenses amounted to more than $4,000 a year, which Frank's salary plus whatever Emma could pick up from teaching music failed to cover. Beyond that, there was a constant drain from new improvements to the property and new additions to the farm. By the end of 1879 they owed $9,300 in notes, including a mortgage of $8,000 on Woodlawn and $700 borrowed from Lowell Smith. The interest amounted to about $80 a month. Unless the dairy could make a profit, they faced serious trouble.

# CHAPTER 16

*We have had an artesian well bored with great success, on our little farm. Such pure, soft sparkling water in such great abundance is marvelous, and such a blessing.*

Emma Smith Dillingham
November 1881

THE Dillinghams moved to Woodlawn in September of 1879, after three horrible years of sickness. Almost six years later, in the summer of 1885, Frank's life entered a new phase when James Campbell offered to sell him his ranch properties on Oahu. The years between these two events seem at a casual glance to have been quiet and uneventful, filled mostly with domestic happenings and the growth of the family. But with Frank Dillingham, no time was ever quiet and uneventful. A closer look reveals a multitude of projects which he undertook in these years, some of them unsuccessful and most of them now forgotten, but all of them suggesting the direction of his future work.

In the family life these years were crucial: a time when the younger children were born and the older children were growing up in an atmosphere of horses and outdoor living.

Seven months after the move to Woodlawn, Emma gave birth to Alfred Hubbard Dillingham. Abba wrote:

> Our precious baby boy came to us on the morning of April 21st. Now six weeks old, the best and most precious baby in the world. After so much illness and cross bearing the past three or four years can you think what this gift is to us all, but especially to Emma. May and Walter were almost wild with delight. It was beautiful to see them after their introduction to him run to their rooms and bring their hands full of their precious toys and lay them as an offering of love before the little unconscious brother. May is fast becoming a little mother to the

> baby. Emma is wonderfully well considering that she has had no adequate help in the nursery since the monthly nurse left. She has missed the home care she had when the other children came and I was too ill to go to her when she most needed me. But her young nurse maid is beginning to do better now and I trust Emma will grow strong and well.

But Emma had one more trial to face. Six months later the baby died, leaving a grieving family behind.

> I don't know as Emma will feel able to write at all [wrote Abba]. She dreads it so. She already lost eight pounds of flesh tho she does bear up wonderfully and tries to attend to all her duties. There are the awe-struck and broken hearted little May and Walter to be comforted and diverted from their great grief. Poor little dears! How they loved their baby brother. "How can I ever go home from school again and not find my baby," poor little May sobbed out upon my bosom and Walter said, "I play Grandma, but I don't enjoy it as I used to for I think of little Freddie all the time."

The following year Harold Garfield Dillingham was born. "Health and strength were his from the day of his birth," wrote the proud father.

"Frank has grown very stout the past year," wrote Emma in the spring before Harold's birth. Regarding Walter she said that "we cannot help confessing that he is a bright boy . . . affectionate, obedient . . . but such a *driver*." She added the surprising information that he loved to play with dolls. At six he was riding his own pony, Flyaway.

A year after Harold's birth, Frank's brother Charles mounted his horse one day to ride to town. A hundred yards from his cottage the saddle girth gave way and he was thrown violently to the ground. He suffered fatal head injuries and died six hours later without regaining consciousness.

Charles' death dealt a terrible blow to Frank. Abba wrote that "C. had just had his 29th birthday. Since his death a sweet baby girl has been added to the family, making three, all under five years of age. Frank and Emma have assumed largely the care of this little flock."

After the birth of the baby, Charles' widow decided to return to Worcester, Massachusetts. In April of 1883 Emma and May accompanied her and her children as far as San Francisco and stayed on for a few weeks' rest before returning. Abba kept them well posted on happenings at home. Harold was restless at night, but Frank was "as patient and gentle as a mother" with him. Frank had not been feeling well, but went to the dedication of the Y.M.C.A. anyway. Afterwards he "ate four glasses of ice cream, drank a cup of coffee, and felt better!" Frank's love of ice cream was proverbial in the family. Abba also reported "I have just been in to help Walter dress and heard his spelling lesson and 'Roman Numerals' at the same time. Leaving him to draw on his stockings, I took his shoes out to be blacked. Finding the man at the churn, I took the crank and gave him the shoes. I 'brought' the butter by the time the shoes were ready — felt quite proud." Abba was seventy-three at the time.

Emma had good reason for not going further than San Francisco: she was almost thirty-nine and carrying her last child. Marion Eleanor Dillingham was born in September of 1883. Thirteen years younger than May and eight years younger than Walter, she was within two years of Harold, and the two of them became inseparable.

That fall Abba reported to a young cousin that

> May is growing on, lovely in character and person. She is 13 years old. Grown up people who admire true and unaffected childhood are very apt to fall in love with her. Walter is eight years old and is a boy of the best type—handsome and true, but not priggish. Harold is just two years old and can say "My name is Harold Garfield Dillingham" and many other things. As he can never be Pres. of the United States his grandpapa has devoted him to the "gospel ministry." The child is very unregenerate at present but he has a wise mother. When he is under discipline it is impressive to hear him shout "M-a-y, Wal-ter, Fen-ny [the nurse] come help Harold." But no one interferes and he is obliged to surrender at discretion. He is a very precious little boy, but at present fancies that all things are created for *his* pleasure."

To the end of her life, Abba reserved her warmest thoughts for Walter. When he was nine, she wrote that "Walter is the apple of my eye. For all practical purposes of life he is perfection. Quick witted, neat handed and fleet footed, and his inventive genius is wonderful, but he is not yet exactly a bookworm. . . . In her class of 35 your little cousin [May] was marked No. 1 for the first time. In algebra she was the only one that was marked 100. . . . She also took a prize in Rhetoricals."

Abigail ("Abba") Willis Tenney Smith, wife of the Reverend Lowell Smith and mother of Emma Dillingham. This picture was taken in 1882, three years before she died at the age of seventy-five.

In one of Abba's last letters, she had this to say about Emma and Frank:

> I do wish you knew your cousin Emma, in her daily life. She has developed into such a good, I may almost say grand woman. In every particular she is so true, so enlightened, so honest and sincere and unworldly and really so superior in her humility, if that is not a paradox, and withal so full of right ideas and principles. Now I have mused over the character she has developed a great deal, and almost wondered at it. I wanted to have her develop just in this way, but I wanted God to use the means I proposed. If He had done so I wonder if it would have been as well as or if I should have been as well satisfied with the result as I now am. Apart from being mother and daughter, we are such friends. Nothing can go beyond it, I am sure, and our intercourse is so intimate and so precious and Frank has developed into such a *man*. Neither he or she know how it has all come about, but standing a little apart I see it all. Being rightly disposed, he could not help growing rapidly in such good soil and the children have the greatest reverence and love for both their parents.

The Reverend Lowell Smith at the age of eighty. After Abba's death, Lowell Smith came to live with Frank and Emma at Woodlawn.

In January 1885 Abba wore herself out at a series of revival meetings, and went to stay at Woodlawn for a rest. There she developed a fever and in spite of loving care sank lower and lower until she quietly died. Lowell Smith wrote that "she had been so diligent in business, fervent in spirit, serving the Lord of late that she was obliged to stop and rest, and in lying down to sleep, she fell asleep in Jesus without a struggle or a groan."

Abba's death marked the end of an era for Frank and Emma. They were no longer the younger generation, but approaching middle age, with an eighty-two-year-old father to care for. "Mr. and Mrs. Dillingham have adopted me as one of their family," wrote Lowell Smith. "We are all up here at the old homestead for a few days while the 'Woodlawn' premises are being painted and set in order; and if Mr. D. can sell those premises then they would like to come and live with me in this Nuuanu Cottage." The sale of "those premises" never materialized, but instead the Reverend Smith came to live at Woodlawn with Emma and Frank.

Once Frank got Dillingham and Company back on its feet after his illness and established in new quarters, he seems to have to some extent lost interest in it. The conflict with Mr. Castle continued, however. In 1880 Frank was drawing $200 a month, less than what he had been getting before his illness. The old partnership agreement with its prohibition on Frank's engaging in outside businesses had expired at the end of 1878. There are no papers to indicate a new agreement to replace it, and the partners may have gone along for a while on a verbal understanding.

In June of 1880 James Gordon Spencer went to work at Dillingham and Company. A few months later Spencer put $10,000 cash into the firm and became a partner, so that he and Frank each had a one-third interest, and Ellie Castle and her children each had a one-ninth share. Mr. Castle remained as trustee for Mrs. Castle and the children. Frank and Spencer each drew $250 a month in salary. This arrangement got some desperately needed cash into the business and made it possible for Frank to concentrate more on other projects, but it did increase the overhead of what was still a struggling concern.

Spencer turned out to have a quite different attitude from Frank's toward business, and the history of their long association is full of mutual recrimination. Nevertheless, Spencer remained connected with the firm for close to thirty years.

The next few years were moderately successful for the partnership, but Frank still felt the need to get out from under the Castle interests. He and Spencer agreed on a plan of incorporation, and Frank approached Mr. Castle with an offer to buy him out for $37,000, including some $25,000 owed to the family by the partnership.

As Mr. Castle explained it later, "When I sold to Mr. D., the partnership had almost expired, and I think neither he nor Mr. S. were inclined to renew it. . . . I should have had to take ⅓ of the goods, ⅓ of the accounts, & assume ⅓ of the debts. In the very depressed state of business, it was doubtful I could have paid the debts out of the assets. Besides, I still stand responsible for the original $13,000. Mr. D. made a fair offer, expecting to raise cash by sale of corporation stock but it didn't sell."

In lieu of cash, Mr. Castle took Frank's note for $37,000 dated 1 November 1884. The interest at 8 percent—almost $3,000 a year—would support Ellie and the children, if it could be collected.

The problem lay in collecting it. A year later Frank, who was badly overextended, had not paid a cent of interest or principal. Ellie was then living in America, and Mr. Castle kept sending her remittances out of his own pocket, without telling her that Frank had defaulted.

Mr. Castle's irritation was no doubt increased by items such as the newspaper article which stated that Mr. B. F. Dillingham had purchased a splendid horse, "Billy Wobum," from Mr. Porter for $1,500. The story seems greatly exaggerated; Frank certainly didn't pay cash for the animal, and he did give a note for $500 to J. H. Porter. But the effect on Mr. Castle must have been unfortunate in any case.

The actual incorporation of Dillingham and Company took place early in 1885, and at the same time the company took over the hardware business of Frank's old friend Sam Nott, paying for it with $19,000 in stock in the new company. Frank had incorporated his dairy business a year earlier and had found it possible to sell a little stock at that time, but by 1885 the price of sugar had fallen so low that Hawaii was suffering what Mr. Castle called "unprecedentedly hard times." The Pacific Hardware Company, as the business of Dillingham and Company became known upon incorporation, had to struggle along without an infusion of capital—or rather, Mr. Castle had to struggle along without payment on the note he was holding.

As Frank's interest in the hardware business declined, his preoccupation with other activities grew. The original Daisy, the beautiful little Jersey who gave such wonderful milk, multiplied to twenty, then eighty, then two hundred, but the dairy business proved no easier a road to fortune than the hardware business—even though it did supply unlimited quantities of homemade ice cream.

At the end of 1880 Frank leased the Punahou School pasture lands and began to pull his dairy operations away from Woodlawn itself. The following year he began to invest in ranching operations at Waimea and Kawailoa, at the far northern end of Oahu. His partner in these operations was John H. Paty, the son of his old skipper and a banking partner of Charles R. Bishop. This operation led to Paty's coming into the Woodlawn Dairy. The partnership document recites that Frank and Paty each contributed $4,600 in capital. A third partner, R. H. Graham, contributed about $1,150 and also gave notes to the other two partners for about $1,150 apiece. Graham was to manage the dairy at a monthly salary of $100.

This partnership lasted only twenty-eight months. For reasons unknown, Frank and Paty split their interests, Paty ending up with the Kawailoa and Waimea ranches and Frank with the dairy plus some property Paty had bought in the Punahou area. Soon afterwards, in early 1884, Frank incorporated the Woodlawn Dairy and Stock Company, the name advertising the fact that besides selling dairy products he imported and bred horses and cattle. Among the stockholders was Thomas H. Hobron, founder of the Kahului and Wailuku Railroad, the first public railway in Hawaii.

At an early directors' meeting, Frank noted that he had paid $500 for two bulls in Syracuse, New York, and was having them shipped to Honolulu—no mean feat. At a later meeting he reported their safe arrival and the sale of one of them for $575, remarking with some pride that the bull was giving "great satisfaction."

As the dairy business grew, it required more land than Frank could find in Manoa Valley. Shortly before he incorporated the business, he signed an agreement to buy from John H. Wood a large and attractive estate in Nuuanu. He took possession early in 1884 and proceeded to develop it as a dairy, but a flaw in the title prevented an immediate consummation of the sale. The entire transaction later aborted and led to an acrimonious lawsuit, described in a later chapter, which was not finally settled until the middle of 1887. Meanwhile the dairy business chugged along in desultory fashion, contributing little besides milk, cream, and headaches to its owner.

Frank never really learned to cut his losses. This tenacity stood him in magnificent stead later when almost no one else thought his railroad could survive, but in smaller enterprises it cost him a great deal of time and money. Mr. Castle apparently washed his hands of the ramie business back in 1877, but not Frank. In 1884 Frank went into partnership with Mr. Castle's son, William R. Castle, in the Hawaiian Ramie Company. The details of the enterprise are lost, but apparently the partners went into it more thoroughly than before, because over the next five years they lost about $18,000. W. R. Castle had put up the money and had also discounted a note which their manager had given Frank, so it ended up with Frank owing him more than $10,000. Nevertheless they remained on close terms through the ups and downs of the next thirty years.

But it was real estate that really occupied Frank's attention in the early 1880s. In 1881 Punahou School started to sell off lots carved out of its lower pasture, and Frank picked up one, of almost an acre and a half, for $200 down against a total price of $1,000, which worked out at a little more than a cent and a half a square foot. Frank knew the price was too low; when he was ready to make his move the following year, he got more than six cents a square foot for two pieces on Beretania Street. These lots, together with the one he had previously sold to his brother Charles, amounted to about three acres out of the original fourteen and a half, and returned to him approximately his total original purchase price. Later in 1882 he sold four lots to John H. Paty and four to Henry J. Agnew.

Also in 1882 Frank leased for ten years a sizeable piece of property called "Marshfield" on the southwest side of Waikiki Road, now known as Kalakaua Avenue, near the present intersection of Kapiolani Boulevard. John Paty was associated with him in the lease; perhaps they wanted it for winter pasturage. But in 1883 Frank bought for $1,000 almost twelve adjoining acres, which he named "Marshfield Annex." A good part of Marshfield Annex was under water, but Frank immediately made an agreement with one Asam to fill in with dirt more than two acres for a total cost of $900. The subsequent sale of this property, together with the other land, provided the means for Frank to go to London in 1887. Marshfield Annex has its own niche in history as the first Dillingham reclamation project.

In 1884 he purchased for $1,100 another eleven acres, known as "Mauna Pohaku," which fronted on what is now Wilder Avenue and ran from Punahou School to Metcalf Street. The low price of this property reflected not only its hilly terrain but also a cloud that rested on the title. Frank cleared the title by paying the trustees of the estate of Bernice P. Bishop $400 for their claim, turned the hill into an asset by rechristening the property "Seaview Tract," and sold it off as building lots in 1885 and 1886.

The success of these ventures compared to the generally unsatisfactory record of the dairy and the hardware business must have made a strong impression on Frank's mind. When he got the Oahu Railway and Land Company under way, one of its first programs was the sale of lots at Pearl City.

His venture with Paty into the ranching business, beginning in 1881 and lasting for more than two years before they split, gave him insight into another form of land investment involving hundreds and even thousands of acres. For perhaps the first time he became familiar with the western part of Oahu, and we can well imagine how its possibilities excited his creative faculties.

In his own back yard Frank already held the key to making money out of vast acreage: his artesian well, completed in 1881. With government water available at Woodlawn, he did not really require an artesian well, but it was something so new and revolutionary that he could not resist having it dug. Land, water, and transportation made up the formula that he eventually parlayed into a fortune, and he was beginning to get a grasp on the first two elements in it.

# CHAPTER 17

*There is an old adage that we cannot get blood out of a stone that I think will apply equally in saying that we can get no money out of a dairy. . . . as I have been running this institution now for about 30 years, it has certainly afforded me a very good sinking fund, a fund sunk so completely out of sight that no one would ever find it.*

B. F. D. to F. C. Smith,
secretary and treasurer of the Woodlawn Dairy
18 February 1909

LIKE many other entrepreneurs, Frank Dillingham bloomed a little late. In early 1885 at forty years of age, he had come a long way from his first clerkship with Henry Dimond, but he had a long way to go before he became a power in Honolulu. In many ways his life had been only a preparation for what was to come. He had learned to buy and sell; he was a skilled accountant; he knew something about the law, and a good deal about real estate; he knew stock raising, and something about agriculture and irrigation; he understood the use of corporations; most of all, he knew human nature and motivations. He was, in fact, ready for the great commercial adventure in his life.

Meanwhile, he faced one problem which would continue to plague him for most of the rest of his life: he was in debt to an extent which would have caused many men to lose heart. At the end of 1879, just after he moved into Woodlawn, he owed notes totaling $9,300, mostly against a mortgage on the property. Four years later this figure had jumped by $30,000, and he owed people and firms all over town. By the beginning of 1885, he owed well over $100,000, including the $37,000 to the Castle interests, and he was no longer promising Mr. Castle to pay the principal, but only saying that he hoped to be able to pay a portion of the interest. Most of his debts carried 9 or 10 percent interest. By 1881 his interest expense exceeded his salary from Dillingham and Company, and it grew steadily heavier until by 1885 it must have run close to $1,000 a month. In addition to these personal debts, both the dairy and the hardware company owed substantial sums of money and were under considerable pressure from creditors.

Frank was genuinely conscientious and idealistic, and this terrible burden of debt must have deeply troubled his New England morality. By 1885 he realized quite clearly that his only hope of ever paying his creditors lay in some large-scale enterprise far beyond the daily occupations of himself and his friends. At the same time his astonishing resilience and optimism enabled him to live with the pressures of insolvency until he saw his chance to escape them.

By 1885 he had his real estate operations at Seaview and Marshfield Annex far enough along to promise a measure of temporary relief, but he still had one sticky problem at hand: his dispute with John H. Wood.

At the end of 1883 Frank had agreed to buy for $18,000 the Wood property in Nuuanu Valley, consisting of 650 acres "more or less." He paid a thousand dollars down and agreed to pay another four thousand on tender of deed on 1 July 1884, and the balance over the next five years. The property in question consisted of what is now known as the Dowsett tract, beginning at the upper end of Queen Emma's summer estate and running close to a mile along the Pali Highway and in to the top of the ridge at the Waikiki side of the valley. Frank took immediate possession and started to improve the property with barns for his dairy.

Since Mr. Wood had never had the property surveyed, Frank hired a surveyor to do the job. Wood, meanwhile, had found a cloud on his title and was forced to apply to the government for relief before he could present a deed to the property. While the title was still pending, the surveyor brought in his report: the property contained not 650 acres but 258.

Frank went to Mr. Wood and requested a reduction in price based on the deficiency in acreage, but Mr. Wood flatly refused to make any accommodation at all. Wood finally secured a clear title to the property and in November of 1885 tendered a deed which Frank and his attorney refused to accept. Wood thereupon filed suit for specific performance to compel Frank to carry out the purchase as agreed. Judge A. Francis Judd heard the case, beginning in March of 1886.

The defense responded that the agreement called for 650 acres, that the price had been figured on a per acre basis, and that the complainant had represented the tract as containing at least 650 acres or more. The defense further pointed out that the complainant had owned the piece since 1861, and "well knew or had the means of knowing" the area, since his deeds to the property cited a total of only 301 acres, out of which he had sold off a portion previously. Justice Judd remarked, however, that defendant's counsel had used the same deeds in drawing up the agreement.

The complainant flatly denied that he had ever represented the piece as containing 650 acres, or that he had ever discussed the price on a per acre basis, and testified that he had gone over the property with the defendant and had pointed out the boundaries, which were clearly visible.

Justice Judd declared that he would not hesitate to annul the contract on grounds of mutual and gross mistake, except that the actions of the defendant in the meantime had made such a course impossible. The judge referred here not only to the improvements which Frank had placed on the property but also to the fact that he had resold it to the Woodlawn Dairy and Stock Company.

Frank's case rested basically on his claim that Wood had cheated him, but the court evidently felt that he had not been cheated too badly, as he had turned around and resold the property for $57,500 in Woodlawn Dairy stock. Sanford Dole, Frank's attorney for the case and a minor stockholder in the dairy, claimed that that figure included about $22,600 in improvements and cattle, but even so the resale involved a paper profit to Frank of about $17,000.

A disgruntled stockholder in the dairy testified that Frank had put the property into the company at too high a figure, and Frank agreed that he had given the minority stockholders a 20 percent stock bonus on account of the transaction. The only reasonable conclusion is that Frank was running up the paper value of the dairy company to aid him in either selling out at a profit or borrowing substantially against his stock.

The question arises as to why Frank should have so determinedly refused to accept the property. From our vantage point in time, it appears that he had an outstanding bargain. At 258 acres, most of them usable, the price works out at less than $70 an acre. In getting it surveyed he had the surveyor lay it out into lots so that he could subdivide and sell it in case it proved unsuitable for the dairy. It was close to town and had a cool climate, and it would appear that he could have sold off the lots at a good profit. In reselling the property to the dairy company—and by that time its true acreage had been established—he defended its value to the dairy.

The reason for Frank's intransigence seems to be simply that he got mad at Wood and allowed the whole affair to become a moral issue in his own mind. He had agreed to buy 650 acres and he was not going to settle for less, unless the price was reduced accordingly. Wood had directly contradicted his word on their negotiations, and Frank was going to make him pay for it.

At any rate, Justice Judd decreed that Frank should have the choice of either accepting the deed and paying for the property as agreed, or annulling the agreement and immediately vacating the premises, with the complainant in that case required to reimburse him for the enhancement of the market value from the permanent improvements he had erected.

Frank's memoir tells of his choice.

> After many months the judgment was rendered against me, with the alternative of leaving the property if I preferred! It appeared as though the underlying opinion was that it would be impossible for me to do this; and that I was fairly cornered. But "God helps those that help themselves." I was enabled at this time to sell 200 head of my stock to parties who were just starting a dairy on the Island of Maui! The cows were brought from the valley through town to the point of shipment in the cool and early hours of morning, two and three o'clock before anyone was stirring. In like manner the remaining 160 were taken back to the Woodlawn dairy, together with all the moveable outfit, and I in one day had the pleasure and satisfaction of informing Mr. Wood and his counsel that I "accepted the alternative and returned the property!"

Eventually the court awarded Frank about $3,600 for the value of his improvements, but by that time he and Emma were on their way to London to seek money for his great land scheme.

The Woodlawn Dairy and Stock Company survived the lawsuit, moving to 513 acres in Manoa Valley where Frank had laboriously assembled the fractional interests in a beautiful piece of mountainside property. Thrum's *Almanac* for 1886, written when Frank still had the Wood property, called it the largest milk dairy in the Hawaiian Kingdom, with more than 600 head including Durhams, Devons, Ayrshires, Holsteins, and Jerseys.

But in spite of all efforts, the dairy never made money with any consistency, and the finishing blow came when the Board of Health condemned and destroyed a large number of the milking cows. In 1910 the last of the animals were sold off, the dairy operation closed down, and the property subdivided and sold. The name "Woodlawn," carried over first from the Dillingham home at Punahou and Beretania streets and then from the dairy company, still attaches to this tract of land on the Koko Head side of Manoa Valley.

# Part III
# Working on the Railroad

# CHAPTER 18

*The subject of colonization is not entirely a new one in the Hawaiian Islands, but it has recently been brought forward in an able and practical manner by Mr. B. F. Dillingham, who has succeeded in creating greater interest in the question, by a few weeks of earnest application, than had been excited by all other agencies in the previous history of the country.*

Excerpt from a letter in the
*Pacific Commercial Advertiser*
10 December 1885

IN the last section of his fragmentary memoir, Frank Dillingham wrote that in the summer of 1885

> there was a considerable business depression at the islands over the low price of sugar. One day I listened to the talk of a number of men who were taking a gloomy outlook into the future, and turning to one, James Campbell, who owned 60,000 acres of land on Oahu, said "If I had such a magnificent landed estate as you have, I'd build a railroad around it and open it up and do all I could to get settlers to take it up. I'd give away half of it, if necessary, to make the other half valuable."
>
> A few days later this same James Campbell came to me and said "I'd like to make you an offer. I will sell you my 10,000 head of stock for $200,000 and lease you my 60,000 acres for 15 years." "Oh," said I, "15 years is too short a period of time. What will you sell it for?" "$600,000" was the reply. This amount staggered me. That I should ever have to do with properties and values that would outrank this figure was farthest from my thoughts.
>
> Mr. Campbell said "You have a dairy now. You will need land to

run your stock on, and there is the land.'' ''Well'' I said, ''I will think it over.''

On going home that night I told my wife of the whole affair, and then added the thoughts and schemes which had flashed through my mind during my ride home, which were to cover those beautiful stretches of country with settlers, who . . . .

Frank abandoned his memoirs in midsentence at the decisive turning point of his life. Before his talk with Campbell he had been a small-time businessman, ingenious and hardworking but financially unsuccessful. Campbell's lands offered him the key to financial salvation, the means to extricate himself from the morass of debt into which he had fallen. Much more, they gave him the chance to use his creative faculties on a project of magnificent proportions, a project beyond the comprehension of most of his contemporaries. In this almost chance encounter with Campbell he found the moment for which he had been preparing all his life.

Of Scotch-Irish ancestry, James Campbell was born in Londonderry, Ireland in 1826. He went to sea at an early age and after various salty adventures landed in 1850 in Lahaina, Maui, where he supported himself by carpentry.

The Hawaiian sugar industry was then in its infancy. Campbell sensed an opportunity and learned the business from the ground up, literally. Along with Harry Turton, whom he later bought out, he became the owner of Pioneer Mill, which eventually proved extremely profitable. The 1876 Treaty of Reciprocity made the sugar business even more lucrative, and Campbell found himself rich enough to spend more and more time in Honolulu. Near the end of 1876 he bought Kahuku Ranch, at the northern tip of Oahu, for $63,500, and the following year he bought the immense Honouliuli Ranch in central Oahu for $95,000. The latter property included the great Ewa plain from Pearl Harbor to Barber's Point and Kahe Point and stretched inland toward Wahiawa as far as the present Schofield Barracks boundary, between the top of the Waianae Mountains and Kunia Road. The area around Iroquois Point (on the port side as you enter Pearl Harbor), known as Puuloa, had previously been sold off and had come into the possession of James I. Dowsett.

(Puuloa was the Hawaiian name for Pearl Harbor, but it also applied to the landing on the western side of the harbor entrance. One

James Campbell offered to sell Frank Dillingham his Honouliuli and Kahuku ranches, consisting of more than 60,000 acres in fee simple on Oahu, for $600,000. Luckily for the Campbell heirs, Dillingham could never raise the money. Later Campbell leased the lands to Dillingham for fifty years at a fixed annual rental of $50,000; it was this lease more than anything else which made the Oahu Railway and Land Company a profitable enterprise. (Courtesy of the James Campbell Estate)

of the original stations on the O. R. and L., not far from the present main gate of the Pearl Harbor Naval Shipyard, was named Puuloa, presumably because of its proximity to Pearl Harbor. Later, the Honolulu Plantation established a camp near the station and called it Puuloa Camp. Thus the name Puuloa became associated with the area to the east of the harbor entrance, as well as to the west.)

These properties gave Campbell more than 60,000 acres in fee simple on Oahu, land which at that time was considered good only for raising livestock.

Campbell immediately set out to fence his property, to build up his herd, and to improve the value of his land. In 1879, in California, he met James Ashley, a well-borer by trade, and brought him to Hawaii. Working with a crude, hand-operated rig, Ashley dug for almost three months behind Campbell's ranch house at Honouliuli, and on 22 September 1879 brought in at a depth of 273 feet the first artesian well in Hawaii. *Waianiani,* the Hawaiians called it: "sparkling water." It was a momentous day in Hawaiian history, for it opened the way to irrigation and cultivation of areas which up to that time were not even prime grazing lands.

When Campbell first went to Lahaina, he had boarded with a part-Hawaiian family named Maipinipini. To celebrate the arrival of a new baby girl in the family, he made for her a wooden cradle, still in existence. Some twenty years later, when he was almost fifty, he married the former occupant of the cradle, by then grown into a beautiful young woman. The couple had four daughters, but their only son died in infancy. Thus at the age of about sixty, Campbell found himself extremely wealthy, with a young wife and four daughters to provide for and no son to inherit his property. He had worked hard all his life, and was ready to enjoy some leisure at the Cleghorn property he had purchased on Emma Street in Honolulu. Probably these circumstances explain why he was willing to sell the estates he owned in rural Oahu. He had come to a point where he wished to lighten his own responsibilities and know that his wife and children would in any case be well provided for.

He would sell, but only at a price. He wanted cash, and he wanted more than three times what he had put into the property in less than ten years.

James Campbell was a reserved, secretive man. Men who did business with him found him shrewd and hard. Nothing in the record suggests any degree of intimacy between him and Frank Dillingham. To put it baldly, he would do business with Dillingham because Dillingham was the only man in Honolulu willing—if he was able to raise the money—to pay Campbell's price.

Yet it is easy to suppose that Campbell must have had great faith in the younger man. Certainly he went to extraordinary lengths, then and later, to keep the door open for Frank's plans, during times when almost everyone else had lost faith.

Frank was fortunate on two counts. First, he was dealing with a man who was under no financial pressure. Campbell had paid cash for his ranches, and his income afforded him an elegant style of living. If Campbell had needed to sell property to meet a note, Dilling-

James Campbell bought this fine residence on Emma Street in Honolulu from Governor Archibald Cleghorn, the father of Princess Kaiulani. It later became the home of the Pacific Club. (Photo by Ray Jerome Baker, Bishop Museum)

ham would have been squeezed out of the bidding at an early stage. In the second place, Campbell had a high opinion of the worth of the property, and no disposition to compromise on it. If Campbell had offered the property at $300,000, which would still have given him a good profit, other men would undoubtedly have taken it. At $600,000, only Dillingham recognized it as a magnificent bargain.

Frank was not one to dilly-dally. The two men first talked "in the summer"; on 3 August 1885 Campbell gave him a one-year written option to purchase the Kahuku and Honouliuli ranches including no fewer than nine thousand cattle for $600,000. In the same month Frank issued a printed "Memorandum Relating to Honouliuli, Kahuku and Kawailoa Ranches," followed in short order by a proposal and then by a preliminary prospectus for a "Great Land Colonization Scheme," offering stock in a corporation to be called the "Hawaiian Colonization Land and Trust Co." which would control the properties.

In other words, Frank, having no money of his own to buy the

Campbell properties, was proposing to sell stock in a publicly held corporation to buy them, taking his own profit in the form of cash and promotional stock. The Kawailoa and Waimea ranches, which were owned principally by Frank's friend John H. Paty and in which Frank had once held an interest, were included in the scheme. These two ranches, held under a twenty-four year leasehold, covered some 43,000 acres, bringing the total acreage involved to more than 115,000 and assuring a practical control of the Honolulu beef supply.

Campbell was to be president of the new corporation, Paty vice-president, and Dillingham general manager. Additional directors were to include Samuel G. Wilder, A. J. Cartwright, William F. Allen, S. B. Dole, W. R. Castle, and W. Austin Whiting. The capitalization was set for the time being at $1.2 million, of which the promoters were subscribing for $400,000 and offering $800,000 to the public. The capital was to be used as follows:

| | |
|---|---|
| Purchase of 63,250 acres in fee | $ 822,250 |
| Capitalized value of leased land, 52,500 acres | 65,750 |
| 15,000 head cattle at $20 each | 300,000 |
| 260 head horses, etc. | 12,000 |
| | $1,200,000 |

Campbell insisted on $600,000 cash for his land and livestock, and John Paty apparently agreed to take mostly stock in payment for his leaseholds and animals. Since Frank held an option on Campbell's property at $600,000, he apparently expected to make a profit of $200,000 in cash and $222,250 in company stock, less whatever Paty got for his animals.

The prospectus listed the present net income of the ranches at slightly more than $60,000 per year, or 5 percent on the capital, and explained in some detail how this amount would be raised to more than $220,000 per year, through increased sales of animals, rental of land for rice and sugar growing, and sale of land in moderate amounts for "colonization"—that is, the settling of small farmers in the country.

Frank, or "B. F.," as he was more generally known among the businessmen of the town, always appreciated the value of publicity. As soon as he had his scheme well in hand, he organized a safari of all the newspaper people in Honolulu to view the property. This trip resulted in extensive and favorable publicity in Honolulu and eventually in the United States and even England. It aroused a great deal of interest among people who wanted to buy the small farms projected in the development. Evidently, however, it aroused very little interest among people who had money to invest in the landholding company.

No record remains to show how long the stock subscription stayed open, or how many shares were subscribed for, but it is clear that the project fell flat. In the 1880s, $800,000 was a great deal of money, especially in capital-starved Hawaii. The projected return—about 18 percent when the property was developed—was not high enough to get prospective investors excited, especially in a time of depression when ready cash could always command a bargain. The Great Land Colonization Scheme stirred up a great deal of public interest and helped to make the name of Dillingham known in Honolulu, but it did nothing to pay the Dillingham creditors.

# CHAPTER 19

*I want him [Charles R. Bishop] and other people to remember that it was once my privilege to have purchased the whole of Honouliuli and Kahuku with all the cattle and horses running thereon for the sum of $600,000, a property which could not be bought today for $5,000,000.00.*

B. F. Dillingham to W. H. Chickering
9 May 1902

IN the Honolulu of 1886, B. F. Dillingham occupied an anomalous position. On the one hand, he was well known as the principal owner of a leading hardware store and of the largest dairy in the kingdom, and as a land developer and the man behind the Great Land Colonization Scheme. Men respected him for his industry and for his practical knowledge on a variety of subjects. Charles R. Bishop sought his advice on the matter of well-digging. He had been invited to Kalakaua's coronation ball in 1883, and he was one of a "committee of 13" selected to plan the opposition to the king's party in the election of 1886. Through his wife he had ties to the missionary families and to the brotherhood of Punahou School. On the other hand, his most zealous efforts in business kept miring him even more deeply in a morass of unpayable debts.

By 1885 Ellie, the widow of Charles Alfred Castle, had remarried on the mainland, but old Mr. Castle continued unabated his efforts on behalf of her and her children. By the end of the year he was writing to Frank Dillingham: "By next mail I must again remit to Ellie. . . . I have advanced all that you are in arrears and must depend on your paying before the next mail." When Frank replied that he was unable to do so, Mr. Castle reminded him that when the Pacific Hardware Company was incorporated in 1884, the heirs of Alfred

Castle were supposed to receive their $37,000 in cash at an early date. "I wanted to help," he said, "and haven't pressed but did expect a prompt payment of the interest. Please send me a careful and accurate statement in writing of the exact position of your affairs and your liability in connection with each of your enterprises. Make it clear so that Ellie can understand it if I send it to her. She may think it strange that you have paid your own family expenses and Mr. Spencer his, when you knew she had no other resources. I have not told her that I was making the advances for you."

At the end of February 1886, Mr. Castle was repeating his demand for a statement, without results. In May he wrote Ellie that he had received no money for more than a year, but he believed that Mr. Dillingham was doing his best. Times were very hard and there had been many failures, but he felt that Mr. Dillingham would pull through. By June he was demanding that Frank pay him $50 every week; $200 to start would be satisfactory. In August he wrote Ellie at length to justify the course he had taken in trying to protect her interests.

Frank, meanwhile, had managed to stave off his creditors with the profits from his land ventures, but he came no closer to success with the one project which would give him a fresh start in life: the Great Land Colonization Scheme. A severe depression, caused by the low price of sugar, continued to plague Hawaii, and it became obvious that money to float such a large enterprise would have to be sought elsewhere. Because of this need for money, Frank Dillingham's affairs became caught up in the sweep of public events in the little kingdom.

In the 1880s, up to 1886, the strange triumvirate of King Kalakaua, Claus Spreckels, and Walter Murray Gibson ruled Hawaii, to their own personal profit and advantage. Spreckels, the sugar king from California, sought many favors from the Hawaiian government; he used his money to place Kalakaua and Gibson in a position where they could hardly refuse his requests. By the beginning of 1886, Spreckels held $700,000 out of a total Hawaiian public debt of about $1.3 million. He was exerting his influence to hold down public spending, but if the kingdom had to have a public debt, Spreckels wanted to control it himself.

At that point one Abraham Hoffnung of London contacted Gibson with the suggestion of floating a Hawaiian loan in London. Hoffnung's firm had for several years been acting as the kingdom's agent for Portuguese immigration. On receiving an indication of interest,

Hoffnung dispatched H. R. Armstrong to Hawaii, representing the firm of Skinner and Company, successors to A. Hoffnung and Company. As the proposed loan would pay off the existing government debt, it ran into strong opposition from Spreckels, who wanted to hold control in his own hands. Kalakaua meanwhile had grown disenchanted with Spreckels, whose crude dictatorial ways were infringing on the prerogatives and dignity of the crown, and threw his support wholeheartedly behind the London loan. In a memorable struggle the Kalakaua forces in the legislature routed the Spreckels interests and voted approval of the loan on Kalakaua's terms. The enraged Spreckels returned the royal orders which Kalakaua had bestowed on him and sailed away to San Francisco, never again to become a political power in Hawaii. By December of 1886 Skinner and Company had floated the loan with huge success; the bonds, or at least the scrip which had been issued to represent the bonds until they could be printed and signed, quickly rose on the London market.

Hawaiian capitalists could hardly fail to read the message: London was the financial center of the world and the place to go when you needed money.

Samuel G. Wilder, already deeply involved in shipping, had bought the Kahului Railroad on Maui from the Thomas H. Hobron family in 1884, and had built the Hawaiian Railroad to connect the port of Mahukona, Hawaii with seven small sugar plantations on the North Kohala coast. Wilder also held a franchise to build a railroad from Hilo, Hawaii, up the Hamakua coast. He controlled the Wilder Steamship Company and had served as minister of the interior and *de facto* premier, but he had no luck in raising locally the $1.8 million he believed necessary for his new railroad scheme. Wilder turned to London as a source of funds. William R. Austin had secured in 1885 and again in 1886 a franchise to build and operate a street railway in Honolulu; the London firm of Skinner and Company was backing the scheme. Franklin H. "Frank" Austin was working on a plan to buy up and consolidate some sugar plantations on Hawaii; he likewise sought help in London. In this atmosphere it is not surprising that the enterprising Frank Dillingham should have cast his eyes in the same direction.

Borrowing $1,000 to pay Emma's way, and leaving the children in the charge of Lowell Smith, Frank left Honolulu in April 1887 bound for the financial capital of the world. On 3 May he left Emma temporarily in Auburndale, Massachusetts, at the home of his cousin Isaac Dillingham, and took ship from New York.

On the eve of his departure from Honolulu, Frank signed a personal financial statement showing assets of $168,000 and liabilities of $123,000, leaving a respectable net worth of $45,000. His liabilities consisted of notes payable totaling $111,000—mostly in fairly small amounts, except for the $37,000 owed to the C. A. Castle estate—and open accounts of $12,000. The joker was in his list of assets. The bulk of them—$130,000—consisted of stocks in companies, mostly Pacific Hardware and Woodlawn Dairy, which would have found little or no market at any price. Frank was simply insolvent.

Mr. Castle had the last word. "Mr. D. Starts for London today," he wrote to Ellie, "under advice of businessmen, to push his scheme. I am less optimistic than many others. Have received only $400 in 25 months. It is due to the hard times. When they will be better, I don't know. We have long looked for it, but sugar is falling lower and lower, and the consequence is, people are driven to the wall themselves, instead of buying from others and helping them."

# CHAPTER 20

*The new constitution has clipped off the King's wings, and put him into pretty close quarters. I hope the London capitalists will now remove the blocks from the wheels of your colonization scheme, and also from Mr. Wilder's railroad scheme and bid you both God speed.*

The Reverend Lowell Smith to B. F. D.
28 July 1887

FRANK Dillingham did not leave for London on an entirely cold scent. He presumably had met H. R. Armstrong, who had helped to negotiate the Hawaiian government loan and who now basked in the title of Hawaiian Consul General in London. He had written to Abraham Hoffnung as early as October 1885. He had been corresponding with Thomas Wallace of Birmingham, who took an interest in his project. W. L. Green of Honolulu, a partner in Theo. H. Davies and Company and a former premier of the kingdom, gave him a letter of introduction to his brother, Joseph Green of London. Thomas May, a sometime resident of Honolulu and a fellow member of the "committee of 13" a year or two before, was living at Banbury, near London. And Colonel Jonathan Austin of Honolulu, an uncle of Frank Austin, had given B. F. a letter to a Colonel James T. Griffin, an American who lived in London and was said to have excellent financial connections.

According to his own fashion, Frank charged into London eager to seize the bull by the horns. We do not know whom he contacted on this first pass, but something evidently went wrong, as he speedily retreated to Thomas Wallace's home in Birmingham, muttering that "the square thing was not being done." Mr. Wallace got him a conference with two lawyers and two chartered accountants. Frank in his outline had put himself down for a promoter's profit of $475,000. One of the lawyers suggested that the scheme might get taken up more quickly if he reduced his immediate amount to $250,000 in cash and preferred stock, with the balance paid in deferred stock which would eventually be retired through excess profits after the preferred stock was earning 10 percent. Frank accepted the suggestion with alacrity. The men also told him frankly that London was the place to find his money. Frank accepted the advice and was back in the capital three days after he had left it, picking up Tom May on the way.

Frank had hit London in the midst of the Jubilee, the celebration of Queen Victoria's fifty years on the throne. The city was thronged with visitors, and the ladies of the night were ready to do their part. The man from Honolulu was amazed. "Well dressed and *sometimes* quite fine looking women, do not hesitate to invite a man on the street, in the evening to take a walk with them. Coming from the Theatre with Tom May one night, I stopped a moment to look into a shop window, and when I turned to go on, *imagine* my astonishment at seeing a woman snuggled up to Tom as close as if she had been his wife! In an instant I took her by the arm, saying you have got my place madam. She looked up in astonishment and said 'most *extraordinary*.' We passed on leaving her behind."

The two gentlemen did taste the more sedate pleasures of the city. Tom took Frank to his tailor, and they went to see the original company of *Ruddigore,* and Sir Henry Irving as Shylock. But business moved slowly, in the British fashion, and after a few preliminary maneuvers Frank retired again to the Wallace home at Birmingham, where he reworked his prospectus and made arrangements for its printing.

Mr. Wallace's sisters had friends in for cards one evening and insisted on his playing. "I soon got the idea," he reported, "and came within one of beating the crowd." The next day the family took him to Church of England services: "a beautiful church and very pleasing service, a good sermon."

But in spite of the pleasant company, Frank was desperately lonely for Emma. He had hardly reached England when he began to look for letters from her. He began to keep a diary—the project lasted for ten days—and filled it mostly with complaints that Emma had not written. According to his own account, he had written Emma on 14 May, then sixteen pages more on the same day, on the seventeenth from Thomas May's home, on the eighteenth nine pages closely written, on the twenty-third ten pages plus a short letter; also from the Windsor Hotel in New York and a postal from Sandy Hook, sent back by the pilot. "If I have *overdone* the thing, I am willing to be pardoned." After two weeks in England he cabled Emma to know whether she was well. "I felt when I cabled that I could not go on with my business much longer, with the interest and care I ought to bestow, without knowing of Emma's welfare and safety." When he received the cabled reply that all was well and three letters on their way, he began to fret that he had not received the letters. On 27 May he waited at the printer's until 7:30 P.M. to get the first copies of his new prospectus, then called in vain at the post office. "No letter from Emma! . . . if accustomed to swear I should certainly say *damn,* or something else."

Back in London by himself, he felt worse. "My social nature," he wrote, "shrinks from all society which would not be tolerated in my home and among my friends."

But suddenly and unaccountably things began to move. Colonel Griffin introduced him to a Mr. Maclean of the New Oriental Bank, and the two men began a serious consideration of Frank's scheme. The answer came with surprising swiftness: Yes, they would float the Great Land Colonization Scheme. The paperwork on the project would take a couple of weeks, and Dillingham would have time for a fine tour of Scotland and Ireland first, or perhaps Paris. Frank rushed to cable Emma, who was still in Massachusetts, to join him.

Frank left London for Ireland on 23 June, "feeling free to breathe the air of heaven." Wilder's bonds were to be marketed on the twenty-eighth and were all spoken for. Hawaiian government bonds were going at a 7 percent premium. But at that moment of near triumph a cloud appeared on the horizon.

Hawaii had no cable at that time; the fastest communication with London was by ship from Honolulu to San Francisco and then by cable. News was slow to come and unreliable. In the middle of June, the London newspapers began to carry stories of shipments of rifles and ammunition to Honolulu, in anticipation of an imminent revolution. The Hawaiians in London scoffed at these stories as obviously untrue. Then a new rumor circulated that the German residents of Honolulu had appealed to the British and American consuls for protection. Maclean of the New Oriental Bank was worried, but decided that the rumor must be false, and promised to cable San Francisco in time for payment of $50,000 in earnest money to be forwarded to James Campbell in Honolulu by the ship sailing on 1 July.

Still walking on air, Frank went to Queenstown, Ireland, to meet Emma, going 12 miles offshore in the tender to greet her. Together they went to Dublin to plan their celebration, and there they found a cable from Colonel Griffin saying that confirmation of the rumor of trouble in Honolulu made it quite impossible to do anything more until it was officially contradicted.

"Really," Frank wrote, "this is the *bitterest* pill I have had to swallow, the most trying experience, the most deadly obstacle."

Giving up their intended tour of the country, Frank and Emma went back to London to study the situation.

The rumors, of course, had been substantially correct. Hawaii had gone through a bloodless revolution. Led by the Hawaiian League, a society dedicated to ending the corruption and extravagance of the Kalakaua–Gibson regime, and backed by the Honolulu Rifles, the only effective military force in the kingdom, a group of citizens took control of Honolulu. On 28 June Kalakaua beat a strategic retreat by dumping Gibson and his colleagues, and on 1 July he appointed W. L. Green to form a new cabinet. Reform was firmly in the saddle, and on 7 July Kalakaua found himself obliged to promulgate a new constitution which stripped him of most of his cherished royal powers.

When he first heard news of unrest in Honolulu, Frank called it a "useless, senseless squabble which I am afraid will never amount to anything but empty words." But when news came of Gibson's overthrow and subsequently of the new constitution, he was delighted. "It is better under the present situation to let David [Kalakaua] be a figurehead, or blockhead (which he is) . . . the native Hawaiian is not yet ripe for a good republican form of government." He set about to write his friends in Honolulu, starting with S. N. Castle, begging them to cable assurances of firm government to reassure the London financiers.

The extent of Frank's emotional involvement with his scheme can best be gauged from a letter he wrote to James G. Spencer at a time when the issue still hung in doubt. "I have felt *very keenly* at times," he wrote, "the remarks that have been made about me and my 'wild goose scheme.' I have been *bound* to *succeed* if I *died* in the effort, not for the *profit alone* (which is by *no* means to be despised by one in my financial position) but to prove that *I* was not the fool." Citing the enthusiasm he had aroused and the compliments he had received on how well he had worked up the scheme, he felt that he was now vindicated. "I shall not be cast down *now* if I fail for I have *tried* to do my *duty*, and I do not *now* see what *more* I could have done."

For a while it appeared that he would not fail, in spite of the bloodless revolution. Dispatches from Honolulu told of peace and quiet, of firm government in the hands of well-known, responsible men. Confidence began to return in London. Wilder, who had been left waiting at the church door in June, became bold enough to give his group of financiers an ultimatum: Come up with the money now or I shall turn my proposition over to Dillingham's group.

But fate had one more cruel trick to play on Wilder and Dillingham.

The reform government in Honolulu began looking more closely at the London loan, and were appalled at what they saw. A loan of approximately a million dollars had cost the government more than $200,000, exclusive of interest, and of this amount $75,000 was entirely unaccounted for. Moreover the loan had been negotiated in English pounds, although the loan act specified payment in United States dollars. A new loan bill would be necessary to cure the defect, and the legislature would not meet again until September. Meanwhile, the Britishers who had bought bonds and paid for them were still holding the scrip which they had received in place of the bonds. According to the rules of the London Stock Exchange, if the bonds were not delivered before the end of the year, the issue would automatically be delisted, which would certainly bring a drastic drop in their market value.

In Honolulu an uproar arose over the apparent swindling of the government in the bond issue. Gibson by this time was in a sanitarium in San Francisco; in his absence the newspapers and politicians went after Armstrong and Hoffnung and Skinner and Company. Some men declared that Hawaii should repudiate the loan entirely, others that she should merely refuse to pay the part represented by the missing $75,000. Obviously such statements had no reasonable basis; the British public had invested in good faith, and Hawaii's recourse ran against the agents, not the bondholders. No responsible voice in the government advocated repudiation. But the loose talk was enough to create a minipanic in London.

Samuel G. Wilder, who failed as a sugar grower but made a fortune in shipping and railroads. Wilder undoubtedly enhanced Dillingham's knowledge and appreciation of railroads when the two were together in London in 1887. (Bishop Museum photo)

Wilder was still pressing for an answer, and had been told that he could have his money if no disturbing news arrived by the ship which was to reach San Francisco on 8 August. The London newspapers of the ninth were full of "repudiation"; one man alone backed out of a commitment to take £50,000 in Wilder's bonds. "Wilder was a pretty sick looking man last night you may be sure," wrote B. F. "I shall succeed before I return, but oh! the delay is enough to drive one less cool, quite mad. I am calm as a clock compared with poor Wilder!"

On the other side of the world, the Reverend Lowell Smith had loving thoughts of Emma and Frank. "I think it is wisely ordered," he wrote, "that you, Emma, are with Frank during this time of suspense." On 12 August he reported a splendid camping trip:

> Only Mr. Langley, Guss, Mr. Frear, May, Walter, Miss Sorenson and one or two boys of Walter's age, all left us on the 3rd. inst. on a camping party. They left at midnight, full moon, Tuesday night, all on

horseback except Mr. Langley. He had a two horse carriage, load of provisions, boxes, pails, food cooked and uncooked, and a large tent on top of all the rest and set off for Waialua. At 8 a.m. May telephoned that they had arrived safely at Waialua, but they returned about four miles and found a place near a stream of water and a place to graze their horses and pitched their tent or tabernacle.

August 5th your mail arrived from London, so when they telephoned to us we told them that a long journal from Emma and a joint letter to Walter from his parents had come to hand. Having some wants that could not be supplied in the country, Walter and one of his mates came to town and got the mail and filled their saddle bags with provisions at the grocers and returned as far as Ewa and spent the night, and on up to their tent the next morning. Yesterday Mr. Langley rode 4 miles to a telephone and reported to his wife that they were all well, having a good time, and that they were coming home tomorrow, Saturday, the 13th. "Variety is the spice of life." May and Guss will tell you all about how they enjoyed dwelling in a tent, camping down on the hard earth, riding their horses by day, bathing, talking, laughing, etc. etc.

May, who was seventeen at the time, unquestionably enjoyed the trip very much indeed, since one of the other campers was Walter Frear, age twenty-three. Frear had returned from Yale to teach at Punahou, where May was known as the brightest student in the school. Soon their obvious interest in each other became something of a joke on campus. It may well have been on this camping trip that they became engaged, because Frank was soon writing to her to give his approval of bringing another Walter into the family.

Engagement, of course, did not mean an early marriage. May had set her heart on going to college, and Frear was to study law. Their wedding finally took place six years later, in 1893.

Griffin blew hot and cold. On 21 August he wrote Frank from Lucerne that he had full confidence in him and Wilder, but could do no more for the present. Wilder sailed for home, leaving his scheme in Frank's hands; Frank and Mr. Wallace saw him off at Southampton. By the twenty-seventh Griffin was optimistic again, and on 9 September he authorized Frank to cable Wilder to expect a definite proposition cabled to San Francisco to reach him about the eleventh, but nothing came of it.

The pressure began to tell on Frank. To keep busy he began to buy

Christmas merchandise for the Pacific Hardware Company. Then Mr. Wallace put him on the track of something called the Transparent Wire-Wove Roofing Company, and he talked himself into an exclusive franchise for the entire United States. Finally he took Emma sightseeing, visiting Oxford, Kenilworth Castle, Warwick Castle, and Stratford.

Admitting defeat was not Frank's nature, but he finally and reluctantly decided that he could no longer remain in England. He gave Colonel Griffin his power of attorney to finance his project and sailed for America on 15 October, five months after he arrived in England.

# CHAPTER 21

*If there is any one thing in the world that cannot be done in a hurry, it is to raise money.*

B. F. D.
27 June 1902

No other development of the nineteenth century so caught the imagination of America as the railroad. The railroad became the symbol of power, of riches, of commerce, of adventure, of romance. All over America small boys went to sleep to the sound of a locomotive whistle, and dreamt of the far lands where the train would one day take them.

In 1859 Frank Dillingham sailed from Boston to San Francisco on the *Southern Cross* by way of Cape Horn. When Emma and her family went from Honolulu to New England in 1865, they were able to eliminate several thousand miles by crossing the Isthmus of Panama. But when Frank and Emma journeyed to London and back in 1887, they crossed the United States with comparative speed and comfort by railroad; the golden spike had been driven at Promontory, Utah eighteen years earlier. By 1887 the oldest railroad in America had been running for sixty years, and the whole country was bound together by bands of iron stretching from the Atlantic to the Pacific and from Canada to Mexico.

But railroads came late to Hawaii. Not until 1879 did Waiakea Mill near Hilo, Hawaii, become the first plantation to use a steam locomotive to haul cane. In the same year Thomas H. Hobron opened the Kahului and Wailuku Railroad on Maui, the first common carrier or public utility railroad in Hawaii.

Public railroads in Hawaii might have been further delayed if the legislature of 1878 had not passed a Railway Act providing for their charter with broad powers of eminent domain. Samuel G. Wilder, as minister of the interior (and *de facto* premier), helped to make this act become law. The legislature of 1880 amended this act to provide a subsidy; the day after he signed the amendment, Kalakaua dismissed Wilder's cabinet, leaving Wilder free to pursue his pet project: a railroad on the island of Hawaii.

Wilder chose a most unlikely place to start: the miniscule, bone-dry, windswept port of Mahukona, on the northwest coast. There Wilder's interisland steamers tied up at offshore buoys, while passengers and freight were lightered ashore. From this desolate jumping-off spot, where even the water for the locomotive boilers had to be brought from Honolulu, Wilder drove his little railroad mile after tortuous mile around the northern tip of the island, until by the beginning of 1883 he had completed his 20 miles of railroad almost to the impassable valley of Pololu. Along the way the road passed seven tiny plantations and sugar mills. It boasted one straight stretch of track half a mile long; the rest of the line consisted of curve after curve, and passenger trains averaged about 10 miles an hour. The sharpest curve had an incredible radius of 81 feet; as one newspaperman wrote: "the hind carriage can shake hands with the locomotive and chaff the engineer."

In 1883 King Kalakaua honored the railroad by riding in a special train from Mahukona to Hawi for the dedication of the statue of Kamehameha. A contemporary account notes that the king and his chamberlain returned to Mahukona on horseback.

The locomotive *Kinau* hitched to three "Kalakaua cars" at Mahukona on the northwest coast of Hawaii. They were called Kalakaua cars because the king had ridden in one of them in 1883. Sam Wilder's little railroad provided a valuable service to the district of Kohala. (Photo by A. A. Montano, Bishop Museum)

But in spite of all the difficulties of terrain and the extreme thrift with which Wilder had built his road, the Hawaiian Railroad Company did provide a needed service for the people of North Kohala. Soon the railroad, together with the Wilder Steamship Company, enjoyed a practical monopoly of freight in and out of the region, and was making a modest profit. According to Wilder's own figures, 20 miles of railroad, fully equipped, cost him about $227,500 net after subsidy, and in the early years returned an annual profit of about $20,000. Of course Wilder also profited from his related steamship and merchandising activities.

In 1884 Wilder bought the Kahului Railroad, thus becoming the owner of both public railroads in the kingdom.

Having cut his teeth on the Kohala line, Wilder set out after bigger game. The original charter of his railroad had proposed to extend the line from Mahukona to Kawaihae and from there through Waimea to Honokaa and Laupahoehoe. Wilder at that time believed that a railroad could not be built from Hilo to Laupahoehoe. By 1886, however, he realized that Hilo was the only real harbor on the island, and he had become convinced from his experience in Kohala that he could build from Hilo up through the Hamakua coast. He had come to appreciate, moreover, the tremendous size and fertility of the Hilo and Hamakua districts, as compared with Kohala. In January of 1886 he completed a quite detailed prospectus for a railroad from Hilo to Kukuihaele, together with wharves at Hilo and a merchandising, shipping, and banking business, for a total investment of $1,800,000 including $200,000 to take over the existing line in Kohala. He estimated the cost of the new railroad, fully equipped together with three wharves in Hilo, at $1,115,800. The basic line of reasoning behind his prospectus was the same used by B. F. Dillingham when he built north from Hilo some twenty-five years later.

Wilder failed to obtain his money in Honolulu and New York, but a trip to London early in 1887 produced promises of support from Abraham Hoffnung and Skinner and Company, subject to engineers' verification of the statements in his prospectus. Wilder returned to Hilo in April 1887, with two railway engineers, who rendered a favorable report to London. Thus it happened that Wilder was back in London to conclude his deal when the revolution of 1887 broke out in Honolulu.

Wilder and Dillingham had little contact in London when things were going well for both of them, but through the dreadful days of

July and August they were brought together by their shared anxiety. When Wilder left for Honolulu near the end of August, he entrusted his scheme to Frank Dillingham to carry through in his absence. Undoubtedly the two men spent many hours discussing each other's projects.

Up to this point Frank Dillingham had thought largely in terms of increasing the value of the Campbell land through subdivision and irrigation. The prospectus of the Great Land Colonization Scheme made no provision for money to build a railroad. It is logical to suppose that Frank's talks with Wilder opened his eyes in this direction. By 15 July he was writing that "it is not my proposition to have the (rail) road taken up independent of the rest of the scheme. The land is essential to the success of the road, and the road is very *important,* tho' not *absolutely* essential to the financial success of the landed interests." And when Frank finally left London, he gave Colonel Griffin a power of attorney to represent his interests not only with regard to the land and colonization scheme but also "the twenty miles of railroad which I proposed to build on the Island of Oahu." Clearly, Frank's horizons were widening from a purely land-development scheme to one in which a railroad would play a major part.

The first half of 1888 must have been a particularly miserable time for Frank Dillingham. He and Emma had returned at the end of November 1887 in time for a late Thanksgiving, but when the joy of the family reunion wore off Frank had to face the fact that his mission had failed.

Frank never quit without a fight, however. Wilder on his return to Honolulu had persuaded James Campbell to give Dillingham a "final" extension of his option to the end of 1887, but before the end of the year Frank had talked Campbell into another extension to 1 April 1888. The ship on which Frank had returned to Honolulu in November 1887 had brought news of President Cleveland's ratification of a "supplementary convention" to the Reciprocity Treaty, which extended the treaty for seven years and also gave the United States "the exclusive right to enter the harbor of Pearl River in the island of Oahu, and to establish and maintain there a coaling and repair station for the vessels of the United States." This Pearl Harbor concession actually meant nothing, because it terminated with the life of the treaty itself, and the United States would never under these circumstances have spent the large sum necessary to dredge a channel through the Pearl Harbor bar. Nevertheless the concession did focus attention on Pearl Harbor as a center of real estate speculation and it made Frank Dillingham nervous that Campbell would raise the price of his option.

Frank continued to write Colonel Griffin in London—he could not afford to let his friends in Honolulu think that the scheme was completely dead—but even his great spirit faltered at times. "It is going on three years since I started working on this scheme," he wrote. "I am growing weary."

Mr. Castle obviously felt the same way. In January he wrote Frank: "I trust you will be able to settle the whole of the balance of interest in a few days. I note from the papers you have bought McCully [Judge Lawrence McCully, owner of Pawaa Dairy, near Woodlawn]. I hope this is a good move, and that the Colonization Scheme will bring you a good income. What news do you get? I wish you to send me a statement of your assets and liabilities, and how secure. . . ."

"I cannot possibly comply with your request," Frank replied, but he promised another payment at the earliest possible moment. Yes, he continued, it was true that Woodlawn Dairy had bought the Pawaa Dairy, but the Honorable William R. Castle would bear out his view that Woodlawn Dairy could not afford to let Pawaa Dairy pass into other hands. He should hear very soon of the floating of the Colonization Scheme. Colonel James G. Griffin is taking up his scheme, Wilder's, and Frank Austin's all at the same time.

By February, Mr. Castle was confiding to his son Will that "if this mail does not bring a favorable answer [from London], we shall be compelled to resort to some other measures." In March he wrote to Ellie: "Have rec'd from Mr. D $250 and hope to get more soon. Have on the whole sent about twice what Mr. D. has paid to me. I hope he gets good news from London. If not, I fear bankruptcy might follow and leave no dividend or very little, if stocks and debts due were closed under pressure. And I still owe the $13,000 borrowed to buy out Mr. Dimond."

In May he wrote Ellie again: "Have received nothing from Mr. D. He continues to receive encouragement from London. I hope his hopes are not in vain. I earnestly hope Mr. D. will pull through. I think I hold all the security it is in his power to give, and any attempt to collect by force will be at the sacrifice of nearly every dollar, while the course I am pursuing I hope will ultimately save what is due Alfred's heirs, as well as the $13,000. . . . I rather think he will not fail. . . . will probably hear from London in June or July."

Meanwhile, Frank had been as busy as usual. "I have talked up the importance of having a paper," he wrote on his return from London, "to enlighten the world about this little spot of dust, and the result is a paper called the Paradise of the Pacific. . . . Thousands of copies go abroad on this steamer all over the world." Since the first issue carried a strong plug for his Great Land Colonization Scheme, in connection with the treaty renewal and prospective opening of Pearl Harbor, it is quite possible that he did inspire the founding of this magazine.

Other ventures were aimed at making money. On his way home he had looked up Walter Murray Gibson, who was dying of tuberculosis in a San Francisco hospital, and obtained from him a purchase option on most of the island of Lanai. Frank disapproved completely of Gibson's politics, but he was perfectly willing to do business with him. His best efforts, however, never located a purchaser, though he wrote, "This Island could be made a *lovely* place for tourists, or an exclusive English Colony, or the Isle of Wight of the Pacific."

Likewise, Frank's franchise for Transparent Wire-Wove Roofing never resulted in anything more substantial than a sidewalk awning covered with the stuff in front of the Pacific Hardware Company store.

And still no word from London. "We wait from month to month," Emma wrote, "for the mail to bring us news of success to Frank's enterprise, but still we wait in vain. The strain is hard."

# CHAPTER 22

*Power and authority are hereby given to the Minister of the Interior . . . to contract with B. F. Dillingham, his associates and successors and their assigns, or such corporation as shall be formed or organized by him or them under the laws of this Kingdom, providing for the establishment of private corporations for the constructing and operating on the Island of Oahu a steam railroad or railroads of not less than 3 feet gauge, for the carriage of passengers and freight.*

An Act to Authorize and Promote the Construction of Steam Railroads on the Island of Oahu. 1888.

AT some time during this difficult period, Frank came to the perfectly reasonable conclusion that he could not afford to wait for action from London. His option from Campbell expired on 1 April, and he did not immediately secure another extension. London in any event was a long way off, and there were disquieting indications that the financing of all the Hawaiian schemes might be blocked by squabbles among the London promoters. Circumstances forced Frank to look closer to home for a solution to his problems. Stymied in his attempts to develop the Campbell lands, he turned to the Pearl River railroad project as his way out.

Frank realized, however, that in order to raise money for such a project and profit by it personally, he would have to control something at least potentially valuable, just as he had held an option to purchase the Campbell lands for nearly three years. This time he turned to politics as the means to accomplish his ends.

On 29 May the regular legislative session of 1888 opened. Nine days later William R. Castle, who had won election as a noble the previous year, introduced a bill "to authorize and promote the construction of steam railroads on the island of Oahu."

Castle's bill went far beyond the general Railway Act of 1878 in that it specifically empowered the minister of the interior "to contract with B. F. Dillingham, his associates and successors and their assigns, or such corporation as shall be formed and organized by him or them under the laws of this Kingdom . . . for constructing and operating on the Island of Oahu a steam railroad or railroads of not less than three feet gauge, for the carriage of passengers and freight." The bill allowed B. F. Dillingham eighteen months in which to give "satisfactory guarantees" to the government that he would build a steam railroad to connect Honolulu with Pearl River lagoon within three years of the passage of the bill; he would have exclusive rights to whatever territory (excluding Honolulu) the railroad covered within three years. The bill provided for tax exemption for a period not exceeding twenty years on property necessary to the operation of the railroad, but no subsidy.

After first reading the bill was sent to committee.

Regardless of its merits, the fact that this rather extraordinary bill gained serious consideration was due to a combination of circumstances at the time.

The Reform Party, which amounted pretty much to an extension of the Hawaiian League which had forced the new constitution on Kalakaua, had swept the election of 1887 and completely dominated the legislature. Its backbone consisted of American businessmen and sugar planters. B. F. Dillingham not only shared their outlook and interests, but he had actually served on the committee which started the reform movement in 1886. He could at least expect a respectful hearing from members of the party.

With regard to encouragement of railroads in general, this was already well-accepted public policy in Hawaii and met with little opposition from any quarter. When it came to giving an exclusive franchise to B. F. Dillingham, controversy was inevitable.

But B. F. had another source of strength. He not only stood well with Will Castle and Lorrin A. Thurston and others who were leading the government, but he had friends on the other side of the fence as well. He had an inborn courtesy and—especially in his younger days—an uncommon quality of disagreeing without offending. Also, he had been far away during the crisis of 1887 when tempers ran high. He had remained friendly with Kalakaua, and he was generally popular with the Hawaiians, who responded to his warmth and enthusiasm. In the days ahead he would need all the strength he could muster.

As it happened, Frank could point to a direct and recent precedent for granting an exclusive franchise to an individual. The legislatures of 1885 and 1886 had granted to William R. Austin the exclusive right to build and operate a street railway in Honolulu. Austin had assigned his franchise to the Hawaii Tramways Company, Ltd., an English concern, which had given a contract to build the line to Skinner and Company of London. As the legislature met, Skinner and Company, represented by an engineer named T. Graham Gribble, was even then starting construction of the tracks.

On 11 July, four days after the introduction of Castle's bill, the legislature took a day off for a cruise to Pearl Harbor on Mark P. Robinson's side-wheeler *Ewa,* whose draft was shallow enough to pass over the bar at the mouth of Pearl Harbor. Feature of the day was a grand *luau* at the old Robinson homestead near Waipahu. In view of his long and close association with Robinson, B. F. undoubtedly had a hand in this affair, with the idea of showing the legislators the benefits of a railroad to that part of the country.

But on 7 August the committee handling Castle's bill dropped a bombshell: in place of the Dillingham bill, it brought in a new Oahu railroad bill which left out both the Dillingham name and the exclusive feature of the proposal.

Immediately it came out that the committee owed its change of heart to the urgings of T. Graham Gribble, who proposed on behalf of the tramway company to build a steam railroad to Pearl Harbor as an extension of the street railway, without subsidy and without an exclusive franchise.

Luckily for Frank, Gribble lacked common sense and good manners. In defending his project in the public press, Gribble managed to antagonize local businessmen by declaring that "thus far no capitalist here has ventured to risk one dollar either in the Tramway or the Oahu railway. The domestic investments made in those directions appear to be largely composed of vituperative epithets and self-laudation." And try as he might, Gribble could not disassociate himself from Skinner and Company and from H. R. Armstrong, who the leaders of the legislature believed had defrauded Hawaii out of $75,000 on the London bond issue.

Frank Dillingham restated his belief that domestic capital should build the road, and denied the rumor that he intended to sell the franchise. "I have already arranged with good reliable residents of this country, men of capital and landed estate, to form a company here, for the purpose of carrying out at least a part of my long-cherished enterprise."

The *Pacific Commercial Advertiser* was less restrained, stating that the committee's bill would open the way for foreign monopolists —that is, Skinner and Company.

At this juncture, with the issue very much in doubt, Dillingham received strong public backing from Charles A. Brown. Brown (known to his friends as "Cabby," from his initials) had married Irene Ii, the only child of John Papa Ii, a high *ali'i* and staunch supporter of the early missionaries. Through her, Brown controlled the immense estate of Waipio, including Waipio Peninsula in Pearl Harbor. Brown's prestige with the Hawaiians was thought to be immense.

The decisive vote came on 20 August, when the legislature sent both bills back to committee with instructions to report out the version favorable to Dillingham. A considerable number of *haole* legislators voted against the Dillingham bill, but it received solid support from the Hawaiians.

A little more oratory remained, but the issue was settled. On 4 September, Frank's forty-fourth birthday, the original bill passed third reading and was sent to Kalakaua for signature.

Frank Dillingham was gratified, but he preferred to live in the future rather than gloat over the past. "One year from today" [or words to that effect], he told his friends, "I will give you all a ride on my new railroad."

One sad event of the summer perhaps diminished Frank's joy at his triumph. At the end of July his friend and mentor Sam Wilder had died at the age of 57, following a stroke. Frank believed that Wilder's failure in London had hastened his end, and for years he pointed to Wilder's disappointments as an example of why it was necessary to establish an international market for Hawaiian securities.

On 9 August, when the railroad issue was hanging fire in the legislature, Frank wrote to Mr. Castle to thank him for some fatherly advice. "God knows I am trying to do what I can," he added, "not to be rich or great in this world, but to pay my just debts. Oh I have prayed God that your life might be spared to see me out of debt."

Mr. Castle has left no record of what he thought of this reason for his continued longevity.

At first glance, and in the light of his future career, Frank's statement seems unbelievable or even laughable. But taken in the context of his circumstances at the time, it begins to make sense. Frank was no hypocrite, though he was a great salesman. He did have an emotional nature and lived his experiences very intensely. Undoubtedly, he did feel at the moment he wrote Mr. Castle that he was aiming not at becoming rich or great in the world but at paying his just debts.

# CHAPTER 23

*Your withdrawal was damaging in the extreme and cost me no little hard work and much delay. A man of less backbone than Robinson would have followed your example, which would have killed the scheme dead as far as home capital was concerned.*

B. F. D. to C. A. Brown
11 April 1889

ON 11 September 1888 Kalakaua signed Dillingham's railroad bill, and Frank had what he needed to launch his project: a definite and exclusive legal right which represented a potential value and which could serve as his investment to control the enterprise. Having no money, Frank used his own time, effort, brains, imagination, experience, powers of persuasion, and fighting heart as substitutes for capital.

Actually, all he needed to be in business—aside from money—was a survey, a right-of-way, road bed, bridges, trestles, track, fencing, cattle guards, locomotives, cars, stations, shops, tools, machinery, turntables, engine houses, car sheds, warehouses, coal, water, supplies a telephone system, trained employees . . . and some freight and passengers.

Compared to the railroad that Mr. Wilder built in Kohala or the one he planned from Hilo to Hamakua, Frank's project must have seemed either visionary or foolhardy. Wilder went into districts already developed enough to support a railroad and offered a service far superior to what they had. Frank planned to open up a whole new district and make its economy thrive on account of the railroad. The satirist who described the Oahu railway as ''starting nowhere and ending up a tree'' was really not far shy of the mark.

Oahu in 1888 produced little sugar. At the eastern end of the

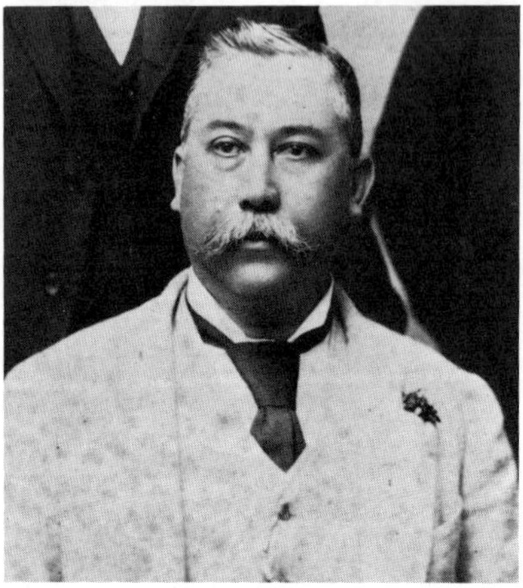

Mark P. Robinson, heir to family estates in the Ewa region, backed Frank Dillingham's railroad plans by putting extensive properties into the O. R. and L. in exchange for stocks and bonds. He served as treasurer of the O. R. and L. for many years and remained a close associate of Frank Dillingham until the failure of the Puna Sugar Company soured their relationship. (Bishop Museum photo)

island, John A. Cummins lived in lordly style on Waimanalo Plantation; near the opposite end Hermann Widemann had the Waianae Sugar Company. In between were tiny sugar mills at Kaneohe, Heeia, and Laie, and the Halstead Mill at Waialua. All of these plantations were small scale. The sugar they produced was carried in longboats to schooners or small steamers lying offshore and then taken to Honolulu for reshipment.

The Pearl Harbor area produced no sugar at all. Chinese planters grew considerable rice around the northern edge of the harbor, where water gushed out of the ground in great streams and provided not only irrigation but also power to run the Waiawa rice mill, Aki's mill at Kalauao, and Ah In's at Aiea. Mark Robinson and others grew bananas for export, and Hawaiians raised taro for local consumption wherever the ground was wet enough. The great dry plains of Ewa produced nothing but cattle and firewood.

Such was the territory into which B. F. Dillingham proposed to drive his railroad.

Kalakaua's signing of the railroad bill signaled the start of a year and a half of frenetic activity during which B. F. Dillingham changed the map of Oahu forever.

From all indications, Dillingham had no real plan for financing the railroad when he was seeking the franchise. His statement that "I have already arranged with good reliable residents of this country, men of capital and landed estate, to form a company," probably meant only that he had had preliminary talks with some of his friends. His usual method of operation was to put off decisions until they became necessary, to think on his feet, and to examine a situation from all sides before committing himself.

His first interest had always been in land, and he still saw land as the key to making a go of the railroad. James Campbell had gone on an extended trip, and anyway he still wanted cash for his property; Frank put that project aside for the time being and concentrated on other possibilities.

The Ewa district had two other great landholders besides Campbell: Cabby Brown and Mark Robinson. Both proved receptive to Frank's gospel of building a railroad which would multiply the value of their holdings.

The Ii lands controlled by Brown—about 18,000 acres in fee simple—stretched from Waipio Peninsula in Pearl Harbor far up into the great central plateau behind the Koolau Mountains. Mark Robinson, from the Robinson homestead between Hoaeae and Waipahu, managed the family estate surrounding it, and also lands which he personally held in leasehold at Waiau, Waiawa, and Waimano-uka and in fee simple at Manana and Waimano.

Evidently Frank's thoughts revolved first around the Ii lands. A month after getting the franchise he made a proposition to Brown under which Brown would put into a new corporation the bulk of the Ii lands, at a valuation of $250,000, payable with $50,000 in cash and $200,000 in stock or bonds of the corporation. Frank would receive $100,000 for his franchise, presumably in stock, and Mark Robinson would get $75,000 for his lease lands and cattle, payable with $30,000 in cash and the balance in stock or bonds. From the sale of bonds, $300,000 cash was budgeted to build and equip the 15 miles of railroad.

According to Frank's later account, Cabby Brown stated publicly that he was going in with Dillingham on the project, but Frank never succeeded in bringing him to the point of committing himself in

Charles A. "Cabby" Brown, who through his wife, Irene Ii, controlled the valuable lands of Waipio. Frank Dillingham flew into a rage when Brown failed to back his plans for a railroad, but later buried the hatchet when he needed part of Waipio to form the Oahu Sugar Company. (Photo by Taber, Bishop Museum)

writing. By 26 October Frank had grown tired of Brown's "unbusinesslike procrastination," as he put it, and demanded an answer by noon the next day. Brown complained that Frank had not given him time to consult Colonel Spalding on Kauai and said that he could not give an answer within the deadline. Frank broke off negotiations.

Mark Robinson meanwhile had evidently agreed to the scheme which Frank had presented to Brown. Brown's withdrawal left Robinson as the financial kingpin in the enterprise, and a new scheme of course became necessary. Apparently Robinson and Dillingham did not reach a final definite agreement until the end of the year, but Robinson meanwhile gave Frank to understand that he would back the project wholeheartedly.

The total uncertainty as to money and corporate structure did not deter Frank from taking the first steps toward building the railroad. Obviously, first of all he needed to know just where the railroad would run, and for that survey he required a more experienced engineer than Hawaii could produce at the time.

About a week after gaining the franchise, Frank wrote to an old friend, George E. Wilhoit in Stockton, California, to ask him to find an experienced railway engineer. Wilhoit knew a man for the job who proved to be unavailable but who recommended instead Charles H. Kluegel. Fortunately, Kluegel was available, and by November was surveying the line from Honolulu to what became Pearl City. The work took him sixteen weeks and four days, at a total cost to Frank Dillingham of $1,856.28. It proved to be the beginning of a long association between Dillingham and Kluegel.

(In 1931 George P. Denison, then general manager of the Oahu Railway and Land Company, wrote that "Kluegel also did a great deal of engineering work for the other railways and for a number of the plantations either in new construction work or in betterments, so that a very large percentage of the railroad mileage of the Islands had the benefit of his splendid engineering ability.")

Kluegel did not approve of all the compromises adopted in locating the line. Looking at the problem as an engineer, he wanted to run the line from Honolulu *makai* ("by the sea") along the Palama rice fields, but Frank overruled him on the grounds that by going inland close to the government road (King Street) they would pick up more traffic. Frank also found it necessary to compromise with J. S. McGrew at Aiea and later with Cabby Brown at Waipio, who objected to Kluegel's survey line. The new railroad would have the power of eminent domain, once it was organized, but an unhappy landowner could stall progress indefinitely. Kluegel was right, as an engineer; over the years the line was gradually straightened to eliminate the difficulties he complained of. But Frank got the line built.

Even before sending for Kluegel, Frank had decided on three-foot gauge for the track. This was the width used by narrow-gauge railroads in the western United States; it would serve the purpose and would save substantial amounts as compared with a standard-gauge (4 feet 8½ inch) road.

When he had finished laying out the line, Kluegel estimated the cost of construction and equipment for 15 miles of first-class railroad, three-foot gauge, at $241,000, or just a little more than $16,000 a mile—"a full and safe estimate," he called it.

As fast as Kluegel surveyed the line, Dillingham followed up with letters to the landholders through whose properties it passed, asking for right-of-way. Luckily for him, most of the line went through a few large estates, limiting the number of parties with whom he had to deal, but what the landowners lacked in numbers they made up in obstinacy. Frank later called this acquisition of right-of-way "the most tedious and disagreeable task I ever undertook to perform, to get right of way where on to build the line. With few notable exceptions I have been compelled to pay for right of way several times the value of the land, to avoid a law suit and injunction being served to stop the progress of the road. The idea of some landowners in this country seems to be that a railroad company ought to cover the ground they take with twenty dollar gold pieces for having the privilege of increasing the value of land and making its owners rich."

At the same time that he was sending for a civil engineer, Frank was preparing to procure the cars, rails, and especially the locomotives he would need. He had decided on a pair of "American" (4-4-0) type engines (that is, engines having four pilot wheels in front, followed by four driving wheels, with no trailing wheels under the cab), made by the famous Baldwin works in Philadelphia: one 12½-ton and one 14-ton. In an effort to get the best price, he wrote to two agents as well as direct to the factory, but he did not actually place the order for six months, presumably because it required hard cash which he did not have.

He also wrote about rails for his road, and found that he could get the best price by ordering from Germany through H. Hackfeld and Company. By pledging half of his franchise as security and offering a commission of 2½ percent in stock, he induced Mark Robinson to guarantee payment of the order, and then after lengthy negotiations on prices and terms he pressured Hackfeld into accepting $5,000 in railroad bonds in part payment. By 19 December he wrote Will Castle that the rails were ordered and the road would be running in six months.

Meanwhile he was using his position as a potential buyer to try to lure investors into the railroad, starting with Samuel C. Allen. Sam Allen was one of the very richest men in Honolulu, in a class with Charles R. Bishop and Samuel N. Castle. He owned the lumber firm of Allen and Robinson, in which Mark Robinson had formerly been a partner, and was married to Mark's sister Bathsheba. In September of 1888 he was in San Francisco; Frank wrote him that Lewers and Cooke would take a good slice of the railroad bonds, but they wanted the lumber and supplies business in return. Frank wanted Sam to have the "inside track" on the "lumber racket." Allen replied that he would take some bonds if he could make some business out of it.

In answer to a question of Frank's, he added: "I do not believe you can do much with Jim Campbell. He is a hard nut to deal with and wants all the cake himself. He should assist you all he can, as it is for his interest to do so."

By the end of the year Frank decided to try C. Brewer and Company. He asked P. C. Jones of that firm to serve as president of the railroad and to help float the bond issue, offering to pay a 10 percent commission in stock, either to him personally or to his firm, if he would sell $100,000 in bonds. Joseph O. Carter replied for C. Brewer that they considered it unwise to enter into a business so entirely new to and so little understood by their directors.

To make it easier to raise money, Frank sought to sign freight contracts with the Chinese rice millers. A. H. Loo Ngawk, of Aki's Mill, replied bluntly that no Chinese would sign a freight contract, and Sing Chong and Company added that they would ship the cheapest way.

On another front Frank was more successful. After tortuous negotiations he managed to buy, in Mark Robinson's name and with Mark's money, 75 acres of the Manana Peninsula in Pearl Harbor for $50 an acre. (Another 145 acres were added the following year.) Rechristened Pearl City Peninsula, this land was to play an important part in his development schemes over the next several years.

Dillingham evidently cut Robinson in on a quick profit on this land, as the 75 acres ended up on the railroad company books at $200 per acre. Robinson received $12,500 for his share and Frank $2,500.

In spite of all obstacles and setbacks, Frank's year ended in a blaze of hope and solid achievement. On Christmas Eve he wrote to Mark Robinson: "My dear friend—I take the occasion at this season to send you a little token of my esteem, a slight expression of the gratitude I feel for you for your kindness, sympathy and solid support, and cheerful cooperation with me in my land and railroad scheme which has occupied so much of my time and thoughts during the past 3½ years. Now no one but God himself knows what disappointments I have experienced, what discouragements I have had to endure during those long many years. I feel sure of success now and I want to assure you of my most hearty appreciation."

One week later, on the last day of the year, Frank was writing to Mark again, this time to confirm the details of the agreement which they had finally made. Mark had committed himself to put into the railway company, in exchange for stock and bonds, 2,010 acres in fee simple at $25 an acre, a paid-up lease from the Bishop Estate for twenty years on 18,000 acres, one thousand head of cattle and fifty horses, 45,000 *'ōhi'a* railroad ties, and the steamer *Ewa.* At least in Frank's mind, the success of the railroad company was now assured.

# CHAPTER 24

*We are having splendid weather this month . . . for the 150 men who are making a rail road to Pearl Harbor. Frank says the ties and rails are now laid about 1/2 mile per day and engineers say it is a good substantial road. He seems to be very happy superintending the work.*

The Reverend Lowell Smith
22 October 1889

IT was time for Frank to organize his company, so that he could go to the public for money. He had already entered into a contract with Minister of the Interior Lorrin A. Thurston, as authorized by the Oahu Railway Act; now he and Mark Robinson applied for a charter for the company, which Thurston issued to them on 4 February 1889.

This charter ran for fifty years, provided for an original capitalization of $700,000 increasable to $5 million, and empowered the corporation not only to build and operate a railroad but also to purchase, own, develop, sell, lease, and otherwise deal in lands ''along and near the line or lines of the railway . . . for the purpose of inducing the settlement of population along or near said line.'' The charter, however, limited the right to acquire and deal in lands ''to such lands as shall be at the date of this charter of an agricultural, pastoral or waste character, and to such 'made land' so called as said Company shall fill in or reclaim from the sea or other places.''

In other words, the ''Oahu Railway and Land Company'' (O. R. and L.), as the charter designated it, got the green light to act as a land development company as well as a railroad.

Even before the charter was issued, the company held its organizational meeting, which set the tone for the management of company affairs for years to come.

B. F. Dillingham's overriding need at that point was to raise cash by selling bonds to the public. He chose as officers and directors men who could themselves bring money into the company and who bore such high reputations that their presence in the company would inspire public confidence.

First, he prevailed on his old friend Will Castle to serve as president. In accepting, Castle noted that he might have to absent himself for three or four months. By the end of the year he had resigned, perhaps because of a conflict of interest when he organized Ewa Plantation, and John H. Paty took his place as president; Will's brother, James B. Castle, at that point became a director.

The other original officers were James I. Dowsett, 1st vice-president; W. C. Wilder, 2nd vice-president; Mark Robinson, treasurer; George C. Williams, secretary; and Colonel William F. Allen, auditor. Additional directors were Sam Allen, Robert Lewers, and T. Rain Walker. Williams bowed out shortly in favor of W. G. Ashley, the superintendent of the railroad, but the others kept their connections for years, in many cases until death. When Paty died in 1897, Sam Allen took his place as president; after Allen's death in 1903, B. F. Dillingham finally became president.

The original trustees for the bondholders were William G. Irwin, Thomas R. Foster, and John A. Cummins. Trusteeship turned out to involve considerable work and responsibility and no pay; turnover in the office remained high until much later, when the bonds had become recognized as gilt-edged investments and two "in-house" representatives, Walter Frear and Robert W. Atkinson, took over the job.

For himself, B. F. Dillingham took no title at all. He had decided that he would act as contractor for building the railroad and presumably felt that he should not sit on both sides of the fence. He had put together a strong board of directors, one that would not be likely to rubber-stamp his decisions, but with or without a title, he was the heart and soul of the road. Later, after the first contract was completed, he took the title of general manager, but he did not become an officer or director until 1903. Walter Dillingham, however, was made a director in 1901, at the age of twenty-six.

Frank took himself off the payroll at the Pacific Hardware Company about the time the railway was organized, and he drew no salary from the railroad until he became general manager more than a year later. Presumably, his living expenses came out of his profits as contractor for the line. Frank believed devoutly in making money for his enterprises, but he never loaded down his companies with high salaries or expense accounts. He made his money as a promoter, by turning worthless paper into valuable securities.

Actually the O. R. and L. was launched without cash payment for any stock. For the properties which he turned over to the company, Mark Robinson received $39,350 in bonds and $57,400 in stock at par. B. F. Dillingham was credited with $200,000 for his franchise and $353,250 for other items, mostly expenses he had paid or undertook to pay on behalf of the railroad. Of the original 5,250 shares of stock, 574 were allocated to Robinson and the balance to Dillingham, but by the time the first certificates were issued, B. F. had apparently sold or given away 605 shares, including a number given as 10 percent bonuses on the sale of bonds.

In one of their first acts, the directors authorized $300,000 worth of 7 percent bonds to build the line from the Old Fish Market in Honolulu to Manana (Pearl City). This amount included the $39,350 promised to Robinson. Public subscriptions opened in March, with a dull thud. Investors held back from anything so new and untried. Mr. Castle broke the ice by subscribing for $15,000; such was his prestige that others followed. In early April cash started coming in in substantial amounts: $5,000 from E. Bond, $5,000 from C. Afong, $6,000 from Mr. Castle, $5,500 from Lowell Smith, $2,000 from Lewers and Cooke, $10,000 from Annie Parke, and so on. Frank had enough to make a start.

Actually, of course, he had started already. Regarding Frank's proposed contract to build and equip 15 miles of railway for $260,000, the directors had consulted a noted railway engineer from Boston named Lincoln Cabot who had worked with S. G. Wilder trying to get his Hilo railroad financed and who was one of the two engineers who had come out to make an on-site inspection, along with T. G. Gribble of Hawaiian Tramways. Cabot had assured them that the price was high enough to include a handsome profit, but that it was not extravagant, since Frank proposed to take his pay in bonds and would assume all risks from whatever causes. By the time the directors received this assurance, Frank was hard at work building the line.

The formal groundbreaking took place on 8 March 1889 at Moanalua, with seven-year-old Harold Dillingham turning the first shovelful of earth. Moanalua was chosen as the starting place because the cuts necessary there would provide fill for the watery parts of the line.

A contemporary account says the work also started "near Waller's," which presumably referred to the slaughterhouse managed by Gilbert Waller near the present intersection of Middle Street and Kamehameha Highway.

A subcontractor by the name of Ng Fawn began the actual grading, and by the end of March Kluegel certified that he had completed work to the amount of $1,878. Lack of manpower held back the job, but by May 148 men were working.

One important point remained to be straightened out. The original plans placed the Honolulu depot on the waterfront at the foot of Queen Street, across from the Old Fish Market, but the site was obviously too small to provide a proper terminal. Also, Frank had probably come to realize the advantage of controlling land around the terminal which would become valuable for warehouses. Frank served notice of intention to take 22 acres of government "land" for his terminal, consisting of Kuwili Pond on King Street, across from the present Aala Park.

At this point Frank ran afoul of Minister of the Interior Thurston, who defended the public interest with vigor and verbosity. Thurston said 4 or 5 acres would be plenty: "The reference to the size of the railroad yards at Buffalo seems about as germane to the question as the relative amount of oxygen necessary to keep the sun warm as

View across Kuwili Pond toward Punchbowl and the mouth of Nuuanu Stream, with the O. R. and L. terminal in the left background. (Photo by Kent Cochrane, Bishop Museum)

compared to that of a tallow dip." Frank had to swallow his pride and settle for 5 acres plus the right-of-way.

Frank never gave up easily. Within a few months he had persuaded the Bishop Estate to sell him 15 adjoining underwater acres at $1,000 an acre, two-thirds payable in bonds and one-third in cash, and shortly thereafter he picked up another 10 acres at the same price. He also wanted the nearby Kawa Pond at the mouth of Nuuanu Stream; the estate did not want to sell it, but feared his possible use of the power of eminent domain. Finally, in 1898, the estate got off the hot seat by trading Kawa Pond to the government for some land in Kakaako; Frank then got hold of the pond as part of a deal with the government.

On 9 April 1889 Frank took time out from his pressing affairs to acknowledge an old debt, in the following letter:

Hon. S. N. Castle, Honolulu
Dear Mr. Castle,

It is now twenty years since you made it possible for me to start in business with your beloved son, Alfred. During all those years you have been an endorser for the firm of Dillingham & Co. and have also through many errors of judgement of *mine,* been called upon to support and assist in matters of finance. Your treatment of me has *always* been most considerate in the *extreme,* you have been more like a *father* to me, than a business acquaintance or friend. I can make you *no adequate* return for all your kindness to me. But I venture to ask you to accept my deepest heartfelt thanks, and the trifle which I beg to enclose, viz. 50 shares of stock in the Oahu Railway and Land Company, Ltd. As I was offered $10,000 by Mr. Afong for the same stock at par last Saturday afternoon, I think it may be regarded as worth its face. I am not willing to sell without a large premium, though it is possible that I may sell, as soon as the line is completed at a lower rate than its real value for the sake of paying off all my debts. I expect to pay over to the old firm of Dillingham & Co. by the first of July next an amount sufficient to cancel *all* your endorsements. Thank you again for your great kindness to me and mine, I shall ever remain dear Mr. Castle your grateful friend,

B. F. Dillingham

Frank left for San Francisco at the beginning of May; a few days later Mark Robinson, who was receiving bond subscriptions and cash for the railroad, wrote him some good news: "Mr. S. N. Castle came in the office and looking over the list of subscriptions filed he saw, or I showed him, the one filed by J. B. Atherton, so he made up his mind to increase his ($15,000) and so filed a new application for $10,000 more, making it the same figure as J. B. Atherton's.''

The Castle commitment in the railroad continued to grow. By 1892 James B. Castle held $46,600 in railroad bonds as trustee, and $89,200 in the name of his father. Without Mr. Castle's backing the whole railroad project might never have got off the ground.

Mr. Castle was past eighty when he began his investment in the Oahu Railway. He lived on until 1894, just short of his eighty-sixth birthday, when his death deprived Frank of his oldest patron and benefactor.

Before leaving for San Francisco, B. F. took care of two more important matters: locomotives and cars.

He ordered the two Baldwin locomotives through Charles Brewer and Company of Boston, with whom he had had dealings for many years in the Pacific Hardware Company. (The Boston firm of Charles Brewer and Company was started by the same man who gave his name to the entirely separate company of C. Brewer in Honolulu. After making a tidy fortune in Honolulu, Mr. Brewer sold out and returned to Boston, where he re-entered the shipping and commission business.) From Carter Brothers, a railroad supply house in San Francisco, he ordered cars for the new line.

2 hand cars
2 track-laying cars
8 flat cars
1 box car
6 flat cars with tops and seats, suitable for third class passenger or excursion cars
2 second class cars
2 combination freight and smoking cars
4 first class cars
1 first class parlor car with chair seats and one or two lounges, WC on each side for gentlemen and ladies, upholstered in plush, everything finished in first-class style.

Along with the parlor car, he ordered a set of royal purple portable curtains stamped or embroidered with the Hawaiian coat-of-arms in gold, evidently for use when royalty rode the train. Frank christened this stylish conveyance the ''Pearl'' and kept it for his own private car.

Frank took fourteen-year-old Walter with him to California, but the rest of the family apparently stayed home. After Frank's return, Emma took May and Walter for a summer in the East. May was to have her dearest wish: a college education in Massachusetts, at Wellesley. Emma intended to return with Walter after enrolling May in college in the fall, but a letter from her father tells of changing plans:

> Frank tells me that you and he are corresponding about the propriety of Walter going to a Boston school the coming winter rather than coming home to enter Oahu College in September. Dr. Tucker and several other intelligent gentlemen and some intelligent gentlewomen, advise that he by all means stay there at least one winter, and I most heartily "*kokua.*" And not only that, but I give the same hearty advice to you, to prolong your visiting in New England and New York till the spring months of 1890. This blessed recuperating visit has been postponed some 4½ years on my account. Now, my dear daughter, please make haste slowly about returning to your good home at Woodlawn. I have had a talk with Frank, and he says "you just write to Emma and tell her how you feel about her spending the winter there." Can't you have a central station and be near both May and Walter?

The Dillingham family, about 1889. Left to right: Frank, Marion, May, Walter, Harold, Emma. Frank was about forty-five at the time. (Courtesy of the Dillingham family)

Walter did indeed stay for a winter of school in Massachusetts. In fact he stayed for four years, living in the home of his father's cousin, Isaac Dillingham, in Auburndale, a suburb of Boston, and attending Newton High School.

In San Francisco Frank bought a second-hand steam shovel from the San Francisco Bridge Company and also acquired from the same concern John A. Hughes, a feisty Irishman who became the master car builder for the O. R. and L. The steam shovel took six months to get to Honolulu, perhaps because the vendor demanded cash, but when it did arrive it created a mild sensation, being the first of its kind in town, as it rolled off the dock and down King Street under its own power. It was sent to Moanalua, where it dug up enough dirt to fill the depot site and tidewater lands down to the waterfront. Hughes moved with it to Moanalua, where he built a blacksmith shop, car shop, store rooms, and dump cars to carry earth for filling.

Hughes arrived in August, about a month before B. F.'s birthday, on which the backers of the railroad had been promised a train ride. "At that time," Hughes later wrote, "the railroad terminal was on a

Dillingham's first steam shovel loads dirt to fill the watery places around the terminal. The engine is the Sonoma Valley Railroad's *General Vallejo,* bought by B. F. Dillingham in 1889 and renamed *Lanakila* (Victory) and later renamed *B. F. Dillingham.* It is said to have been his favorite locomotive. (Bishop Museum photo)

small strip of dry land on the harbor side of Iwilei Road. A building about 12 by 20 feet of rough 1 × 12 boards served both as an office and as a storeroom. In front of it there was a single track extending across Iwilei Road and connecting with the main track on the other side.'' Early on a Monday morning Hughes reported for work and found B. F. in his shirtsleeves, helping to load ties and track onto the cars. He told Hughes that the railroad would be open on 4 September, and he wanted two cars ready for service. The bodies and trucks were then aboard a ship in the harbor; they had canvas tops, open sides and longitudinal seats.

By the morning of 4 September Hughes had the two cars ready, except that their oil boxes remained to be packed. While B. F. watched, Hughes put an augur to a barrel of oil. The oil spurted out and came down in a shower on Mr. Dillingham. Instead of giving an angry rebuke as Hughes expected, B. F. took out his handkerchief and wiped the oil from Hughes' eyes.

Meanwhile the Baldwin locomotives had not arrived, and B. F. would have failed in his promise but for a stroke of luck. The royal government had ordered a small eight-ton locomotive for hauling crushed rock on Honolulu's mule-car tracks, but by the time it arrived someone had figured out that it would not negotiate the extremely sharp turns on the streets. B. F. Dillingham happily bought it in time for the O. R. and L.'s ''first ride.'' This little locomotive, the *Kauila,* first to run on O. R. and L. tracks, has been preserved and today sits on the Honolulu waterfront beside the restored sailing ship *Falls of Clyde.*

The *Pacific Commercial Advertiser* carried an admiring account of this event under the heading of ''A Successful Experimental Excursion, and the Redemption of Mr. B. F. Dillingham's Promise Given One Year Ago.'' According to the *P.C.A.,* about 150 persons rode, the second car being filled mostly with native Hawaiians. Amid cheers, ringing bells, and tootling from the band the train rolled out of the terminal promptly at 4:00 P.M. and, racing at speeds of up to 10 or 12 miles an hour, got all the way to the Palama rice fields, more than a mile from the depot. The report continued: ''It was not considered advisable to make the return journey owing to the engine being new and previously untried.'' The engine returned later in the evening, ''the passengers in the meantime having come back by other conveyances.''

George Denison has left us a somewhat different version of the

Locomotive number 6, *Kauila,* the first engine to run on the O. R. and L. tracks, shown here in front of the Pearl City station. The *Kauila* has been preserved and now sits on the Honolulu waterfront beside the restored sailing ship *Falls of Clyde.* (Courtesy of the Dillingham Corporation)

story. "The trip started with many prominent citizens present," he wrote, "also the band, but came to an abrupt stop opposite Dowsett Lane. The man employed to erect and operate the engine not having removed the grease from the boiler in the process of erecting the engine, the grease caused heavy foaming and the passengers, who were in open cars, were showered with black hot water from the engine and had to make their way back to town by such means as they could find, with hacks for such as had the price and could find a hack, others, not so fortunate, walked." The name of Dowsett Lane was changed to Akepo Lane in 1923. If Denison had his facts straight, it appears that the "first ride" lasted about a third of a mile.

No doubt Frank had to laugh off a few wisecracks from his friends at this ignominious ending, but on the whole the evening of his forty-fifth birthday should have found him proud rather than ashamed. In one year he had laid out and organized a railroad, financed it, and made a good start toward building and equipping it. Those who doubted his ability to complete it were reckoning without his fantastic drive and will.

# CHAPTER 25

*The terms of the lease were drawn up hurriedly on the eve of my departure for S.F. and I was at that time pushing the construction of my 15-mile contract to build a line to Hoaeae as fast as possible, and my mind was overpressed with work.*

B. F. D. to William R. Castle
25 May 1893

THE "first ride" had been merely a trial run. The real opening of the line came on Kalakaua's birthday, 16 November 1889.

By that time the road had made substantial progress. The Honolulu depot was completed, a handsome two-story frame building with open lanais that continued to serve until the new terminal was built in 1923. The track ran about 8 miles to Halawa by the shores of Pearl Harbor, near the present Aloha Stadium. The two Baldwin locomotives *(Kaala* and *Leahi)* had arrived, as well as conventional passenger coaches. It was time for Frank to show his wares to the public.

B. F. Dillingham had a strong flair for publicity. Instead of inviting a select few to the opening, he announced through the press that there would be free rides for all. Tickets were distributed ahead of time, but everyone who showed up was accommodated. *Kaala* led off, drawing five closed and two open coaches, followed by *Leahi* with one closed and four open. In all eleven trains ran to Halawa and back, carrying some four thousand passengers. Mr. A. F. Cooke enlivened the occasion by impersonating a hawker of refreshments, distributing as part of his act a basket of luscious green grapes.

But opening day proved a tough act to follow. From Honolulu the line still ran only to Moanalua, Puuloa, and Halawa, and none of these stations produced any appreciable amount of passengers or

Opening day on the O. R. and L., with the *Kaala* at the left and *Leahi* waiting at the right. (Photo by Ray Jerome Baker, Bishop Museum)

freight. The line was opened through to Manana (Pearl City) on 1 January 1890, but Frank as contractor did not complete his 15 miles and turn it over to the railroad for another seven months. Meanwhile he ran the trains—three a day each way and four on Saturdays—for his own account, paying the expenses and pocketing the proceeds. The first five and a half months produced a grand total of a little over ten thousand dollars in gross receipts.

From the first, of course, Frank had thought of the railroad as the means to an end, not as an end in itself, and he was stalking bigger game than the freight from a few rice mills.

In June 1889, after a lapse of more than a year, Frank had secured the last in his series of options from James Campbell. As he had feared, Campbell had upped the price for his ranches to $800,000, but he was willing to take the last $200,000 in bonds of a proposed development company, and in a separate unrecorded document he agreed to refund $50,000 of the bonds to Dillingham after the purchase. The option ran to the end of 1889.

Frank was jubilant. On the same day that he got Campbell's signature, he wrote Walter Frear, his future son-in-law, explaining that he

A view across Kuwili Pond to the O. R. and L. terminal. Visible to the right are Punchbowl and the twin spires of the second Kaumakapili Church. The watery area in the foreground has long since been filled in. (Photo by Kent Cochrane, Bishop Museum)

An early O. R. and L. train; photo taken from the famous Damon gardens at Moanalua. Samuel M. Damon inherited the estate of Moanalua from Bernice Pauahi Bishop, wife of his banking partner Charles R. Bishop. (Hawaii State Archives photo)

This photograph taken at Waiau, near Pearl City, with a railway trestle in the right background, shows the type of country served by the first increment of the O. R. and L. (Photo by Alonzo Gartley, Bishop Museum)

intended to form a syndicate to exercise the option and that the scheme was well regarded by Hartwell, H. A. P. Carter, P. C. Jones, Sam Allen, John Paty, Hackfeld and Company, and others. "I want you to come and take hold with me," he said. Evidently Frear decided to stick with his law studies, however.

A couple of weeks later Frank was writing to Mr. Castle that

> Mr. P. C. Jones of Brewer and Company offered to take up the Campbell land scheme and float the bonds, upon condition that I would give him or his syndicate $600,000 of the stock, allowing me to keep the balance, $400,000 of the stock. I have agreed to give them $500,000, half of the stock, and sell them 100 shares more at par, say $10,000 to be paid me in U. S. gold coin. H. A. P. Carter, George Wilcox and Charles M. Cooke all seemed satisfied with my offer and told me they thought Mr. P. C. Jones would be. They have all gone for a visit to the volcano and I believe are expected to return on the *Kinau* a week from tomorrow, when I hope to close with them. Mr. Harry Glade of H. Hackfeld and Company told me yesterday that they would like to talk with me in case I did not close with C. Brewer.

But however much interest in his project he may have stirred up, Frank failed to get final agreement from any of his moneyed friends. Perhaps he demanded too much for himself, or perhaps it was simply a case of Honolulu being desperately short of capital. At any rate, he began to think in terms of getting money from San Francisco. To nail down his presentation, he had soil analyses made of the Ewa plains, prepared estimates on the cost of pumping water, and hired Sereno Bishop, a former missionary and an able surveyor, to make a report on surface water in the area around Pearl Harbor. (Sereno Bishop later, as editor of *The Friend,* requested Frank to omit from his advertisements in that publication any reference to trains running on Sunday.) Bishop's report impressed Frank sufficiently that he buried the hatchet with Cabby Brown, with whom he had had a brief but heated argument, and secured from him an option on all the water in Waikele Stream.

B. F. also brought to Honolulu from California two civil engineers, James D. Schuyler and G. F. Allardt, whose reputations would command the respect of bankers and capitalists. Schuyler and Allardt prepared for him a comprehensive report on the water resources of both Honouliuli and Kahuku ranches, concluding that ample water for sugar plantations existed at both Ewa and Kahuku and could be developed at a cost well within the margins of profitability. Appended to their report is a map showing the water sources

A *luau* at the residence of C. A. Brown, who appears at the extreme right. B. F. Dillingham is third from the right, and beyond him, May, Emma, and Walter. The picture must have been taken not long before Walter went east to school in 1890. Aloha attire had not yet penetrated Honolulu society. (Bishop Museum photo)

of Honouliuli, based partly on surveys by Kluegel; one interesting feature of the map is the fact that it shows the proposed route of the O. R. and L. past Pearl Harbor extending to Waialua and Kahuku over the central plateau rather than around the Waianae coast.

Allardt, who was a brother-in-law of C. H. Kluegel, remained in Honolulu after completing the water report as a consulting engineer for B. F. Dillingham and also made a report for the government on dredging Honolulu bar. Dillingham retained Allardt again toward the end of the decade, when he drafted the plan for developing the west end of Honolulu Harbor. Allardt also in 1897 suggested to Mr. Dillingham that the O. R. and L. acquire its own dredge; B. F. followed his advice a couple of years later, and the dredge which he procured was the one that Walter Dillingham later leased from the railroad to start his spectacular career in land reclamation. Mr. Allardt thus may be considered a distant progenitor of Ala Moana Center.

Renewed interest in the Campbell lands pointed up another necessity for the little railroad: if it was going to handle sugar, or any other export or import commodity, it needed to connect with deep-water docks in Honolulu Harbor. B. F. Dillingham had spent years in ships, and he recognized the overwhelming advantage of being able to spot freight cars right alongside a docked vessel. The city of Honolulu cut off his railroad from access to the existing docks, but if the railroad owned its own wharf it could collect tolls from others rather than pay them itself.

The 25 acres of fee-simple "land" which Frank bought between the terminal and the harbor gave him the position he wanted; he planned to get the harbor line established at the edge of it, build a retaining wall, and dredge and fill until he had his dock.

Here again he ran afoul of L. A. Thurston, minister of the interior, who believed that the government should control the waterfront. Frank got approval to fill his 25 acres and run a railroad track onto it, but he had to agree to Thurston's terms: the government retained ownership of a narrow strip of land between the railroad property and the harbor, and of the site of the dock itself, which would stretch out into deep water. The best that Frank could get was a ten-year lease on the site, with the privilege of building the retaining wall and dock.

By the end of 1890 the railroad had invested $100,000 in its wharf division property, plus $12,800 in extending the main line of track to the wharf. The sea wall had been erected, 6 acres of company land reclaimed, and a wharf 60 by 210 feet built on government leasehold

The first railway dock in Honolulu, built on land leased from the government for ten years. About 1890. (Hawaii State Archives photo)

land. The railroad had also built a scow and scow landing, both equipped with tracks, so that a freight car could be put alongside any ship in the harbor. Early the next year the railroad completed an iron warehouse for the storage of sugar on its own property near the wharf.

To pay for these improvements, the railroad directors in 1889 authorized $250,000 in Terminal Division 7 percent bonds—that is, bonds secured by a mortgage on the terminal property. These bonds were sold or given as payment for work over the next seven years, until the consolidated bond issue took their place at the beginning of 1897.

By November of 1889 Frank evidently realized that he was not going to get the money to buy out Campbell before the end-of-the-year deadline, and he turned therefore to another means of accomplishing his objective. Talks with Campbell began again, and on 19 November the two men signed a lease for fifty years covering Mr. Campbell's two ranches.

Without doubt the signing of this lease represented the greatest single step in B. F. Dillingham's entire business career. By a stroke of the pen he gained control, for a fixed annual rental and without investing a dollar in cash, of some 60,000 acres of land, much of it ripe for development—the same land that he had been scheming and struggling to acquire for four and a half years. Now his railroad would have a real reason for its existence; now the docks that he planned for Honolulu Harbor would handle something besides bananas and a little rice.

Hard on the heels of this triumph came another. Now that he had something tangible to offer, a plantation site at Honouliuli, he gave the first refusal to his old friend Will Castle. Castle got together with his family and friends in Castle and Cooke; they studied B. F.'s facts and figures on soil and irrigation until they convinced themselves of the merits of the proposed plantation.

Frank as usual was in a hurry. He had his railroad to finish, and what probably mattered more at the moment, Emma was still in the East and Frank was getting lonely. On 14 December 1889 he and Will Castle agreed on a sublease covering what would become Ewa Plantation. On the afternoon of the same day, on top of the world, he sailed for San Francisco to meet Emma for Christmas.

# CHAPTER 26

*Frank's prospects now are far more promising than they would have been had he succeeded in getting a loan of money in London for his railroad.*

The Reverend Lowell Smith
March 1890

THE lease executed by Dillingham and Campbell is a brief, simple document which describes in legal phraseology the lands involved, gives the term as running from 1 January 1890 to 31 December 1939, and sets out the rent as being $20,000 for the first year, $30,000 for the second year, and $40,000 per year thereafter. Based on Campbell's own price for his land—$800,000 including livestock, less a $50,000 rebate, or about $650,000 net for the land—the rent starting with the third year represents about a 6 percent return. Dillingham of course paid the taxes. The extraordinary feature from today's point of view is the setting of a fixed lease payment for fifty years, during which time the increase in value of the property accrued to Dillingham's benefit. Within a few years subleases on portions of the Campbell properties were bringing in more than the rent paid to Campbell. The amount of rents received increased steadily and by the 1920s ran well over $300,000 a year. The total rent paid to the Campbell interests over the life of the lease amounted to a little less than two million dollars, while rents received on the same property must have come to at least ten million.

Dillingham also agreed to buy, and Campbell to sell, all livestock on the ranches: cattle at $8 a head, horses, mares, and colts at $35 a head, and two stallions at $500 apiece. The price worked out to about $88,000.

B. F. continued to run the Campbell properties as ranches, though the best portions of the land were quickly leased out for other purposes. Along with the livestock, B. F. secured the services of Harry

M. Von Holt. Von Holt, who managed the ranch properties, was the young nephew of Cecil Brown, a lawyer who helped Mr. Campbell with his business affairs. B. F. always gave Von Holt full credit for the railroad's enlightened policy of fencing the forest lands to keep out cattle, thereby preserving and enhancing the watersheds for the whole area. Von Holt served as a director of the railroad from 1890 to his retirement in 1926, when his son, Herman V. Von Holt, took his place on the board.

The sublease to Will Castle, which Castle assigned to Ewa Plantation Company as soon as it was organized, called for payment of $5,000 a year or 4 percent of the value of the sugar produced by Ewa, whichever was greater. (This is an early example, possibly even the earliest, of a percentage lease in Hawaii.) Ewa got possession of the lands of Honouliuli between the coral rim and an elevation of 200 feet, plus 2,500 acres of coral land and a large lot fronting on the west loch of Pearl Harbor. Ewa would depend on artesian wells for irrigation, and the 200-foot elevation boundary represented the maximum height to which it was considered feasible to pump this water. The lease included a freight contract with the O. R. and L. at $1.25 a ton from the mill to Honolulu.

Will Castle drew up the lease, acting for both parties. He was an eminently fair and honorable man and a leading lawyer of his time, but two opposing lawyers might have produced a happier result. The lease as written served as a springboard for endless arguments between the plantation and the railroad; in justice to Castle, these disputes were probably nurtured as much by clashing personalities as by ambiguities in the lease.

At the same time that he made the lease with Will Castle, Frank offered a similar arrangement at Kahuku to Will's younger brother, James B. Castle. On Frank's return from San Francisco, Jim Castle signed his lease, which in later years provoked a bitter confrontation over the issue of exactly what lands the plantation held under it. Also, the Kahuku lease specified a 5 percent rental rather than 4. Although probably no one realized it at the time, the Kahuku lands were vastly inferior for sugar and much less able to support a high rent. Possibly, Frank's 4 percent to Will Castle reflected his friendship and appreciation for past favors.

B. F. inserted an unusual feature in these subleases by having them run for forty-nine years and eleven months, instead of the fifty-year term of the basic lease. When the leases expired in 1939, this feature gave Walter Dillingham substantial leverage in dealing with the problems of the termination.

Frank could have kept the Campbell lease as his personal holding, but he chose to put it into the railway company. For doing so he received another $175,000 in railroad stock, making a total of $700,000 in stock issued. The two leases actually went on the books at a valuation of $350,000, and an adjustment was made in the way that Frank's original stock was charged.

Out of this $700,000 in stock, about $130,000 had been issued in payment of tangible assets or for the actual expenses of getting organized. The remainder, about $570,000, represented intangible assets, principally the purported value of the franchise and of the Campbell lease. In other words, the railroad was capitalizing the future value of unproved earnings. Frank Dillingham knew in his heart that the road could earn a handsome return on its capital, but he was very much on a spot to prove it.

The year 1890 must have given him great encouragement, as he made progress on several different fronts. In California he made contact with the San Francisco and North Pacific Railway Company, which was converting its Sonoma Valley division from narrow gauge to standard, and bought from them two locomotives and a number of cars at bargain prices.

At home the Palama branch—half a mile upstream to a rice mill—was installed, and the main line pushed steadily on until by 1

The O. R. and L.'s first "roundhouse," with the depot in the background. Photo evidently taken soon after the railroad opened. (Photo by Harry L. Dennison, Bishop Museum)

July Frank had completed the original 15 miles to Hoaeae and turned the line over to the railroad to operate. Allardt and A. M. Sproull reported to the directors that "the contractor has performed his work in a thoroughly good manner . . . he has interpreted the terms of the contract most liberally in the company's favor."

Always looking ahead, B. F. wrote the legislative committee on railways to ask for a government guarantee of bond interest plus a subsidy of $2,500 per mile for an extension to Waianae, also for a line from Honolulu around Koko Head and up the windward coast to Kahuku. For good measure he threw in a line from Hilo to Hamakua. The Koko Head idea remained alive for many years, and the railroad spent more than $30,000 on surveys and leases before finally abandoning it.

A new Railway Act did pass in September of 1890, extending the exclusive feature of the franchise for fifty years with respect to all territory covered within five years. It made no guarantee of bond interest, but did provide a subsidy of $3,500 per mile payable at $700 per year for five years, on new track built, excluding the original 15 miles. Within six weeks the main line was finished to Ewa Mill, and the directors authorized a new bond issue of $250,000 to extend the line to Waianae.

To celebrate the completion of the first section, the railroad held a Fourth of July Grand Excursion to Pearl Harbor, with trains leaving Honolulu every hour from 7:00 A.M. to 5:00 P.M. Adults paid 50 cents for a round trip, children 25 cents. This event set off a perfect orgy of Grand Moonlight Picnics! People's Excursions! and so forth. Fares on "those delightful canopy-top open cars" were cut to 35 cents a round trip. Baseball games were organized at Pearl City, and regattas on the "lagoon." Professor W. S. Maltby, "the undisputed Champion Scientific and Artistic Cyclist of the World," performed.

At Pearl City, 22 acres were set aside for Remond Grove, a park with a pavilion, baseball diamond, and picnic area. The Oddfellows held Family Day there with an all-day picnic, an event marred by the girls' baseball team beating the boys', 17–8. The *Kaala* was decorated with branching antlers for the occasion, as a salute to the Oddfellows. The less folksy Arion Society hosted His Majesty Kalakaua at a dance, with lancers, waltzes, polkas, schottisches, and "nice cool lager beer." The railroad even built the eight-room Grove Hotel, a humble predecessor of the Haleiwa Hotel.

All this hoopla served not merely to publicize the railroad but also

The Pearl City station at an early date. A branch line down Pearl City Peninsula joined the main line at this point, making it possible to commute easily to Honolulu from the attractive homes which were built on the peninsula in the 1890s. (Photo by Harry L. Dennison, Bishop Museum)

The Oahu Railway set aside 22 acres of land at Pearl City for picnic grounds and athletic fields, known as Remond Grove, and built the tiny Grove Hotel there. Pearl City land sales suffered, however, from competition from districts closer to the center of town opened up by the new streetcar lines. (Bishop Museum photo)

to build up interest in the coming Great Land Sale! at Pearl City. A sizeable section of Manana had been laid out as an entire new town, including land on both sides of the railroad, the tip of the peninsula, and a section going up the hill *mauka* from the railroad. A special committee had chosen the name "Pearl City," after passing over such suggestions as "Dillinghampton," "Dillingmania," and "Benville." A railway branch line running from Pearl City station a mile down the peninsula was on the drawing boards as an inducement to buy peninsula lots; it was completed in 1891.

The railroad offered building lots of about 9,000 square feet in the new town at about $300 each, with a one-third down payment required and the balance in three and five years, at 7 percent interest. As an additional inducement, purchasers had the right for nine years to buy special commuters' tickets to Honolulu at 1½ cents a mile first class or one cent second class. Two Grand Sales at the end of 1890 resulted in about $75,000 worth of land changing hands.

In spite of this promising start, Pearl City was not an overwhelming success. Completion of the tramway lines boosted the outlying parts of Honolulu proper for residences. Many speculators bought Pearl City lots with the idea that the United States would build a naval base at Pearl Harbor, but when the channel was finally opened many years later, the base developed near the mouth of the harbor, miles away from Pearl City. The section of the new town that

View from Pearl City Peninsula toward Honolulu, with Diamond Head in the center background. The railroad track is the short spur which ran down the peninsula. (Photo by T. A. Jaggar, Bishop Museum)

stretched up the hill *mauka* from the railroad had a splendid view but no transportation; practically no one built there, and the land was eventually "de-subdivided" and put into sugarcane to wait for a later building boom.

The peninsula section of the new town, on the other hand, and particularly the waterfront lots, quickly gained a popularity which lasted for two generations. Many families built unpretentious but charming and comfortable houses there, in some cases occupying them as full-time residences and in others merely as vacation homes. Many *kama'āina* ("native-born") families still recall with delight and affection the joys of living on an unpolluted Pearl Harbor. World War II ended this happy way of life when the U.S. Navy commandeered the entire rim of Pearl Harbor.

Early in 1891 Frank Dillingham presented "with peculiar pleasure and no small degree of satisfaction" a report on the O. R. and L. for the period ended 31 December 1890; almost two years from its date of incorporation, but only six months after Contractor Dillingham had turned the line over to the company to operate. (Frank called this the Second Annual Report, but it was the first public report and the first report on operations.) Against all laws of probability, the little railroad company showed a profit of $62,000 after six months of operations.

In round figures, the railway department earned $16,000, the ranches $27,000, and land sales $60,000, for a total of $103,000. Against these earnings were charged property taxes of $3,000 and interest, principally on bonds, of $38,000, leaving the net profit of $62,000. While this made a splendid showing for the first year, little of the interest was properly chargeable against the ranches or against land sales, and though the figures included only six months of railway operations, they did include more than $12,000 paid to the railroad as track rental by B. F. Dillingham, contractor. In other words, the little railroad was not yet paying its own way and had been bailed out principally by the Pearl City land sales.

In the clear light of hindsight, a more serious threat emerges from the dry figures of the report. Little by little the sums spent on capital improvements were adding up. Reclaiming land at the terminal, building machine shops and car shops, rebuilding those delightful canopy-top cars into conventional coaches, branch lines, sidings, filling in land at the wharf site, thoroughbred stock for the ranches, improvements at Pearl City, water works, office furniture—item after

The Honolulu depot in 1891. Note the mourning bands for Kalakaua hanging from the tower. (Photo by Harry L. Dennison, Bishop Museum)

item the total mounts—until the capital expenditures for twelve months reach a sum of $325,000, with only $170,000 in bonds sold during that time to pay for them. As the gap widens, notes payable and "sundry creditors" stretch to fill the gap.

Yet by and large the little railroad was in remarkably good shape. The bondholders received their interest on time and Mr. Campbell his rent. Railroad stock found a market; a few shares sold at 105. And as the railroad prospered, so did B. F. Dillingham.

In January of 1890 Frank returned from California to finish the signing of the leases and to complete the railway line as specified under the original contract. Then someone suggested that he run for Noble—at that time an elective seat in the legislature—and he immediately zoomed off on a political tangent.

Frank ran under the banner of the Reform Party, which had scored such a smashing triumph in 1887. But by 1890 the party had lost prestige through quarrels within its own cabinet and had failed to enlarge its narrow base of support. It continued to dominate the outside islands, but on Oahu the National Reform Party, beating the drums of anti-*haole,* anti-American and anti-missionary sentiment, mustered a majority of voters. Frank Dillingham ran a dignified campaign, emphasizing stability in government and proclaiming pride in his association with the O. R. and L., "whose contractor paid the Hawaiians and Portuguese $1.25 a day, when the London and Hawaiian Tramways paid only 87½ cents a day."

In the February elections not a single Reform candidate for Noble won one of the nine Oahu seats. Frank got the most votes of any Reform Party candidate, but lost by fifty-three votes to the lowest National Reform man. The election as a whole left the legislature about evenly divided between the two parties. In spite of his defeat, Frank retained considerable political influence; the railroad bill that passed late that summer gave him a great deal of what he wanted in the way of legislative aid.

To meet the requirements of running for office, Frank took an oath of allegiance and became a naturalized citizen of the Hawaiian Kingdom, without renouncing his American citizenship. There is no reason to suppose that he took the oath with tongue in cheek. Along with most foreigners then resident in the kingdom, Frank undoubtedly supported the continued independence of Hawaii.

Frank did well on his railroad contracting, at least on paper. The railway paid him in bonds, and as long as he could sell them or give them in payment to his suppliers he was able to keep going nicely. On 1 April he took in Will Castle and Mark Robinson as partners in his contracting business, under the name of the Hawaiian Construction Company. They each acquired a one-quarter interest and he retained one-half out of a total capital of $60,000. Eleven months later the three of them incorporated the company, after adding $71,000 in profit earned by the partnership.

From time to time, Frank sold off a few shares of railroad stock to raise some cash, but he carefully kept a majority of the outstanding shares for himself. As his fortunes rose, even Charles R. Bishop began to believe in him; at one point in 1890 Frank owed the bank of Bishop and Company the astonishing total of more than a quarter of a million dollars.

His new-found prosperity enabled Frank to free his mind of what had undoubtedly been a terrible burden: his debt to Ellie Castle and her children. Frank paid them the original note of $37,000 plus accrued interest of $15,000, in full satisfaction of the debt. Frank's prayer was at least partially answered: Mr. Castle lived to see the note paid, and if Frank was not exactly out of debt, at least he was out of debt to Mr. Castle's grandchildren.

But amid the heady excitement and real progress that marked the year 1890, one warning note cast a cold chill over future prospects for

Hawaii. On 1 October President Harrison of the United States signed into law the McKinley Tariff Act. This act in effect nullified the Treaty of Reciprocity by removing all import duties on sugar and by instituting a bounty of 2 cents a pound to be paid to domestic sugar producers. No longer would Hawaiian sugar planters enjoy a favored position in the American market; now they would have to compete with the rest of the world on even terms, and with American beet and cane producers at the double disadvantage of ocean freight and domestic bounty. The act cut $40 a ton out of Hawaii's receipts in her only major market. Although the sugar schedule in the tariff would not go into effect for six months, as soon as news of the act reached Honolulu the banks began to cut back on loans and gloom settled over the business community.

# Part IV
# STRUGGLE AND TRIUMPH

# CHAPTER 27

*I cannot help but look back at times and feel almost crushed down; then I think of you and your indomitable faith and courage when things looked gloomiest.*

Albert Raas to B. F. D.
8 January 1901

THE McKinley Tariff Act of 1890 marked the beginning in Hawaii of an era of depression, distress, and uneasiness about the future. The illness and death of Kalakaua, whose role of "Merry Monarch" had helped his subjects to forget their problems, contributed to the general feeling of malaise and foreboding. Liliuokalani ascended the throne in January 1891 under inauspicious conditions; her reign proved short and stormy.

Whatever her merits or shortcomings as sovereign, Liliuokalani warmly supported the endeavors of B. F. Dillingham. She called at his home to congratulate him in person on his "courageous undertaking" to plan the building of a railroad, awarded him the Royal Order of Kalakaua, and invested money both in the railroad and in building lots at Pearl City peninsula.

Unfortunately the three lots which Liliuokalani bought in October of 1891 were among the last sold for a long time. As the depression deepened, business came to a standstill and the railroad sold not a single lot during 1892.

The railway had managed to show a modest profit of $19,000 for 1891. B. F. evidently started to cut back on capital spending, as the main line of track pushed along no farther during the year, but certain ongoing projects had to continue. The Pearl City peninsula branch was built, the sugar warehouse erected, more tide land reclaimed at the dock and by the depot, lots at Pearl City cleared, graded, and fenced, the Pearl City waterworks completed, the tug *Frolic* purchased to handle the railroad scow, Halemano Ranch, comprising 12,000 acres in leasehold and 200 acres in fee simple bought for $12,000, and so forth, to a staggering total of $225,000. New bonds sold during the year amounted to only $122,000, leaving a gap of more than $100,000 which the company could bridge in only one way: by not paying its bills as they came due. Notes payable and "sundry creditors" jumped to $223,000.

By 1892 the brakes were on fairly tight; the only sizeable capital expenditure involved a long-planned coal elevator by the dock. Charles Brewer and Company of Boston sent out Lucius Eugene Pinkham to act as consultant for building the elevator. Pinkham stayed in the islands and remained associated with B. F. Dillingham for many years, finally becoming governor of the territory.

This coal elevator marked the beginning of an important business for Dillingham interests. The sugar plantations used coal to run their irrigation pumps and locomotives and as a supplementary fuel for their factory boilers, and the O. R. and L. supplied and delivered the coal. When oil began to replace coal in the early 1900s, Mr. Dillingham secured the agency for the Union Oil Company and remained a dominant factor in the business.

But in 1892 the railroad had fallen on hard times. No longer were people flocking to gala picnics at Remond Grove or taking a Sunday excursion to see the marvelous pumping works at Ewa Plantation. The year ended with a catastrophic loss of $76,000 which nearly wiped out the surplus accumulated up to that time. B. F.'s absence on the mainland served as a welcome excuse not to issue a report which would only have confirmed what many people guessed: the little railroad was insolvent.

For 1890, its first year, the Campbell lease called for a rental of $20,000. The railroad made both semiannual payments promptly. In 1891 the rent increased to $30,000; the railroad paid the first half on time, after B. F. borrowed $5,000 from Campbell a few days before (he paid the interest on it eight years later). The second half and the rent for the following years remained largely unpaid for two and a half years. Early in 1894 Campbell accepted a series of notes for $5,000 each, payable one every six months, in settlement of the overdue rent, which by that time totaled about $84,000.

Oddly enough, in the middle of all his trobles in collecting rent, Campbell acquired two hundred shares ($20,000 par) of stock in the O. R. and L. from Mark Robinson. There is no record of what he paid for it, but he must have thought it was worth something.

The pumping station at Ewa Plantation. The whole plantation was made possible by irrigation water pumped from artesian wells. The O. R. and L. in its early days advertised Sunday excursions to see the great pumping works. (Hawaii State Archives)

Ewa mill station, the terminus of the O. R. and L. until the Waianae section was opened in 1895. Ewa mill can be glimpsed in the background. (Photo by Ray Jerome Baker, Bishop Museum)

Campbell had plenty of company in trying to collect from the O. R. and L. The Bishop Estate trustees protested that they could not buy bonds in order to get the Waiawa rent paid. The Department of the Interior threatened to turn its lease rentals over to the attorney general for collection. In 1893 the payroll fell three months in arrears, and the men "submitted cheerfully" to a cut in pay. At the end of 1892 the O. R. and L. directors sent a committee to Castle and Cooke to ask them to waive demand of payment on the bond coupons due 1 January and to pay the Ewa rent in cash on that date; they also asked Bishop and Company and others to waive demand of interest for three months.

Possibly the most serious delinquency of all was the failure to pay interest on the bonds. The trustees for the bondholders held mortgages on the assets of the company and could have taken over at any time during 1893 or 1894, freezing the stockholders out entirely. Obviously, no one wanted the headaches involved.

O. R. and L's miseries at this time were increased by the troubles of its prime tenant, Ewa Plantation. Will Castle and his friends had started Ewa on a small capital and had got it operational at a time of low sugar prices. Worse, they had installed an unproved diffusion system for the extraction of cane juice, in place of the traditional crushing mill. Diffusion had worked beautifully for beet sugar, and sixty years later it proved itself on sugarcane, but at Ewa it worked not at all. In desperation the directors finally threw the system out entirely and installed a conventional crushing plant at great expense.

Castle and Cooke, as factors for the plantation, had become deeply involved. At the same time the firm had backed the new Union Iron Works, formed to compete with the Honolulu Iron Works. Union Iron failed and so too, very nearly, did Castle and Cooke. On Honolulu's own "Black Monday," the bank of Bishop and Company dishonored a Castle and Cooke check. W. G. Irwin came to the rescue with a loan that tided them over until J. B. Atherton could make more permanent arrangements in San Francisco.

This crisis had one aftermath which figured in B. F. Dillingham's subsequent career. Castle and Cooke had been factoring Haiku and Paia plantations on Maui and held large notes given by Mr. Samuel T. Alexander and Mr. Henry P. Baldwin. In their hour of need, Castle and Cooke sold these notes in San Francisco, thereby losing their hold over the Alexander and Baldwin plantations and opening the way for Alexander and Baldwin to establish themselves in the sugar factoring business. The firm of Alexander and Baldwin (A & B), operating first as a partnership and later as a corporation, had many dealings with B. F. Dillingham in the years ahead.

In 1892 and 1893 Ewa's crisis severely hurt the O. R. and L. Ewa's crop for 1892 totaled less than 3,000 tons, and H. P. Baldwin sniffed that Ewa would never amount to more than a 4,500 ton plantation and advised Castle and Cooke to write off the $400,000 the plantation owed them. Ewa's low tonnage damaged the O. R. and L. in two ways: the railroad got less sugar to haul, and the percentage rental based on the value of the sugar barely exceeded the $5,000 minimum.

During this time there began also a seemingly endless series of disputes between the O. R. and L. and Ewa Plantation, arising ostensibly from a lack of clarity in the lease. If the original disputes had not surfaced at a time when both parties were suffering a terrible strain, the two sides might have resolved their differences on a friendly basis; as it happened, they got in the habit of squabbling and the arguments continued for a generation.

This particular imbroglio started innocently enough near the end of 1891 when Will Castle wrote to Frank Dillingham to remind him that Ewa Plantation would soon be making sugar and would want to ship it from the factory immediately, so that the railroad would have to store it at the dock. As a common carrier the railroad would remain liable for the sugar until it was loaded aboard ship. Castle sug-

Ewa mill, with the plantation store and an O. R. and L. locomotive at right. Ewa Plantation started out as a near-disaster, but by 1898 it was paying annual dividends of 70 percent on the original investment. (Hawaii State Archives)

gested that with the the dock full of kerosene, the insurance charges would eat up the profit on the freight. In view of the narrow margin or no margin at all on sugar, he added, the plantation would pay nothing it was not required to pay by law.

Frank shot back a testy reply to his old friend, complaining that in drawing the contract Castle had failed to guard the interests of the railway company on at least one point. "It has been my policy," he added, "always to be liberal in business, a policy that works well when dealing with the public at large, but I am beginning to get my eye teeth cut in my old age by coming in contact with sharp businessmen, and I shall endeavor to be more careful in future and see that the railway gets every dollar that it is entitled to 'by law'."

"Of course," Castle replied, "I am pleased and interested by your courteous hint that acting as your attorney and that of the railroad company I neglected or betrayed you or its interest." After declaring that in the lease he had embodied exactly the terms worked out by Frank in conference with J. B. Atherton, C. M. Cooke, E. D. Tenney, and W. A. Bowen, he added, "I am sorry about your eye teeth, and will only say that I was under the impression from my own experience that they were pretty well cut some time ago."

Frank, in the meantime, had discovered a point of leverage: the contract called for the Ewa mill to be built within 1.5 miles of the Honouliuli ranch houses, whereas it stood in fact 2.4 miles beyond. Frank therefore proposed to charge Ewa freight at $1.64 per ton instead of the contractual $1.25.

On the eve of Frank's departure for the United States in 1892, the parties resumed the dispute, without making any progress. Frank by that time had thought of another line of attack: the clause in the lease giving Ewa the right to use the O. R. and L. tracks did not mean free use, and Frank was determined that they should pay for it. The whole argument simmered while Frank was abroad, but came to a boil again in the middle of 1893. Frank tried to settle directly with J. B. Atherton, who had fallen heir to a good deal of the aloha that Frank felt for old Mr. Castle, but Atherton no longer had complete control of the situation. "I find it impossible to induce Mr. Cooke or Tenney to accede to the terms of your letter," he wrote. With Atherton's help, however, the parties finally reached a compromise to avoid a lawsuit, and the situation settled down until the next argument should arise.

An argument also arose with Kahuku Plantation over quite different issues. Jim Castle had taken the sublease on Kahuku and turned it over to a company headed by Alexander Young. As development of the plantation proceeded, the promoters began to agitate for a reduction in rent to 4 percent of the value of the sugar crop, the same figure as in the Ewa lease, claiming in justification that Kahuku had less cane land than Frank had claimed and that the mill which they had erected consequently represented an overinvestment for the property. Frank denied absolutely that he had made any representations regarding the area of cane lands available, and expressed the opinion that if the promoters had spent $100,000 too much on equipment, as they claimed, it only reflected unfavorably on the business judgment of those involved.

The dispute dragged on interminably and was not settled until 1895, when the O. R. and L. agreed to reduce the rent to 4 percent in exchange for a $4,000 bonus and a two-year loan of $15,000. Three years later Kahuku was complaining that nonpayment of the loan was interfering with their payment of dividends.

The railroad's disastrous financial showing beginning in late 1891 was only one of Frank's problems. He already knew that the railway could not really succeed until it pushed on and tapped new markets, but now the depression made it impossible to get the money to continue building. In March of 1891 he incorporated the Hawaiian Construction Company, getting in some additional cash from his old friend Tom May and from F. M. Hatch and others, but eight months later the company had to suspend operations. Since the start of the railroad, first Frank and then the Hawaiian Construction Company had taken payment in railroad bonds and had financed further construction by selling the bonds to the public. Now it became impossible to market the bonds and work ground to a halt, leaving Hawaiian Construction holding a large quantity of unsaleable bonds and owing a large amount in notes and accounts.

Frank's personal position became even tighter than usual. In the fall of 1891, he had to consolidate some loans at Bishop and Company into a note for $150,000, and the bank required Emma to cosign the note. This action rankled Frank for years to come. It was the last time that he permitted Emma to cosign one of his notes, and from then on he made a point of trying to increase the property she held in her own name, as a protection for her in case of disaster to him.

At the end of 1891, Frank personally owed notes totaling $246,000, with interest running at the rate of about $18,000 a year, compared with his salary from the railroad of $3,600. Only if his railroad stock became valuable could he escape from the crushing burden of debt.

To top it all off, the Board of Health destroyed about half of the Woodlawn Dairy's milking herd, costing that company some $30,000.

At the beginning of 1892, Frank had one more try at political campaigning. Probably, he felt that as a legislator he could work more effectively toward a government guarantee of railroad bond interest, which would break the ice jam and allow construction to start again.

The 1892 campaign was confused in the extreme, with four parties in the field and several independent candidates. Frank chose to stand for representative with the Native Sons of Hawaii, a new party which strongly supported the monarchy and opposed the Liberal Party's demand for a new constitution. His principal opponent was C. W. Ashford, who had gone from the Reform to the National Reform to the Liberal Party.

Reflecting the temper of the times, the campaign was not only confused but vituperative. When the Native Sons nominated Dillingham, *Ka Leo o Ka Lahui,* a newspaper edited by Ashford's political associate, John Bush, in a remarkable bit of early Marxist dialectic declared that "The attitude of the O. R. and L. Co. is now clearly exposed as being allied to the reform or plutocratic sugar-barons party and against the party of the people." Ashford charged that the missionaries controlled Dillingham and he had used coolie labor to build his railroad. Furthermore, Thurston (who was campaigning for Dillingham) had taken $500 in railway stock and had given away half the harbor. "Every time you take a bite of poi," he added, "you are paying a tax to Dillingham."

Frank began the campaign on a high plane, but Ashford quickly got under his skin. The firm of Ashford and Ashford, he declared, had done a big business; C. W. Ashford brought charges as attorney general, and V. V. Ashford defended the clients against the charges.

Evidently, legal skullduggery failed to match *poi* as a popular issue, for Ashford polled 358 votes to Frank's 263. The election was as confused as the campaign; no one party dominated the legislature, and Frank succeeded principally in alienating some of his former supporters on railroad matters.

Stymied at home at every turn, Frank determined to rescue the railway with an infusion of capital from abroad. At the end of March 1892, he sailed for the United States to sell the bonds that would put the line on its feet.

# CHAPTER 28

*While I believe in economy, I never economize in traveling by taking second class roads anywhere. . . . I always take the best. I landed once in Boston after having paid first class fare, with 27 cents in my pocket. I borrowed some money until I was in a position to pay it and I would do the same in every account under similar circumstances.*

B. F. D. to his nephew Frank T. Dillingham
26 May 1908

WHEN Frank Dillingham sailed away in March 1892 in search of money to keep building his railroad, Emma stayed behind to look after Harold and Marion. Emma had suffered a double loss the previous year: her beloved father died at the age of eighty-eight, followed five months later by her brother Gussie. Emma's life revolved around her family, and Frank's departure, with May and Walter already away at school, must have left her lonely and depressed.

In later years, after Charles R. Bishop moved to San Francisco and became associated with the Bank of California, B. F. Dillingham preferred San Francisco over any other city, both for business and pleasure, but in 1892 he apparently made no headway at all there. He turned his efforts to New York and Boston, where at least he was close to May and Walter and also to his mother and sister Abbey in Worcester.

Very little record of his trip remains, but evidently progress was agonizingly slow. B. F. tried, he said, every banking source in New York. Finally, he contacted the Lancashire Investment Company, an outlet for English capital in America. This firm eventually agreed to take a consolidated bond issue of the railroad which would provide funds to refinance the existing bonds and extend the line of track to

Waianae and around Kaena Point to Waialua and perhaps Kahuku. Before a final commitment, however, the company decided to send General H. I. Willey to Honolulu to examine the O. R. and L. and report back on whether B. F. had stated his case accurately.

Frank had been through this before. While Willey made his way to Honolulu, Frank stayed in the East, ready to close the deal as soon as Willey's report reached his principals.

By November of 1892, Willey had arrived on the ground and was attending a special meeting of the O. R. and L. stockholders called to approve a new bond issue of $1.75 million (shortly afterwards increased to $2 million). He admitted for publication that he found everything at the railroad exactly as Mr. Dillingham had described it.

Optimism soared at the railway. The stockholders voted B. F. Dillingham full power to make contracts, float bonds, buy materials, and pay such commissions, premiums, and bonuses as might seem best to him. The larger bondholders signified their willingness to exchange their bonds for those of the new issue. The cabinet of the kingdom approved the location of the proposed extension from Ewa Mill to Waialua. The *Daily Bulletin* quoted General Willey as saying that the only thing necessary to make a start in the new enterprise was the passage of a bill before the legislature to validate mortgages and other conveyances of its franchise by the O. R. and L. This act duly passed the legislature and became law.

But General Willey was reckoning without B. F. Dillingham's record of frustration at critical moments. On 14 January 1893, after a most difficult and acrimonious session, Queen Liliuokalani prorogued the legislature. On the same day, she announced to the cabinet her intention of immediately promulgating a new constitution which would restore the royal prerogatives and power pretty much as they had existed before the Hawaiian League had clipped Kalakaua's wings. Liliuokalani was determined not to reign but to rule.

The queen had completely misjudged the temper of the times. Three days later she found herself deposed and a provisional government in power and seeking annexation by the United States. In the aftermath of this revolution, no financial agency anywhere would make an investment in Hawaii until a strong, stable government was assured. B. F. Dillingham's bond issue flew out the window, at least for the moment.

Frank's absence from the kingdom saved him from a personally embarrassing choice. He was a Yankee and he believed devoutly in the republican form of government, at least for the United States.

Queen Liliuokalani backed Frank Dillingham's railroad with recognition, awarding him the Royal Order of Kalakaua, and with investment of her own money. Frank's absence from the country at the time Liliuokalani was overthrown saved him from a painful choice. (Bishop Museum photo)

On the other hand, he had warmly supported the Hawaiian monarchy and had never joined any movement toward annexation. If he had been present at the overthrow of the queen, a hard choice would have been forced on him.

In its first act after securing control of Honolulu, the provisional government appointed a committee of three (enlarged shortly afterward), consisting of Lorrin Thurston, Will Castle, and W. C. Wilder, to go to Washington to negotiate "a treaty of political union between Hawaii and the United States." To carry the committee as far as San Francisco, the government chartered the interisland steamer *Claudine.* As a protection for life and property until the provisional government had time to organize itself, United States Minister

Stevens placed the government under the protection of his country and raised the stars and stripes over government buildings in Honolulu. On 15 February President Harrison sent to the senate a treaty under which Hawaii would join the United States, and its adoption seemed imminent.

But Grover Cleveland, a Democrat, succeeded Benjamin Harrison, a Republican, and on 9 March 1893, before the treaty came to a vote in the senate, Cleveland withdrew it from consideration. His administration dispatched James H. Blount as a special commissioner to Hawaii to investigate the overthrow of Liliuokalani. Blount arrived in Honolulu 29 March; his report did not reach President Cleveland until 18 October, and in the meantime the treaty's fate remained in doubt.

These events left Frank in a quandary. "If the Queen could have deferred her monarchial suicide and kept the Wilcox–Jones cabinet in two months longer," he wrote, "I could have had the money and been at home now paying it out. If the annexation question is disposed of soon, as we hope it may be, not much time will be lost, for everything is ready to go through."

Emma, meanwhile, was growing restless. "A year ago today since I saw you off on the steamer," she wrote on 29 March. Ten days later she declared that "everybody's heart overflows with pity for you in this time of exile." She spoke of "these hard times" being difficult for the children and reported that she had sent off eighteen more fish paintings, for which she had apparently found a market.

At the beginning of May Emma wrote again in the same vein: "I made dresses last summer with an eye to your approval, and they are nearly worn out now. Mrs. Green is making over for me two dresses I had made in London 6 years ago." She reported that she was going soon with the children to Pearl City to wait for Frank's return.

Emma's gentle plaints were reinforced by some plain talk from Charles Brewer and Company. "The writer will say frankly, however," one of the partners wrote, "that we fail to see how you are going to have the time required to give personal attention to the affairs of the hardware company and at the same time proper attention to the O. R. and L. Company's business. We appreciate your ability, but that fails to supply the want of your presence at two widely different points at the same time, say in New York and Honolulu."

Frank at that point had become embroiled in a long-distance confrontation with J. G. Spencer, who had been running the Pacific

Hardware Company ever since Frank had first started talking to James Campbell. Now Frank had heard that Sam Damon was contemplating putting the firm into the hands of a receiver, and he was not pleased.

In May of 1893 Frank admitted not defeat but a temporary obstacle; he went home. Hard on his heels followed May and Walter, finished with their four years of schooling in Massachusetts.

Walter went straight to work on the railroad, doing anything apparently that needed to be done. In later years he reminisced about waiting each night at the depot until the last train came in to pick up the fares the conductor had collected, and rushing to the bank with them the next morning. A year and a half later, not yet quite twenty years old, he was signing the railroad's annual report as acting treasurer.

May's fiancé, Walter Frear, had finished Yale Law School with great distinction. Liliuokalani, in one of the last acts of her reign, appointed him a circuit court judge, and two months later the provisional government appointed him to the supreme court, at the age of twenty-nine. He and May were married in August. His new father-in-law esteemed him highly, and he remained connected with the Dillingham interests in one capacity or another for the rest of his life.

B. F. Dillingham had returned to a railroad not much changed from when he had left it more than a year before. No new track had been laid. Freight receipts were flat, and passenger traffic had fallen off during the revolution. Bills were unpaid, bond interest in default. Together, all departments of the business produced earnings after operating expenses of about $40,000, but from this figure had to be subtracted $85,000 in interest and rent deficit, leaving a loss for 1893 of about $45,000.

B. F. found himself, not for the first time, in a ticklish position. The railroad had issued no report at the end of 1892, during his absence; to come out with two whopping losses in a row might destroy public confidence forever.

Then, someone at the railroad had a bright idea. Bond interest was running well over $50,000 a year, contributing mightily to the deficit. Why not allocate a good portion of it to undeveloped property and, instead of charging it as an expense, increase the value of the property by the amount of the interest allocation? Nothing could be simpler. At the end of 1893 the railway accountant went back to the beginning and capitalized some $76,000 in interest expense, thus turning with a stroke of the pen a $45,000 loss into a $31,000 profit. For some years afterwards, in spite of intermittent criticism by auditors, the railroad continued a policy of capitalizing interest and taxes on undeveloped property.

This policy, though unconventional at the time, had a certain logic behind it, and is actually in line with recent trends in accounting. At the same time, however, the railroad was making no provision for writing off either development costs or the value that had been placed on intangible assets such as the franchise or leases. For that matter, it was charging no depreciation on the rails or rolling stock or any other physical asset. The net result had to be an overstatement of both the railroad's profitability and the value of its properties.

In so far as it is possible to read Mr. Dillingham's mind, it is safe to say that he intended no deceit or fraud on the public. He *knew* the value of his railroad and his bookkeeping reflected it. Against all laws of probability, time proved him absolutely and triumphantly correct.

But accounting methods paid no bills and put no cash in the bank. Mr. E. H. Wodehouse, outraged at not being paid on his bond coupons, accosted B. F. publicly at the post office and again at Bishop and Company; B. F. denied flatly that he had promised him any definite date. Similar incidents must have made life difficult for Mr. Dillingham.

W. G. Ashley, who had served as superintendent in B. F.'s absence, resigned to become marshal of the provisional government, and George Denison took his place. Denison, described as a "dynamo" by one of his fellow workers, continued as superintendent until Mr. Dillingham's retirement in 1915, when he took the title of general manager. His ability and devotion to the job enabled B. F. to concentrate more and more on financial matters, leaving operations in Denison's hands.

Fred C. Smith joined the railroad about this time as general passenger agent and remained with the line until his death in 1918. His duties, according to Denison, included selling tickets at Honolulu Station, dispatching trains, frequently acting as freight agent, occasionally going out as train conductor, and typing the general manager's letters, "which he [Dillingham] would usually prepare at his home at night and leave for Mr. Smith to typewrite."

An incident in September illustrated the rather informal atmos-

George Denison, shown here in his office in the new O. R. and L. terminal, served as superintendent of the railroad from 1893 to 1915, when B. F. Dillingham retired as general manager and Denison took his place. (Bishop Museum photo)

phere of the time. A man on the night shift at Ewa Plantation lost a hand in an accident and required medical attention beyond what the plantation could provide. Unable to reach anyone at the railroad on the telephone, the Ewa manager dispatched a plantation locomotive and car to take the injured worker to Honolulu. The night being moonlit and fine, a number of men from the plantation went along for the ride. When news of the incident reached B. F., he exploded. Only a few nights before, he remonstrated, following an evening entertainment, he had taken a party of friends for a spin down the line. If the trains had met, disaster would have resulted.

Frank Dillingham still knew very well that Pearl City and Ewa Plantation alone did not justify the railroad; the matter of extending the line occupied his mind constantly.

By this time, of course, he had long since given up the idea of reaching the north shore by going over the central saddle between the Koolau and Waianae mountains. The route through Waianae and around Kaena Point was longer, but the road would pick up traffic along the way, and the line would run practically at water level the whole distance. The route over the saddle would involve enough steep grades to require heavier locomotives.

In the middle of 1893 a ray of hope appeared in the shape of letters from A. Feek of Seattle, who described himself as a contractor and financial broker and furnished substantial references. Feek, it seemed, was willing to build the line to Waianae and Kahuku and take his pay in 6 percent railroad bonds. By the end of October, the O. R. and L. directors had approved a contract for 54 miles at $12,600 a mile, a total of $680,400 plus $50,000 for rolling stock. At last the extension would be getting under way.

# CHAPTER 29

*[I] thank my lucky stars that it was B. F. Dillingham with whom I had to deal in a matter of such vital importance to myself and my family.*

Dr. C. B. Cooper to B. F. D.
14 May 1902

FEEK, of course, turned out to be just another disappointment. After many delays he finally sent his son to Honolulu in July of 1894 to start the line. By December the contract was dissolving in mutual recriminations. Considerable work did get done, but Feek never finished even the grading. Frank took over the job personally, and in April of 1895 settled with Feek for what he had done.

Meanwhile, 1894 had its share of other problems. The bond interest remained in default, and the railroad owed, by the end of the year, a staggering sum of $350,000 in notes and accounts, besides the bond interest.

Frank personally was no better off. He was reduced to selling six of the eleven paintings by Joe Strong which he had acquired in 1889 in exchange for a $1,000 O. R. and L. bond. And in July he had to mortgage his private railway car, "Pearl," as additional security on a loan.

When the Oahu tax collector raised the assessment on the O. R. and L. ranch lands, Frank wrote in protest that "the whole income of the company at the present is not quite sufficient to cover current expenses, interest on bonds, and taxes. . . . We are obliged to pay Mr. Campbell $40,000 per annum for his lands—Honouliuli and Kahuku; we have rented nearly all the best lands, and yet they do not pay us nearly enough to pay him; the balance being chargeable to stock raising, which is a very high rent for pasture land, say $5,000 per annum. . . . The lease was made before the passage of the McKinley Bill, when sugar was $100 per ton. I have labored with Mr. Campbell to reduce the rent, but could not get one cent reduction."

In 1894 Frank asked the railway to buy the assets of the Hawaiian Construction Company, which had done no work for three years. It still owned the two locomotives acquired from the Sonoma Valley line, as well as dump cars and other equipment useful to the railroad. Final liquidation of the construction company took place in 1896, when it paid its shareholders handsome dividends in railway stocks and bonds, considered of little or no value a couple of years earlier.

And yet, in spite of all troubles, 1894 actually marked the turning point in the affairs of the O. R. and L. and of Frank Dillingham. It must have been difficult or impossible for anyone except Frank to recognize it at the time, but a faint glow in the sky did herald the approaching dawn.

The bond interest was still in arrears, but by the end of the year the delinquent amount had shrunk to about $6,000. Mr. Campbell agreed to a remarkably liberal schedule for payment of the past-due rent. The road still showed a loss, but less than $5,000 for the year. The railway in 1894 hauled 36,000 tons of freight, up from 25,000 tons the year before; sugar and coal each amounted to almost 8,000 tons, and a new item, fertilizer, close to 7,000 tons.

A sharp eye could see other hopeful signs for the future. Ewa Plantation was working out its problems. Railway grading was complete from Ewa Mill almost to Waianae, and when the line could be built, Frank figured that it would add more than $30,000 a year in net profit. Frank took Admiral John G. Walker and his staff to see Pearl City and Ewa Mill, and accompanied them while they examined Pearl Harbor. He believed that a naval station at Pearl Harbor would increase the population of Pearl City to ten thousand.

In September Frank mentioned for the first time that he had "another plantation site to offer." Ewa Plantation had taken the Honouliuli lands up to an elevation of 200 feet; now Frank had convinced himself that it was possible to pump water higher than 200 feet and still make money out of raising sugarcane. By December he had got out the first prospectus for what became the Oahu Sugar Company.

The great good news of 1894, and the factor which made Frank have faith in a new plantation, consisted of another change in U.S. tariff policy. The Wilson–Gorman Tariff Act repealed the bounty for domestic sugar producers and reinstated the sugar tariff, from which Hawaii was of course exempted by the Treaty of Reciprocity. B. F. figured that this act would mean between $3 million and $3.5 million annually to the Hawaiian sugar industry.

In September of 1894 Frank Dillingham reached the milestone of his fiftieth birthday, though he was probably working too hard to notice it. Almost ten years before, a chance conversation with James Campbell had changed his life radically and permanently. In the interim he had progressed from running an unprofitable dairy and a marginal hardware store to controlling an insolvent railroad.

In many ways, Frank had not changed over the years. He still worked as hard as he had when he was a young sailor trying to educate himself. He still cared as much as ever about Emma and the children, though he might not see much of them for long periods. He still lived at top speed, carrying a dozen different projects in his head at all times. He had a way of catching a bull by the tail and hanging on for dear life, which must have made life in his family far from dull.

Like other men, he was full of contradictions. He could be close and tough in a business deal, especially as he grew older, but he had a warm and generous heart for those less fortunate than himself. He took a particular interest in young people who sought an education, and his files contain many letters from young men thanking him for their start in life. He made his gifts quietly, out of the public eye, without seeking credit for his benefactions.

Frank's brother-in-law, Guss, died only a few months after getting married, without making a will. Frank was named executor of his estate, which consisted almost entirely of some property on Fort Street where Guss had kept his store. Under the law, Guss' property went in equal shares to his widow and his sister, Emma. In order to help the widow, Frank induced Emma to forswear her portion. He had the property appraised by two eminent men of business, who came up with a figure of $13,000 less a mortgage of $6,000. Knowing that the appraisal was far too low, Frank personally paid off the mortgage, paid the widow $20,000 for the property, and gave the property to Emma. In this case fair dealing incurred no penalty, as Emma later sold the property for $30,000.

Frank was full of small, personal kindnesses, especially toward those who worked for him. When John Hughes made his first trip back to the mainland, Frank learned that he had no overcoat; he quietly called home and had his own coat delivered to the dock and put in Hughes' cabin. On another occasion, Frank and Elmer Paxton were together on business in San Francisco. When Paxton came down with a painful bout of rheumatism, Frank insisted that Paxton take his bed, and he himself slept on a cot in the living room so that he could help Paxton if needed during the night.

From the day of their marriage, Emma remained the center of Frank's life, even though they spent long periods apart. Harold wrote of his years at Punahou that "while I labored over Latin vocabulary, I would hear him telling my mother in minute detail his efforts, plans, and disappointments of the day, on and on far into the night." When Frank and Emma were apart, he would write her at length on business. One has to marvel at Emma's strength of character to bear up under the strain of Frank's setbacks and disappointments.

Frank enjoyed people's company, but his commitment to business was so intense that he had little concern for a conventional social life. He found his greatest pleasure and relaxation in listening to Emma play the piano, for which she had both talent and training. In 1884 Frank and Emma opened Woodlawn for a large "lawn party" to raise money for Punahou's first grand piano.

Frank and Emma shared at least one common source of strength; their religion. Frank took a leading role in the Congregational Church, and gave an address on behalf of the trustees when Central Union Church moved, in 1891, into a new building on Beretania Street opposite Washington Place. He became interested in Protestant missionary work among Portuguese immigrants, and served as head of the Portuguese Sunday School until his long absence from the islands in 1892–1893. Walter, he reminisced later, would help him by coming along to play the violin. When in 1930 the Honolulu Board of Supervisors passed a resolution naming Dillingham Boulevard in B. F.'s memory, one of the supervisors, M. C. Pacheco, testified to the inspirational effect on him of Mr. Dillingham's teachings at the Sunday School.

Frank's religion was a quiet and personal one, without bigotry or intolerance. He gave to Roman Catholic charities, and admired the Episcopal service. After Lowell Smith's death, he learned to enjoy a fine Havana cigar, and he liked an occasional glass of good whiskey, though anything approaching loss of control would have been foreign to his character. He had no asceticism; he liked shiny carriages and fast horses and a well-cut Prince Albert. Eating was his vice; his Chinese cook was famous in Honolulu.

But underneath his gusto and enjoyment of life, he had tremendous motivation and strong moral commitment. He believed beyond question that he was doing a splendid thing by opening up western

Central Union Church on Beretania Street, opposite Washington Place. When this church was dedicated in 1891, Frank Dillingham gave an address on behalf of the trustees. Central Union Church later moved to its present location on the site of the Dillingham home, Woodlawn, and the building pictured above was sold to Schuman Carriage Company. It has since been torn down. (Bishop Museum Photo)

Oahu, that by increasing the general prosperity his projects would make people healthy, happy, and virtuous. He believed implicitly in the material values of nineteenth century America, not as an end in themselves, but as a means of achieving a happy and moral state of civilization.

Two things set him apart from other men: his intelligence and his inability to quit. He had the vision and foresight to see what Oahu could become, and the practical ability and vigor to bring it about. And because he *knew* what the future could hold, he never despaired, in the face of incredible obstacles and discouragements.

The year 1895 almost made 1894 seem like a false dawn. It began with the Wilcox Rebellion, an attempt to restore the monarchy, in which Frank served as sergeant of the company of the Citizens' Guard assigned to the Woodlawn end of the city. "Our 13 year old boy [Harold]," Emma wrote, "was permitted the joy of carrying a gun, wearing a belt of cartridges and taking his turn at standing guard for six hours at a time." The rebellion fizzled out rather quickly, but it had a depressing effect on business and particularly on passenger traffic on the railway.

In September an outbreak of cholera required the suspension of all traffic on the railroad for a month, and partial suspension for longer.

In spite of these difficulties, the road showed slightly higher earnings from both freight and passengers. Rent receipts were very low, however, and the company ended the year with a loss of $18,000.

But 1895 marked a real milestone: completion at last of the line to Waianae.

Charles M. Cooke, after amassing a substantial fortune in Lewers and Cooke and other ventures, had retired from businesses in Hawaii and moved to California. (He later returned to head the Bank of Hawaii and C. Brewer and Company.) In California he was keeping his hand in by acting as a purchasing agent. He and B. F. Dillingham agreed early in 1895 on a deal in which Cooke would make a substantial loan to the railroad, and B. F. would buy through Cooke the rails, spikes, and fishplates which were the principal items B. F. needed to complete the line.

Mr. Cooke was a careful man. Welch and Company, he noted, had charged him with 5,314 rails, five more than he had ordered. "I trust you will carefully count the number in each shipment and report to me," he cautioned Mr. Dillingham.

The Waianae sugar mill, at an early date. Hermann Widemann had a well-equipped plantation and factory, with its own little railroad, but lacked an efficient means to ship the sugar to market. The extension to Waianae marked a turning point in the Oahu Railway's progress. (Bishop Museum photo)

Cooke's loan grew to a total of $105,000, and eventually the O. R. and L. assigned to him the Waianae subsidy money as security. B. F. paid a high price for his help, but no doubt rejoiced to get it at any price. The total cost of the extension, including some new box cars that John Hughes built, came to a little over $140,000.

The new line opened with great celebration on the Fourth of July 1895; overall passenger receipts for July were the highest in the company's history. The coming of the railroad made it possible to reach the remote Waianae coast in an hour and a half, instead of by a day's ride on horseback, and ended the isolation of this remote corner of Oahu.

Frank's projections proved correct. The new section of line and particularly the freight from Waianae Mill substantially helped the railroad's earnings. With two plantations to service, the little railway began to look more like a going concern.

# CHAPTER 30

*You have a way of convincing people that things are going to be as you want them to be, that exceeds the ability of any one whom I know.*

W. H. Chickering to B. F. D
30 April 1902

AT the end of 1895, the O. R. and L. was still in extremely shaky condition. It owed mountainous notes and accounts, its loss for the year had exceeded the previous year's, and its total income from hauling freight and passengers amounted to less than $74,000.

Four years later the same railroad had taken in close to $400,000 in one year from freight and passengers, was earning a net profit of better than $100,000 a year, had refinanced its "floating debt" into a new 6 percent bond issue, and had every assurance of more and more business in the future.

In part, this dramatic turnaround came because economic conditions improved significantly and because new sources of business opened up along the right-of-way. In large part, it came because the O. R. and L., in the person of B. F. Dillingham, went out and developed the sources of business and built the line to serve them.

B. F. Dillingham never did things one at a time. At the same time that he was working and scheming to push the track to Waianae, where the plantation was waiting for the railroad, he was laying the groundwork for the Oahu Sugar Company at Waipahu, where the railroad was waiting for the plantation.

Frank had begun working on the Waipahu project soon after restoration of the U.S. sugar tariff in 1894. He already controlled certain O. R. and L. lands not leased to Ewa Plantation which he believed to be suitable for sugarcane, and he had a strong ally in Mark Robinson, who controlled his family lands around Waipahu. By the end of the year, B. F. secured an option to lease the Ii lands of Waipio lying between Robinson's and Waiawa. With these building

The Oahu Sugar mill at Waipahu. Modern machinery hardly changed the rural look of central Oahu. (Hawaii State Archives photo)

blocks, he put together a package which proved attractive to H. Hackfeld and Company, probably the most prestigious of all the sugar factors at that time. In December of 1896, more than two years after he began working up the scheme, Frank signed a formal agreement with Hackfeld under which Hackfeld put up half a million cash for 5,000 shares of stock in the new plantation at $100 par. The total capital amounted to $1.8 million or 18,000 shares. Robinson got 1,500 shares for fee simple property which became the mill site at Waipahu. The O. R. and L. got 2,550 shares for paid-up leases at Honouliuli (above Ewa Plantation's lands) and Waiawa; 1,550 of these shares went to Frank as promoter, and the balance stayed in the O. R. and L. treasury. The railway also got a sixty-year freight contract and the right to supply milk and beef to the plantation. Pacific Hardware Company got the concession to supply tools. The rest of the stock was offered to the public in December 1896 and was immediately oversubscribed. Paul Isenberg, the Hackfeld managing partner, became president of the new corporation, and Frank first vice-president. Hackfeld, of course, got the agency contract.

It proved a very nice pie to divide. The company subsequently needed more capital and sold an amount of stock equal to the origi-

Charles R. Bishop, banker (Bishop and Company) and husband of Bernice Pauahi Bishop, last of the Kamehamehas. After her death Bishop moved to San Francisco, where he continued to work with Dillingham on his financial projects. (Bishop Museum photo)

nal issue, but by October of 1899 the company had paid a 25 percent stock dividend and the stock was selling for $190, making the original $100 shares worth $237.50 on the market, even though the just-harvested first crop had totaled only 8,000 tons. Over the years Oahu Sugar has proved itself one of the best plantations in Hawaii. Also over the years Oahu Sugar had probably less friction with O. R. and L. than any other plantation on the line, except perhaps Waianae, which Hackfeld also factored.

With the exception of the lease to Campbell's lands, no other deal which B. F. Dillingham ever put together did so much to enhance his prosperity and prestige and that of the railroad as did the formation of the Oahu Sugar Company.

In June of 1895 Charles R. Bishop sold the bank of Bishop and Company to Samuel M. Damon and moved to San Francisco, where he continued to keep close tabs on affairs in Hawaii. Frank sent him a prospectus for the Oahu Sugar Company, which he viewed with pessimism. Two years later he was conceding Frank's remarkable success with Waipahu and predicting that he would never be able to repeat it with Waialua.

Waialua indeed offered a tough challenge. The Halstead brothers had a mill in operation there, and Frank started talking freight rates to them in the middle of 1897. At the same time he was again looking for bigger game. With Mark Robinson, he bought from George J. Campbell for $35,000 the same Kawailoa Ranch that he had once owned with John Paty, consisting of 10,000 acres of Bishop Estate leasehold. The value ostensibly consisted of the 2,200 head of cattle, 110 horses and mules, and tools and buildings. Frank believed that the real value lay in the land's potential for sugarcane, once irrigation water reached it. Subsequently, after the Bishop Estate had renewed the lease on reasonable terms, his belief was amply confirmed.

Kawailoa is on the north shore of Oahu, east of Waialua. To the west of Waialua is Mokuleia, where Gaspar Silva had put together a sizeable ranch. Working through Henry Waterhouse, Frank executed a pincers movement on Waialua by getting control of Mokuleia Ranch late in 1897. He later secured a lease on the James Gay estate at Mokuleia, and some smaller properties in the vicinity, so that by the middle of 1898 he controlled 7,000 acres of potential cane land on either side of Waialua.

The Halstead mill at Waialua, Oahu. Waianae and Waimanalo sugar mills had their own railroad systems at an early date, but the smaller plantations like this one depended on ox-drawn carts for transportation. (Hawaii State Archives photo)

Meanwhile, the fortunes of the O. R. and L. had improved wonderfully. Revenues more than doubled in three years. In 1896 the road showed a profit of $28,000 and headed toward a record performance in 1897. Knowing full well the impact that Oahu Sugar Company alone would have on future earnings—he estimated that it would double the road's freight receipts within a few years—Frank determined on a bold and vital step: refinancing in Honolulu of the company's entire debt into a single series of 6 percent first mortgage bonds. At the end of 1896 the railroad had four different bond issues outstanding, totaling slightly over a million dollars, and owed in addition about $350,000 in notes and $220,000 in other accounts. In October B. F. began canvassing the bondholders and creditors of the railroad to get their commitments to take the new issue of bonds in place of old obligations, on the basis of greater security through a single mortgage on all the assets of the company. Just before Christmas the directors authorized the new bond issue in the amount of $2 million, enough to pay off the company debt and extend the line to Kahuku. So persuasively did B. F. present his plan that by January 1897 he had enough bondholders, creditors, and new bond purchasers lined up to almost cover the company debt, and he declared the refunding plan in effect at that date.

This refunding not only reduced the burden of interest payments on the company, but it also eliminated the constant threat, which B. F. had lived with since 1891, that a few unfriendly creditors could put the line into bankruptcy at any time. Also, as excess money dribbled in from bond sales, it enabled the company to begin its extension toward Waialua. At the end of 1897 the company still held $580,000 worth of unsold bonds, but by the end of 1898 less than $60,000 worth remained in a reserve fund in the treasury.

B. F.'s success with the refunding may have lacked in drama, but it enabled the railroad to go forward and at the same time testified to growing public confidence in B. F. Dillingham and the Oahu Railway.

The extension to the Halstead mill at Waialua proved an extremely tough bit of construction. The line around Kaena Point, nicknamed "Cape Horn" by the construction crews, involved 4½ miles of blasting, cutting, and filling to give a solid roadbed 30 feet above the water. It also opened up some of the most beautiful scenery on any railroad in the world; trains would often stop at Kaena Point to let the passengers look back along the Waianae coast.

The line around Kaena Point opened up spectacular vistas. This train has rounded the point and is headed toward Waianae and Honolulu. (Photo by Kent Cochrane, Bishop Museum)

In June of 1898 the line reached Waialua Mill.

B. F. Dillingham, meanwhile, was continuing his efforts to put together a large, modern plantation at Waialua. The Halstead brothers were willing to sell, but evidently they wanted more cash than Dillingham could command. In an effort to find financing, Frank promised the plantation agency to his old friend Jim Castle and offered to let him promote the plantation. Nothing came of it, however, possibly because Castle was beginning to see the outlines of an even larger proposition under which Castle presently became a partner in Alexander and Baldwin by wresting control from the Spreckels family of the immense Hawaiian Commercial and Sugar Company (generally known as H. C. and S.) on Maui; this enterprise absorbed all the capital that Castle and his brother Will and the estate of their late father could muster.

B. F. talked also to John H. Soper, who had served as an energetic marshal of the kingdom under the Reform Cabinet and later as leader of the military forces of the revolution of 1893. Soper represented an American named E. S. Valentine who claimed to be looking for investment opportunities. B. F. offered to let the two men float the plantation, but nothing came of it. Soper and Valentine, however, popped up again in spectacular fashion a little later.

In the middle of July 1898, Castle definitely withdrew from negotiations, and Frank approached in his stead Joseph B. Atherton of Castle and Cooke. By that time Ewa Plantation had recovered from its nearly disastrous start and was busily making its investors rich. A year later its original $100 shares (by then split five for one) had a market value of $700 and were paying annual dividends of 60 percent on the original price. Castle and Cooke was in a position to expand.

Working through A. J. Campbell, Castle and Cooke got an option on the Halstead property at $650,000, bringing the total acreage involved in the projected plantation to 17,850, and then settled down to almost three months of hard negotiations with B. F.

Originally B. F. had asked $150 per acre for his 7,000 acres of land, part of which was fee simple and part under a sixty-year paid-

Colonel John S. Soper, shown here with Sanford B. Dole *(left)*, was one of the leaders of the 1893 revolution. He later sued B. F. Dillingham over the issue of Waialua Plantation stock. (Bishop Museum photo)

up lease, for a total of $1,050,000, plus some promotional stock. He finally settled for $600,000 in stock for the land plus $75,000 worth of promotional stock. He also picked up for the railroad the freight and coal contracts and a limited concession on the meat and dairy business.

Castle and Cooke got $750,000 in stock for the Halstead plantation, plus $75,000 promotional stock. B. F. undertook to sell in Honolulu the balance of the stock, to the value of $1 million. The public offering of this stock resulted not only in an oversubscription, but also in the most spectacular lawsuit of B. F.'s career, of which more later.

Unlike Oahu Sugar, the Waialua Agricultural Company was not an instant success. Its lands stretched over an immense area and required ten years of development before they began to pay dividends. Irrigation proved a particularly difficult problem. The fundamental concept was sound, however, and the plantation ultimately became one of the leading sugar producers in the islands.

B. F.'s protégé and chief financial lieutenant at this time was Elmer E. Paxton, who started out as a bookkeeper at the railroad and became B. F.'s private secretary. Paxton had a marvelous ability with figures and a more orderly approach to affairs than B. F., who concentrated so hard on matters closest at hand that he had a somewhat casual attitude toward note payments and bank balances. Paxton became auditor and a director of the railroad in 1900, but he had enjoyed B. F.'s confidence for some years before then.

When Oahu Sugar was floated at the end of 1896, Paxton cast his eyes at other O. R. and L. lands farther east, above Pearl City and at Waimano and Waiau. With B. F.'s informal blessing, he studied plans for cultivating them and talked both to Ewa Plantation and to Oahu Sugar about milling any cane he might raise there. Early in 1898, however, before his plans had matured, he heard that another group was eyeing the same lands with a view to uniting them with other lands in Aiea and Halawa, thus controlling enough acreage to warrant another sugar mill. B. F. let Paxton have an option on leasing the O. R. and L. lands, which Paxton used to good advantage in helping form the Honolulu Plantation Company, generally referred to as Aiea because of the location of its mill.

Unlike other plantations formed around that time, Aiea was controlled and largely owned in San Francisco. Alone among the island plantations it built its own refinery to supply local needs. In June of

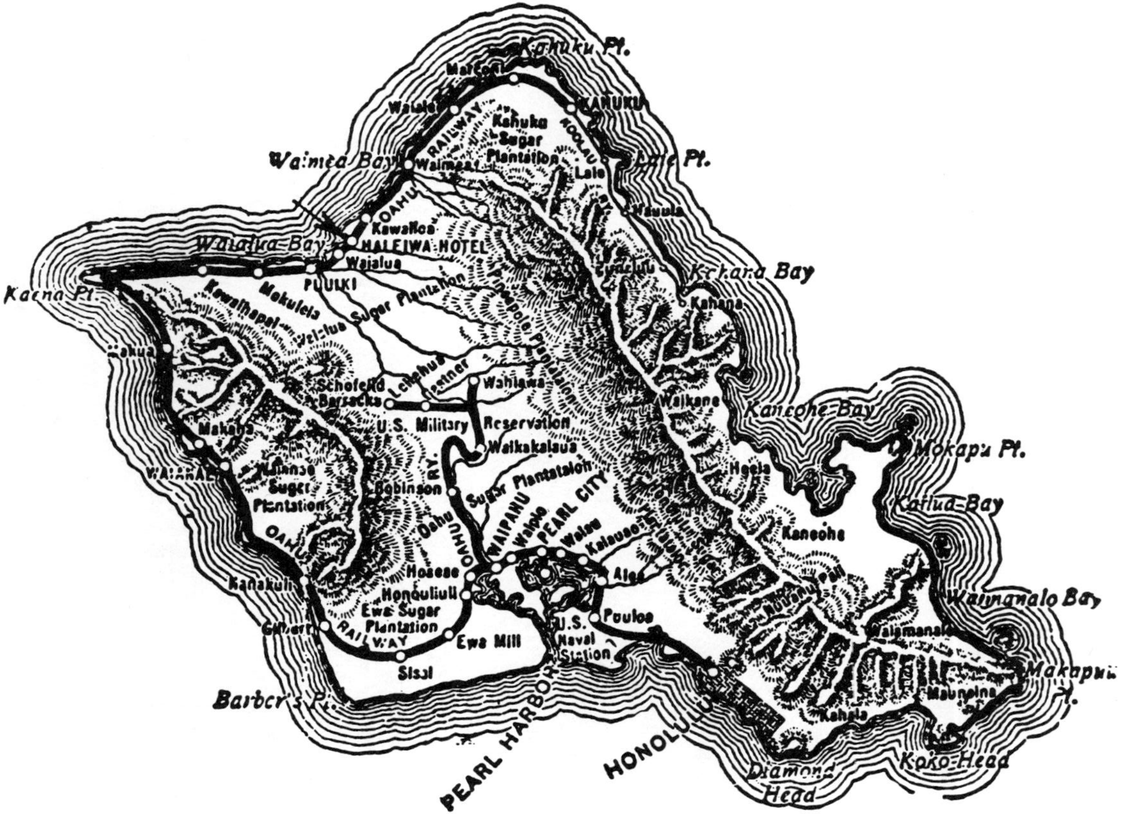


The routes of the O. R. and L. and of the connecting Koolau Railway from Kahuku to Kahana Bay. The O. R. and L. also connected with lines operated by the army and navy and with tracks of the sugar and pineapple plantations. At one time a line was proposed from Honolulu around Koko Head and up the windward coast to Kahuku. (Bishop Museum photo)

1898 it signed a freight contract with the O. R. and L., giving the railroad one more source of receipts.

Early in 1897, with the railroad more than a year away from Waialua, B. F. reached an agreement with Kahuku Plantation on freight rates. In June of 1898 the line reached Waialua, but a prolonged dispute with the government over the location of the proposed extension to Kahuku was not settled until the end of September. Three months later, on New Year's Day 1899, the first scheduled passenger train chugged into Kahuku, 71 miles out of Honolulu, and the main line was at last complete.

The "toy railroad," as Frank liked to refer to it, now served six flourishing sugar plantations and all the thousands of workers who lived on them. During the year 1899 it carried 236,000 passengers and nearly 200,000 tons of freight, and earned a net profit of $212,000. Things were indeed looking up.

# CHAPTER 31

*The conditions in the* Islands *are so* phenominal [sic] *and have been for so many years, the Islanders have gotten to look at them as* normal.

L. E. Pinkham to B. F. D.
2 November 1898

ONE large problem remained for the railroad. Six plantations now expected to ship their sugar by the Oahu Railway to Honolulu and on to America over a dock adequate to handle only one of them.

In 1899 George Denison reminded B. F. of the scope of the problem. Oahu Sugar, he wrote, would be milling 200 tons of sugar daily, Ewa and Waialua each the same, Waianae 50 and Kahuku 55, for a total of more than 700 tons a day, requiring two vessels loading the entire time in grinding season. Each day 300 tons of coal would be coming in, meaning two ships discharging at all times. In addition, the railway docks would be handling fertilizer, lumber, and general cargo. At least five berths were required. Experience had shown that staging cargoes out on scows was very costly.

At that point B. F. had been working on the problem for ten years, ever since the railway started. He believed that the railroad should own in fee simple a big enough chunk of the waterfront to develop the necessary docks; this thinking had led to his original purchase of 25 acres of tidewater land. Lorrin Thurston had temporarily stymied him by insisting on the government's owning a narrow strip along the waterfront, on which he would grant no more than a ten year lease. B. F. accepted the situation for the time being in order to get the first dock, but he had no idea of putting further costly improvements on short-term lease land. During 1894 and 1895 negotiations for a swap of land between the Hawaiian government and the O. R. and L. came to nothing. B. F. decided to try another tack.

In the 1890s, what is now Sand Island in Honolulu Harbor consisted of a reef, known as "Kaholaloa," much of which was barely above water. One end of it was leased to the Board of Health and was known as "Quarantine Island." John K. Sumner and James I. Dowsett owned undivided half interests in the area, which included a mudflat called "Kahaohao" just west of the O. R. and L. tidewater lands. Across from the present site of Aloha Tower, Sumner had built a house on about 4 acres of dry land. With his eye on the mudflat, B. F. induced Sumner to give him and Mark Robinson a ninety-nine-year lease at $5,500 a year on his share of the property, reserving the house site to Sumner. The lease included an option to purchase at any time for $100,000. B. F. also got from Dowsett an option on his half of the property, but the option expired in 1897 without B. F.'s having been able to exercise it. Dowsett subsequently died and his share of the property went into his estate.

Perhaps because his partial control of Kaholaloa strengthened his hand, B. F. finally got just about what he wanted out of the government. In 1896 G. F. Allardt worked up a plan for the development of the west end of the harbor, and after B. F. met with the cabinet to explain his position, the government accepted it as the basis of the official plan. The government and B. F. then worked out a compromise under which B. F. gave up a portion of his original 25 acres in exchange for Kawa Pond and the remainder of Kuwili Pond, adjoining the terminal. The government and the O. R. and L. agreed to dredge an area 700 by 1,200 feet between Queen Street and the sugar warehouse, making room for 7,200 feet of wharf frontage, of which the government would build and own 3,500 feet and the railway 3,700 feet. Thus, Frank finally got the fee simple property on deep water that he had wanted for so long. Allardt negotiated a contract on his behalf with the Pacific Coast Dredging and Reclamation Company, with the stipulation that the railway could purchase the reclamation company's dredger for $25,000 at the completion of the contract.

By 1901 the railway had built docks capable of accommodating eight to ten ships, two warehouses each holding 10,000 tons of sugar and equipped with electric conveyors which could handle 120 tons of sugar per hour, and a wharf shed for inbound freight. The crisis had been met.

This development took place on land already owned by the company. The question of what would happen to Kaholaloa, though it was settled not long afterwards, belongs in another chapter.

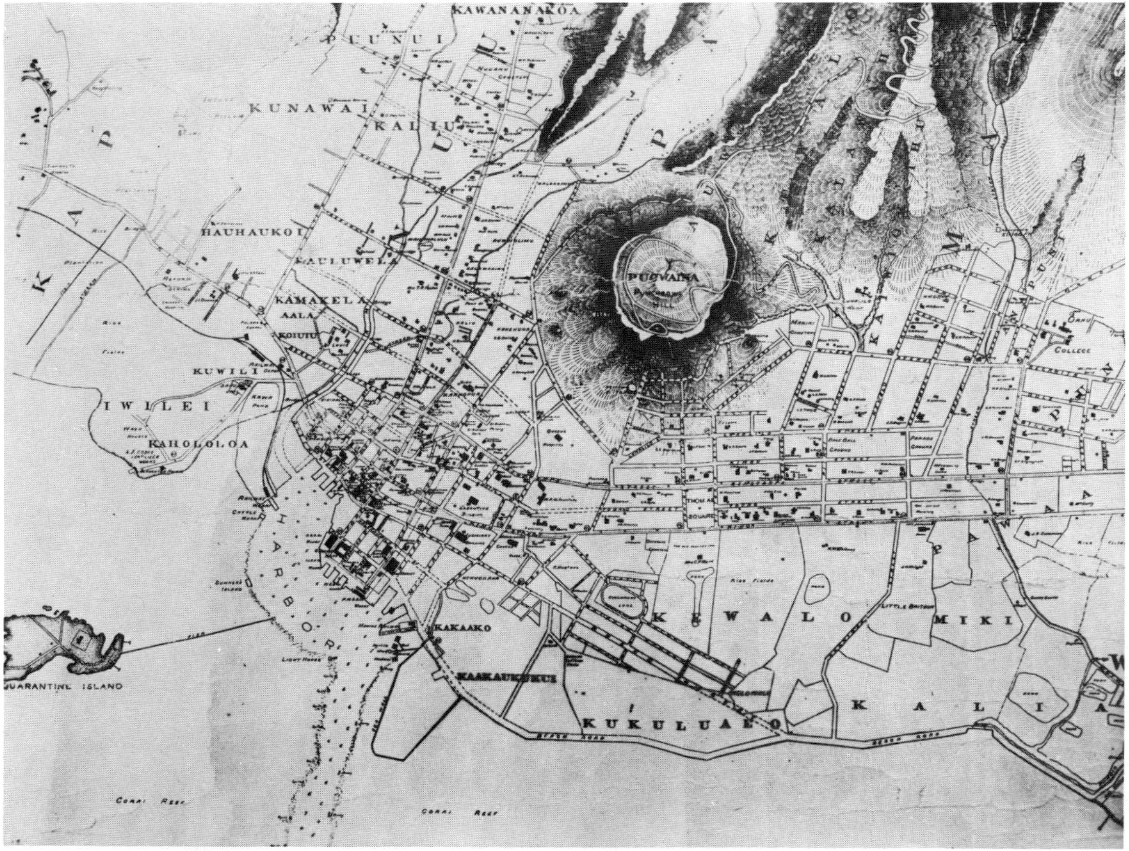


M. D. Monsarrat's 1897 map of the central section of Honolulu shows the B. F. Dillingham estate, Woodlawn, at right center. Above it, just below Oahu College (Punahou School) is marked the site of the Woodlawn Dairy. At the left can be seen the location of the O. R. and L. depot, reclaimed from Kuwili Pond, and Kawa Pond, Kaholaloa, the railroad wharf, Quarantine Island and Sumner's Island. (Hawaii State Archives photo)

The railroad docks at Honolulu in the early 1900's. With five sugar plantations along its right-of-way, the O. R. and L. was doing a booming business. (Bishop Museum photo)

The wave of prosperity which swept over the islands in the second half of the 1890s brought with it at least temporary relief for another problem which had been festering for years: the Pacific Hardware Company.

Pacific Hardware, the successor to Dillingham and Company, was owned largely by Frank Dillingham and James Gordon Spencer, with Frank holding the majority of the stock. Spencer had managed the concern since 1889, when Frank had ceased to draw a salary. During Frank's absence in 1892–1893, the firm had got into financial trouble and the two principals had quarreled bitterly. After Frank's return to Honolulu, they had patched things up enough to continue the business, but without much success.

In 1898 Castle and Cooke decided to dump their mercantile business, and offered it to Frank Dillingham, who was negotiating with them at the same time about Waialua plantation. The price worked out at about $200,000, for which Castle and Cooke took three notes from Frank for $50,000 each, with the balance payable in stock in the reorganized Pacific Hardware. This deal gave the hardware company a capital of $350,000 and a commanding position in the Honolulu market. For the next couple of years, it managed to show a profit.

The railroad also took advantage of prosperity by improving the existing track. Out of Honolulu station the line was straightened to parallel the present Nimitz highway, joining the old line at Waller's slaughterhouse; the old line near King Street became a spur serving the Pacific Guano and Fertilizer Company. The whole main line from Honolulu to Ewa Mill was relaid with 48-pound Bessemer steel rails.

To haul the new tonnage over the extended line, the railroad put into service two beautiful new Baldwin 30-ton "Consolidation" (2-8-0) engines, at a landed cost of just over $10,000 each. One of them, number 76 (for 1876), was named *Reciprocity,* and the other, number 98, *Annexation.* The names were appropriate. The O. R. and L. existed by virtue of the plantations it served, and the plantations existed by virtue of reciprocity and annexation.

Annexation had a very personal meaning for B. F. Dillingham. Restoration of the monarchy had long since become a dead issue, and

With the line finally under construction toward Waialua, the O. R. and L. in 1897 ordered from the Baldwin Locomotive Works two new main-line engines. Number 76 (for 1876) was named *Reciprocity,* and number 98 *Annexation.* For the whole of their careers on the O. R. and L., these two locomotives carried brass stars instead of numbers on the fronts of their boilers to mark them as special. (Photo by Kent Cochrane, Bishop Museum)

The Hawaiian flag comes down on Annexation Day, 1898. Despite sentimental ties to the monarchy, B. F. Dillingham welcomed Annexation once the monarchy had been overthrown. (Photo by Ray Jerome Baker, Bishop Museum)

any lingering sentiment that B. F. may have felt toward the monarchy had dissolved in his belief that union with the United States would best ensure a free and progressive government for the islands. He had worked for annexation, and when it came in 1898 he welcomed it with open arms.

Part of the process of annexation was the framing of an Organic Act to serve as a constitution for the new territory. Congress appointed a commission—partly from its own members and partly from Hawaii—to draft this act, subject to final approval from Washington. Sanford B. Dole and Walter Frear represented Hawaii on the commission, and it is a measure of Mr. Dillingham's standing that the first meeting of the commission, a week after Annexation Day, took place at Woodlawn. Later he gave the commissioners a dinner which included oyster cocktails, salmon wafers, soup, rolls, boiled mullet and mayonnaise, mashed potatoes, brain and mushroom patés, Roman punch, roast turkey, creamed potatoes, French peas, stuffed tomatoes, chicken salad, cheese, crackers, tutti frutti ice cream, cake, coffee, salted almonds, olives, pickled peaches, peppermints and *sauerbrunnen* (''mineral water''). Somehow, the commissioners survived to produce the Organic Act.

Frank loved to spend money on projects which added to the pleasures of life and satisfied his sense of the fitness of things. Soon, his new prosperity reflected itself in additions to the Woodlawn house, in a tennis court and swimming tank, and in a tally-ho coach by Studebaker. He bought the Hassinger property at Pearl City, together with the 15-foot cat-rigged sailboat *Hermit;* many years later Harold wrote that he was ''always grateful for the few precious hours while he taught me the rudiments of sailing.'' Vacations at Pearl City became a regular part of family life. But Frank's greatest gift to the family, and particularly to Walter, was Mokuleia Ranch.

Frank bought Mokuleia Ranch from Gaspar Silva presumably because it included potential cane land which he wanted for Waialua Plantation. But after the cane lands had been sold, there remained a great strip of mountainside and beaches with flat land in between and a homestead in the middle. The railroad ran through it, within

A view of the big house at Woodlawn, after the extensive additions made around 1898. A tennis court and swimming tank were also added. (Courtesy of the Dillingham family)

Interior of the big house at Woodlawn. Turn-of-the-century tastes did not run to understatement. (Courtesy of the Dillingham family)

The B. F. Dillingham property at Pearl City Peninsula. Here Frank Dillingham set aside "the few precious hours" to teach his son Harold the rudiments of sailing. Harold later became the most prominent yachtsman in Hawaii. (Courtesy of the Dillingham family)

easy distance of the homestead. In later years Mokuleia became dearer to Walter Dillingham than probably any other spot on earth, but when his father first bought it he had little chance to enjoy it. In 1898, at the age of twenty-three, he went off to Harvard to resume his interrupted education. Harold went off the same year for two years of school at Oakland before he entered Harvard, leaving only fifteen-year-old Marion at home.

Around this time Frank undertook another project which ultimately gave pleasure to many people, though it never enjoyed much financial success.

On a point of land a mile or so past Waialua, with a charming view of the mouth of the Anahulu River, he secured a fifty-year lease from the Bishop Estate (at $100 a year) and built the Haleiwa Hotel.

O. G. Traphagen, the same architect who built the Moana Hotel, designed a low, inviting building surrounded by lanais, to accommodate about thirty guests. The total cost of the hotel building, including a pumping plant, dynamo, wiring, plumbing, bridge, arbor,

The Haleiwa Hotel in its heyday. Note the horseless carriage to the right of the portico. (Photo by Ray Jerome Baker, Bishop Museum)

depot, powerhouse, three cottages, and a barn came to about $40,000.

For the first manager, Frank got Curtis P. Iaukea, a courtly and well-educated Hawaiian who had served Kalakaua with distinction as chamberlain and special envoy. Iaukea made an investment in the hotel and became Frank's partner and later, after its incorporation, a stockholder.

On 5 August 1899 Frank hosted a press excursion to inspect the new premises. Entertainment proffered to guests included luaus, dancing, swimming in the ocean or pool, boating, canoeing, fishing, golf, tennis, pool, and billiards. We buy our fish alive on the beach, the hotel boasted, raise our own vegetables, fruit, chickens, and eggs, and get our meat and milk from a nearby ranch. Rates were $3.00 per day ($5.50 for two in the same room) or $17.50 per week. The round trip from Honolulu on the *Haleiwa Limited* cost $2.00.

By 1899 Frank had become, by the standards of his time and place, a very wealthy man. With the growth of the city, Woodlawn had become a valuable holding. He also owned property at Pearl City and

Interior of the Haleiwa Hotel, with stairs at the center rear. (Photo by Ray Jerome Baker, Bishop Museum)

Parlor car number 64 with its stylish rear platform provided *the* way to travel to the posh Haleiwa Hotel in the early 1900s. (Photo by Ray Jerome Baker, Bishop Museum)

Mokuleia. He still controlled the dairy and the hardware business, and also the Hawaiian Carriage Manufacturing Company. He had a large investment in the highly successful Oahu Sugar Company, and in Waialua Agricultural. But the cornerstone and foundation of his wealth remained through the years his absolute stock control of the Oahu Railway.

The charter of the O. R. and L. empowered it "to hold real estate and other property not to exceed at any time double the amount of its Capital Stock." By 1896 it was clearly exceeding this limitation, even if the intangible values assigned to the franchise and leaseholds were excluded from the list of properties. For the sake of nominal conformity with the charter, the directors voted an increase in stock from \$700,000 to \$1.5 million, with \$700,000 of the new stock issued as a 100 percent stock bonus and \$100,000 kept in the treasury. To balance the ledger on the asset side, the value of the franchise was arbitrarily increased by \$250,000, freight contracts were put in at \$200,000, terminal division property was written up by \$200,000, and Pearl City property by \$150,000.

At the same time that the directors were voting to increase the capital stock and to refund the company debt into the consolidated bond issue, B. F. made a pitch for his own compensation for extending the line beyond Ewa Mill.

> Your General Manager, [he stated], has from the date said Company was organized, acted not only in the capacity of General Manager, but he has also applied himself to the work of a promoter, financier and broker; and personally, with M. P. Robinson, became indorser for your Company for a large amount during a period of great business depression. . . . I have not only given my whole attention during my waking hours to the business of your Company, resulting in a very heavy loss to me in my other business interests, but I have incurred heavy personal liabilities of over $250,000; and in the latter part of 1891, when all confidence in the business interests of this country was completely shattered, my wife was required to sign jointly with me a note for a heavy amount, secured by railway and other stocks, thus making her liable for her own property and life insurance made in her name.

B. F. reviewed for the directors the failure of A. Feek to finish the line to Waianae and his own successful effort to carry it forward "during the unsettled period following the insurrection of 1895," and reminded them that he had never been paid more than $300 a month as general manager. He asked as payment for the entire job $670,000 in bonds and $66,400 in stock, representing the same price to the company as quoted by Feek.

Two years later, with the line complete to Kahuku, the directors increased the outstanding stock to $2 million (again writing up the assets) and paid B. F. his 664 shares as agreed. At the same time he presented a bill for about $176,000 for extras, which the directors paid by issuing him stock at half its face value, or 3,518 shares, presumably because the work had been undertaken before the two-for-one stock split. About 2,500 shares were held in the treasury.

In 1899 the company offered its treasury stock to the stockholders at par. The stock was not yet selling on the market for par, but Frank took a large block. A month later the company declared a 5 percent dividend, its first, and a good chunk of it went to pay for Frank's share of the treasury stock.

The company undoubtedly treated Frank generously in the settlement. With the stocks and bonds valued at par, he apparently made over a quarter of a million dollars profit on the contract. On the other hand, his efforts put the company in a position where in 1900 it made more than $300,000 net profit; it seems a fair exchange of favors.

In November 1900 the directors of the railway "deeming that its affairs had forever passed the problematic stage" ordered a monthly dividend of one percent. Shortly afterwards, the capital was increased to $4 million by another 100 percent stock dividend, and the dividend was adjusted to one-half percent per month on the new stock.

B. F. Dillingham got as much satisfaction as money out of his railroad's success. His report to the directors at the end of 1898 sums up his feelings.

> It is not too much to say that the development of the sugar industry on this Island since 1890, is directly due to the presence of . . . railway transportation.
>
> The fine large sugar estates which have, within the last ten years, sprung into existence along the line of your road representing a capitalized value of $9,300,000 and a present market value of more than $15,000,000, will, when developed to their maximum capacity, send to market 140,000 to 150,000 tons of sugar per annum, and yield a revenue in taxes, at the present rate, of $200,000 per annum. This large production, greater than the entire output of the whole Islands a few years since insures to this Island a permanent business and adds enormously to the value of all other property, but it especially enhances the value of business and residence property in and around Honolulu. This increased value also greatly augments the revenue receipts to the Government through the increase of taxes.
>
> The total subsidy granted by the Government, to encourage the construction of your road, was $3,500 per mile, after the construction of the first fifteen miles which was not subsidized, which for say 56½ miles would amount to a total subsidy of $197,750.
>
> Not half of the total subsidy has yet been paid. In the meantime the increase of taxes already realized, exceeds the total subsidy paid, and only a few years hence the increase of taxes will exceed annually the total subsidy paid and yet to be paid.
>
> It is an honor to have been associated financially and otherwise with an enterprise which has been instrumental in doing such a vast amount of permanent and lasting good. Every member of this community, and those in other parts of the world who have in any way contributed through the agency of money or moral influence and support to the carrying out of the aims and purposes of your Company are fully justi-

> fied in pointing with pride today at the grand results which have crowned their faith and work.

After due allowance for year-end rhetoric, this report remains a clear statement of Frank's philosophy of business.

At this point B. F. Dillingham had reached the climax of his business career. Nothing that he subsequently accomplished on the outer islands resembled the triumphant results of the Oahu Railway, either in making money or in increasing the welfare of the community.

And yet on a personal basis his subsequent career must be judged a triumph, in spite of the anguish it brought to him and to his family. For sheer dogged perseverance in the face of discouragements of every kind, his latter efforts surpassed even his holding together the Oahu Railway in its formative years.

Frank's star—his ambition and love of adventure—gleamed perhaps less brightly in his later years, but his anchor—his love of home and family—never held more steadfastly. In the last analysis it was for his family, even more than for his personal pride, that he struggled, even to the point of ruining his own health, with the problem of preserving the fortune he had built up.

The story of that struggle is confused and often unedifying. His son Walter once remarked that Hawaiian businessmen of B. F.'s generation spent more time in fighting each other than they did in tending to business. The wealth that showered onto Hawaii in the years after Reciprocity brought with it a generous measure of knavery and callousness. There were those who felt that B. F. himself had wronged them through his business dealings. "Self-preservation," he wrote on one occasion, "is the first law of nature." But his private correspondence clearly shows that he tried "to do the right thing," as he liked to say.

Frank's role was that of a loner. He stood a little aloof from the power centers of his day, the big banks and trust companies and the Big Five sugar factors. From time to time he needed one or another of them and would form a temporary alliance or working agreement, but his private opinions of the people involved were generally unflattering, and he guarded his independence.

Even in social life he was never one of the herd. "I have been such a slave to business for the last twenty years, or in fact all my life," he wrote in 1904, "that I have seemed to have very little time to devote to my friends in a social way."

Always his family provided the core of his life, the reason for his existence. Toward his wife and children and grandchildren he was gentle and affectionate and playful. He gathered them around him physically, so that the entire family lived on the Woodlawn grounds or immediately adjacent to them. And his oldest grandchildren even today remember him with pleasure and affection, as a kindly old gentleman who took a lively interest in their doings.

# Part V
# A Time of Trouble

# CHAPTER 32

Some men *are always saying, "If I get out of this scrape I will never get into another one" when they* know *they would not recognize themselves under any other condition. I am just wondering a little bit if I am not one of those* "some men."

B. F. D.
10 February 1900

IN 1898 B. F. Dillingham sat on top of the world. The railroad had finally achieved success, with excellent earnings that promised to increase steadily. By the end of the year the main line would reach Kahuku. Ewa Plantation, increasing its rental payments year by year, in 1898 would pay almost $52,000 for its share of lands for which the railroad paid a total rent of $40,000. Oahu Sugar was making a promising start, and B. F. had just joined with Castle and Cooke in launching Waialua. Honolulu Plantation would soon be paying both rent and freight. B. F. had signed a contract for the building of the Haleiwa Hotel. Shortly, he would break the log jam that was holding up the development of Honolulu Harbor, and come out of it with about 4,000 feet of deep-water wharves on fee-simple land. On all sides there were opportunities to be seized and work to be done.

If Frank could have restrained himself at that point, the rest of his life would have been quite different. If he had taken Emma and gone to Europe for six months, or perhaps even if he had gone to the volcano to get away from business for six weeks, things might have worked out differently. But he had been starved for success for so long that when it came it unbalanced his judgment. After years of frustration he had proved himself resoundingly and triumphantly correct, and he came perhaps to believe that whatever he touched would turn to gold. In 1898 he started on a series of misadventures which in time broke his health and almost bankrupted him.

Henry P. Baldwin of Maui dominated both Alexander and Baldwin and the huge H. C. and S. plantation. His joint ventures with Dillingham in Kihei and Olaa plantations were both notable failures, but Dillingham was later able to persuade him to bail Theo. H. Davies and Company out at McBryde Sugar. (Bishop Museum photo)

These ill-starred projects had one thing in common: all were located on the outer islands. The first of them was the Kihei Sugar Company on Maui.

According to B. F.'s later statement, he went to Maui with no intention of promoting a plantation, but was so much impressed with the prospects of Kihei that he undertook it. The chief mover in the enterprise was no less than H. P. Baldwin, considered by many the greatest sugar man of his day; associated with him was Lorrin Thurston, now out of the government and eager to make money.

Baldwin contributed 1,576 acres he owned on Maalaea Bay, and he and Thurston put in 8,000 adjoining acres which they owned together. For this land they received $1.5 million in Kihei Sugar stock, or about $156 per acre. The total capitalization was to be $3.0 million, and Frank undertook to raise the remaining $1.5 million through public subscription. He put up seven hundred fifty shares of O. R. and L. stock as a forfeit if he should fail to sell the Kihei stock within four months. If he did sell the stock he would get his O. R. and L. back, plus three thousand shares of Kihei out of the thirty thousand (par $50) which Baldwin and Thurston received for their land.

Frank's later difficulties stemmed to a great extent from the custom prevalent at that time of financing new corporations by the sale of "assessable" stock, that is, stock which was not fully paid for at the time it was issued. Typically, the promoters of a new enterprise would offer $50 par stock at $10 down, with the balance due when called by the directors, generally in increments over a period of as much as two years. Obviously this system made stock easier to sell, but it certainly encouraged speculation rather than investment. Along with those who bought stock as a legitimate investment came those who had no intention of holding it for dividends but who counted on reselling it for a quick profit, usually before they had to pay more than the original assessment.

Theoretically any one who subscribed for stock remained responsible for the debts of the corporation up to the unpaid amount of his subscription in the event of the corporation going into bankruptcy, but this contingency does not seem to have deterred speculation. Usually if a subscriber failed to meet his assessments he lost only what he had put into the stock already.

Sugar prices were high in the late 1890s, and the industry prospered mightily. Annexation in 1898 seemed to assure good times forever by placing Hawaii behind the screen of Uncle Sam's protective tariff. People of little means dreamed of getting rich by buying sugar stocks. Each new plantation that came along was going to become another Ewa and pay 60 percent dividends within a few years.

Speculation centered in Honolulu, the scene of B. F. Dillingham's triumphs. In just a couple of years B. F. had moved in public esteem from a laughingstock to the greatest financier in Hawaii. When he began backing plantations like Kihei, of which the public had little knowledge beyond the prospectus, hundreds of people bought in the belief that his judgment would make them rich overnight. It was a time of frenzied boom, with all the speculative excess of such a period.

B. F. put Kihei on the market in the middle of February 1899 through Henry Waterhouse and Company, and the issue was quickly oversubscribed, with a $2 premium being offered. John F. Colburn wrote to ask for 500 shares for Prince David and Prince Cupid, expressing willingness to pay a reasonable premium. (He referred, of course, to David Kawananakoa and Jonah Kuhio Kalanianaole, nephews of Liliuokalani.) Of B. F.'s 3,000 promotional shares, 378 went for services rendered or in appreciation of past favors; he sold 1,030 shares, mostly on two-year notes, and kept about 1,600. Elmer Paxton became vice-president to represent the Dillingham interest in the company. Alexander and Baldwin got the plantation agency.

From that point on, B. F. had little to do with Kihei. Apparently, he put his stock in Emma's name, as she owned 1,570 shares in 1904.

Like most of the Annexation plantations, Kihei turned out to be undercapitalized. Money that had been earmarked for the Kihei mill had to be used for the irrigation system, and still the plantation had no money to develop water for the good lands above the 400-foot level. The mill which the plantation had ordered went instead to Olaa, leaving Kihei dependent on a milling contract with H. C. and S. At the beginning of the new century sugar prices took a serious slump, and labor costs went up when the Organic Act took effect.

By late 1900 Henry P. Baldwin came to the conclusion that he had received too much stock for his lands and returned $445,000 worth, half his holdings, to the company treasury, and also pressured the reluctant Thurston into turning in another $95,000 worth, representing the estimated increase in the value of Thurston's stock on account of Baldwin's action. This act represented a most gracious gesture toward the other stockholders, but it paid no bills. By 1902 Kihei owed Alexander and Baldwin about $150,000, and the Alexander interests began pressing to get the debt paid.

From today's vantage point, it appears that Kihei failed because of bad timing. The days of starting a sugar plantation on a low budget had passed. Money had become extremely tight in Hawaii, and no one had the means or inclination to invest the additional sums that Kihei needed. Baldwin had his hands full with H. C. and S., which posed many problems in the early years of Alexander and Baldwin control. B. F. Dillingham grumbled about the "grossest kind of bad management," but could do nothing.

Since Kihei had no mill of its own, merger with either Haiku and Paia plantations or with H. C. and S. offered a possible solution. In 1908 Kihei sold out to H. C. and S. at $10 a share, thus passing into history along with American Sugar on Molokai, Maunalei on Lanai, and Kona Sugar on Hawaii, all of which started at about the same time.

As far as B. F. personally was concerned, the failure of Kihei Sugar had no particularly disastrous effects. He had put little cash into the venture, and he presumably recovered it from the eventual liquidation of his promotional stock. It bothered him, however, that friends of his had lost through his promotion, and the failure undoubtedly hurt his public reputation.

Even before he put Kihei's stock on the market, B. F. made a trip to Kauai to organize another plantation.

Duncan McBryde had settled on Kauai in the middle of the nineteenth century and had eventually acquired a large cattle ranch on fee-simple property at Wahiawa, between Eleele and Kalaheo, and on government lease lands at Kalaheo. In 1898, twenty years after his death, the McBryde Estate bought the Koloa Agricultural Company, which owned 2,571 acres on which it raised cane for grinding at Koloa Sugar. At Eleele, August Dreier owned a small plantation of 1,120 acres, partly planted in cane, with a mill of sorts and the country's only electric railroad. B. F. proposed to unite these lands into a large plantation with a modern mill at Wahiawa.

Working with a lawyer named William A. Kinney, who had married into the McBryde family and represented their interests, B. F. arrived at a payment of $1.60 million for the lands, in the form of eighty thousand shares at $20 par in the new corporation, with another $1.85 million to be raised through the public sale of stock. Unlike his Kihei arrangement, B. F. made a large investment in the enterprise by personally buying Dreier's plantation for half a million and then turning it in for an equal amount of stock in the McBryde Sugar Company.

The public stock sale, following hard after Kihei's, met with equal success. J. B. Atherton wanted 1,000 shares and his sons Frank and Charles each 250. Edward Pollitz and Company, San Francisco brokers, took 12,500 shares, and Harry J. Auld of the O. R. and L. machine shop begged B. F. to save him 50 shares as he feared he would never get it through the public offering. B. F. had such faith in the enterprise that he set aside for himself a large block of assessable.

Like the other Annexation plantations, McBryde quickly proved to be undercapitalized. In particular, its founders had underestimated the job of clearing rocks from the former grazing lands. Irrigation also proved expensive to install, and the cost of pumping water excessive. In less than a year the plantation ran up an overdraft of half a million dollars with its agents, Theo. H. Davies and Company, who reacted with shock and consternation. McBryde became a source of concern to B. F. Dillingham in the years ahead.

But B. F. made his major commitment in the area south of Hilo on the island of Hawaii.

Lorrin A. Thurston had long had a lively interest in this region. As minister of the interior he had pushed the construction of a carriage road from Hilo to the volcano, and after retiring from government service he had organized a company which took over the Volcano House and also a tiny hotel at Punaluu in Kau.

The 1890s saw a considerable interest in growing coffee, which was making a promising showing in Kona. Coffee trees grew abundantly in the lands between Hilo and the volcano. Under the Land Act of 1895, the government opened up a large tract in the area as 50-acre homesteads, and settlers moved in with the expectation of making large returns from coffee. They soon found, however, that commercial growing of coffee was completely impractical there because of lack of enough sunshine to ripen the fruit. No other crop had proved adapted to the area, and the settlers faced the loss of everything they had put into their homesteads.

According to Thurston's statement made about twelve years later, the Olaa homesteaders approached him, saying that coffee had proved a failure and had left them in a semibankrupt condition, and asking him to organize a sugar plantation as a way out of their troubles. The matter, Thurston said, was entirely too big for him to handle, and accordingly he laid it before B. F. Dillingham. The district of Puna, he added, was at that time a wilderness, except for isolated coffee planters at Olaa.

In later years B. F. made the rather odd complaint, coming from him, that Thurston had rushed the whole organization of the Olaa Sugar Company. Apparently Thurston made a flying trip to Honolulu and in one Sunday afternoon session with B. F. agreed on the outline of the proposal. B. F. also made the statement later that his own role was supposed to be quite a minor one, with Thurston shouldering the major responsibility, an arrangement quite foreign to B. F.'s character.

Lorrin A. Thurston: public servant, lawyer, firebrand advocate of annexation, long-time business associate of B. F. Dillingham. (Bishop Museum photo)

In 1914 B. F. wrote Thurston of the ship "which we launched one Sunday afternoon when you came down from Hilo enthused with the idea that a sugar plantation should be started at Olaa to save the coffee landowners and the town of Hilo from ruin. . . . I was very loath to go into anything more, having just reached 'Easy Street' after a ten years hard struggle in financing and building the Oahu road. But I finally agreed to put up money to buy a piece of land at Olaa which you said would cost $40,000."

Whatever the original plan may have been, it soon grew into a huge scheme involving thousands of acres of land and millions of dollars. The two men agreed to establish a first-class plantation and sugar mill, and brought Alfred W. Carter, Thurston's law partner, into the project. In order to get hold of the land quietly, without running the price out of sight, the three of them formed a partnership for the purpose of securing options on property, closing the options, and turning the property over to the new corporation when it was formed. B. F. agreed to carry a one-half share of the partnership, Thurston one-third, and Carter one-sixth.

Working through local agents in Hilo, the partnership of Dilling-

Alfred W. Carter, through his association with Lorrin Thurston, became a partner with B. F. Dillingham in acquiring land for Olaa Plantation. Carter later withdrew from the partnership and harassed Dillingham for payment of the resultant debt, much to Dillingham's disgust. (Photo by T. J. Williams, Bishop Museum)

ham, Thurston, and Carter secured the necessary options in February, March, and April of 1899 and incorporated Olaa Sugar Company early in May. Possibly because of Thurston's association with H. P. Baldwin, they signed a fifteen-year agency agreement with Alexander and Baldwin under which A & B agreed to advance as much as $250,000 against operating expenses during the crop season. A & B also bought $250,000 in stock for cash.

The promoters envisioned a huge plantation of 19,500 acres in Olaa and Keaau. The Olaa section would extend on both sides of the volcano road from 9 miles out of Hilo to 22 miles. The Keaau section, mostly on leased lands belonging to the Shipman family, would extend 4 miles from the volcano road to the sea, and the plantation would also take in lands on both sides of the road running south to Puna. The mill would be built near the junction of the volcano and Puna roads, at about the 9-mile mark, where it would be easily accessible for cane flumed from the higher lands and hauled by train from the lower parts.

Almost the entire area has deep volcanic soil, and the region is distinguished by extremely heavy rainfall, averaging about 150 inches a year at the mill site and more than 200 inches at the upper part toward the volcano. No irrigation was deemed necessary, but the promoters planned to develop water resources in order to flume the upper cane to the mill.

The elevation of the upper Olaa lands ran as high as 2,200 feet, giving a cool climate. As cane did not tassel at that elevation, the organizers planned to get seed cane from the tops of the *mauka* cane, thereby wasting little or no sugar.

The promoters came up with an extremely attractive forecast. Citing the opinions of two plantation managers who had examined the area, they estimated 6 tons of sugar for each acre of cane harvested, and calculated on harvesting 8,000 acres a year, for an annual output of 48,000 tons of sugar. At a net return of $70 per ton after deducting expenses of marketing, this tonnage would give an annual revenue of $3.36 million. Using figures from four small plantations near Hilo, they estimated production costs at $30 a ton or $1.44 million in total, leaving an annual net profit of $1.92 million, or 38 percent on the $5 million capital.

Half of the stock, or $2.5 million worth, would be issued to the promoters in payment for the lands, and the balance would be sold as assessable stock, on which 10 percent, or $2, would be payable on each $20 share at the time of subscription.

Like every other plantation stock issue that B. F. handled, Olaa Sugar sold out immediately.

Thurston had given B. F. the excuse he needed to get into the enterprise by citing the good they could do by rescuing the homesteaders, and, in fact, the plantation did give the settlers a chance either to sell out at far more than they could otherwise have got, or to stay on and raise cane to be milled on shares. But in doing good for others, B. F. seldom passed up a profit for himself. The partnership eventually received close to two and a half million dollars in stock, from an original cash investment of less than a quarter of a million. The total cash resources of the partnership, including borrowings, came to about $670,000; after allowing for expenses, including generous commissions in stock to the Hilo agents, it appears that the partners sold the lands to the plantation for more than double what they paid for them. In doing so, however, they paid out a substantial amount of cash (though some settlers took stock in payment of their lands) and received payment entirely in stock of the new corporation.

Having organized the company and sold its stock, B. F. turned his attention elsewhere. Thurston was elected president of the corporation, H. P. Baldwin vice-president, Carter secretary, J. B. Castle treasurer, and Elmer Paxton auditor. B. F. believed that his own participation would be limited to receiving dividends.

South of the Olaa mill site, beyond the last fields of Olaa Sugar, the vast district of Puna stretched away to the east and south coasts of the island. The land was mostly level and a good deal of it fertile, though here and there rough *'a'ā* lava broke up the arable stretches. It was in this area that Mark Robinson, B. F.'s old partner in the Oahu Railway, chose to establish a plantation along with A. J. Campbell. Campbell's brother Will was designated manager.

B. F., along with Thurston and Paxton, was one of the incorporators of Puna Sugar Company, but Robinson and A. J. Campbell were the moving spirits and in fact had been operating the plantation as a partnership for some time before they ran out of money and decided to incorporate. The plantation was capitalized at a million dollars, with $650,000 going to Robinson and Campbell for about 12,000 acres which they had acquired. Only a quarter of a million dollars of assessable stock was sold, and it does not appear that B. F. held more than perhaps a token amount. "I do not hold myself responsible," B. F. wrote later, "for the starting of Puna Plantation nor for the management."

Although B. F. had no personal stake in Puna, he subsequently got himself enmeshed in its misfortunes first by his efforts to help his friend Robinson and then, after Robinson's interest was wiped out, by his efforts to salvage something for Olaa out of the wreckage.

Olaa Sugar Company by itself lacked one thing: a reasonable way to get supplies in and sugar out. Its mill site was 9 miles away from the nearest deep water, at Hilo, and could be reached only by a carriage road that took half a day to traverse. The answer was obvious: build a railroad from the port of Hilo to the mill site and beyond to the settlements along the volcano road, with a branch down to Puna to tap Robinson's plantation. Actually, there was no port of Hilo, but B. F. borrowed a leaf from S. G. Wilder's plan and determined to make one.

And so was born the Hilo Railroad. Walter Dillingham once said that it killed his father, but that was many years down the line, and in 1899 B. F. believed that even the short run to Olaa and Puna would do as well as the O. R. and L.

B. F. capitalized the road at only $50,000, with a bond issue of $450,000. Once work started on the ground, the engineers figured that $419,000 would build the road complete with wharf, warehouses, and rolling stock. B. F. expected a profit of $200,000 or so a year, mostly from hauling for the two plantations. He carefully kept majority stock control in his own hands, allowing Thurston, Carter, and a few others a minority interest.

Early in the game, the decision was made to build the Hilo Railroad as standard gauge: 4 feet 8½ inches, compared with the 3-foot gauge of the O. R. and L. B. F. later came to regret the decision, but in the expansive days of 1899 it seemed a natural step in a program to keep everything first class.

# CHAPTER 33

*I am ready to face the storm and will "fight the battle out." I will try to be a good philosopher and do my duty conscientiously. Will be steadfast in all things. Experience worth more than millions of dollars. A true, perfect nature to be desired above all things.*

Memo in B. F. D.'s handwriting
Undated, probably 1899

BACK in Honolulu, B. F. Dillingham faced a storm which arose from his promotion of Waialua Agricultural Company in 1898.

At one point in his negotiations, B. F. had offered the lands he controlled at Mokuleia and Kawailoa to John H. Soper and E. S. Valentine. Before their option expired, Soper and Valentine exchanged it for the right to sell in San Francisco $1 million worth of stock in the Waialua Agricultural Company, which B. F. by then was putting together with Castle and Cooke.

B. F. believed that Soper and Valentine had forfeited this right by failure to exercise it and that in addition he had notified them of its termination. Soper and Valentine, however, proceeded to sell the entire block of stock at the same time that B. F. was taking subscriptions for the same stock in Honolulu.

If the various subscribers could have known that Waialua would pay no dividend for the next ten years, they might have pressed their claims less eagerly. As it was, however, both Soper and Valentine and the San Francisco subscribers brought suit against B. F. to compel him to deliver the stock, and Soper and Valentine sought damages as well.

The case took most of the year to be settled. In October 1899 Judge Antonio Perry of the First Circuit Court rendered his decision in favor of Soper and Valentine, directing Dillingham to deliver to them the stock in question plus $62,875 in damages.

This decision left B. F. in a most unpleasant dilemma. He believed absolutely in the justice of his case and looked forward to winning on appeal, but he recognized also that Waialua Agricultural as a codefendant was hopelessly stalled until the case was finally settled. Appeal to the Supreme Court would take a year or more, during which time his own interests and those of his friends would suffer. With the case under appeal, he would not have been able to borrow the money he badly needed.

At least Frank had the support of his family. "There never was a more wonderful man than papa *in every way!*" Emma wrote to Marion, who had gone East to school at Dana Hall. "He is not sick or discouraged but is cheerful & clear headed. . . . papa plans to save every one connected with him, & who has shares in Waialua, & do the *square thing by the other side in full*. . . . All this excitement of waiting, & the letters made me have a nervous headache, but it is much better now."

B. F. did manage to work out a compromise under which Waialua issued another million dollars worth of stock, so that both the San Francisco and Honolulu subscribers got their shares. B. F. paid $65,000 in damages and the court costs, and the suits were dismissed. The additional capital actually helped Waialua, but B. F. lost not only the $65,000 but a great deal of prestige and good will as well.

During the time that the Soper–Valentine case was pending, B. F. got into an embarrassing situation with Castle and Cooke, the cofounders of Waialua. First he defaulted on the first of three notes for $50,000 each which he had given Castle and Cooke in payment for their merchandise business. J. B. Atherton helped him to work off this note under a personal arrangement, taking a piece of B. F.'s hide as he did so, but B. F. still owed the firm $100,000. Then B. F. defaulted on assessments due on 1,760 shares of Waialua stock standing in his name, and 500 in Emma's. Paxton, meanwhile, had somehow managed to borrow another $30,000 on B. F.'s account from Castle and Cooke, supposedly for three months. Castle and Cooke eventually took over the assessable stock, but B. F. still owed the company $130,000. Castle and Cooke raised the interest rate to 8 percent and hung on to substantial collateral, but the situation was unhappy for both sides.

A new flare-up of the perennial disputes between Ewa Plantation and the Oahu Railway did nothing to help matters. This time the parties argued about the proper share of land taxes that Ewa Plantation should pay, with the difference amounting to a substantial sum annually. So acrimonious did the debate become that they finally petitioned the Supreme Court for a decision, with rather ridiculous results. The court at the end of 1903 upheld the O. R. and L. position, and within a matter of months the two companies were arguing again over just what the decision meant.

This period saw an increased strain also between B. F. and Samuel M. Damon. Damon had become a man of wealth and power, particularly through his ownership of the leading bank in Honolulu. He had bought out Charles R. Bishop in 1895, thus becoming the sole owner of the banking house of Bishop and Company, and he also served as a trustee of the estate of Bernice Pauahi Bishop. By legacy from Princess Pauahi, he owned the splendid *ahupua'a* (a land division extending from the uplands to the sea) of Moanalua. This was the same Sammy Damon whom Emma long ago had decided to teach "some little sums in Addition."

Frank Dillingham had had great aloha and respect for the Reverend Samuel Chenery Damon, S. M. Damon's father. As far back as 1876 he had gone with Mr. Damon to visit the old Damon house in Holden, Massachusetts, and he had repeated the pilgrimage with Emma in 1887 and would go again in 1906. Mr. Damon had given Frank and Emma the use of his home on Chaplain Lane when they were first married, and Frank served as a pallbearer at Mr. Damon's funeral.

But something in the personalities of Frank and young Sam Damon led to constant friction between them. Frank was outspoken, positive, enthusiastic, and sometimes overbearing and unreasonable. Sam was cautious, cool, noncommittal, and sometimes vacillating and evasive. Sam was a bankers' banker, in the days before bankers had heard of public relations. Frank was enough to give a conservative banker nightmares.

In spite of his bold and visionary schemes, however, Frank had gained the confidence of Mr. Bishop during the last years of Bishop's residence in Hawaii, to the point where Frank owed the bank some $350,000 when Bishop sold out to Damon. Frank had heard that in the sale this obligation had been valued at $75,000 or $100,000, and it rankled that his credit should be discounted so severely.

By 1898 the O. R. and L. was showing good earnings and had refinanced the floating debt into a consolidated bond issue. It came as an unpleasant shock, therefore, when Bishop and Company refused

Samuel M. Damon, who bought the banking house of Bishop and Company from Charles R. Bishop. Something in the personalities of Damon and Dillingham clashed, and they fought sporadically for some twenty years. (Bishop Museum photo)

to continue an overdraft privilege for the railway. The fledgling Bank of Hawaii agreed to lend $25,000, out of $50,000 requested, and the Bishop Estate trustees lent another $20,000. Since Damon served as a Bishop Estate trustee, Bishop and Company's action probably indicated a lack of funds rather than a lack of faith in the O. R. and L., but the incident upset B. F. very much.

In 1899 a group headed by George W. Macfarlane and Cecil Brown (James Campbell's attorney) proposed to start a new bank in Honolulu, and persuaded B. F. to come in with them. B. F. put in for four hundred shares at $100 par but received an allocation of only two hundred, in what was incorporated as the First American Bank of Hawaii. The capital was $750,000, but the trust division broke off a year later with a capital of $250,000, leaving only $500,000 for the bank itself, which by that time was known as the First National Bank of Hawaii. The promoters wanted B. F.'s name for window dressing and persuaded him to serve as vice-president, though he had no hand in running the bank.

This venture proved completely nonproductive for B. F. The new bank lacked enough capital to operate with any effectiveness at all, and the directors seemed unable to agree on a plan for progress. B. F.'s participation in the bank undoubtedly antagonized Damon, without solving any of B. F.'s problems. Ironically enough, when B. F. got into serious difficulties in 1904, the First National Bank of Hawaii proved the least cooperative of all his creditors.

A large bone of contention between Frank and Sam Damon involved Frank's plans for the west end of Honolulu Harbor. Damon opposed these plans, and Frank suspected that he did so because he wanted to develop a new port on his own property. "Sam Damon's peculiar conduct towards the O. R. and L. Co.," he wrote, "the proposed wharf improvements under our control, and his treatment generally of all matters of personal interest to me, passes my comprehension."

B. F. meanwhile had been spending money freely, on improving his homes, on a "billiard parlor outfit" from James D. McInerny, on a new phaeton from G. Schuman, on a seat on the Honolulu Stock Exchange, and on charities. He gave $4,000 to Frank W. Damon for assistance to the Chinese mission work, and $1,000 for improvements to Aala Park. He made what seems an extraordinarily liberal settlement with James G. Spencer of all their accounts to date. He bought the lease of the island of Kahoolawe, which was operated as a sheep ranch. He had always wanted money, and now that he had it he was going to enjoy it and do some good at the same time.

Another project that he had in the back of his mind would require more capital. Frank controlled John K. Sumner's half interest in the reef off Honolulu Harbor and in the tidelands adjoining the O. R. and L. waterfront property, but his option on James I. Dowsett's half interest in the same property had expired in 1897 and Dowsett had refused to renew it. Dowsett died not long afterwards, leaving a large but unliquid estate consisting mostly of ranching operations on leased lands. His fee-simple property included, besides the half interest in Kaholaloa, the lands of Puuloa on the far side of the Pearl Harbor entrance, where he had established a salt works, some property in Kalihi, and the Rose Ranch at Ulupalakua, Maui. It also included the Nuuanu property, known today as the Dowsett tract, over which

Frank Dillingham had gone to court with John Wood. His leased property consisted of ranches at Waianae-Uka (Schofield Barracks), Halawa, Aiea, Kahauiki (Fort Shafter), Nanakuli, Mikilua, Lualualei, and Maunaloa. Apparently this far-flung operation had got out of control, as the rents were seriously in arrears and the Bishop Estate was threatening foreclosure over a debt of about $60,000.

B. F. Dillingham loved to make money and do good at the same time, but those whom he helped often remembered the money he made rather than the help he gave them. In this case, he worked up a plan which saved the Dowsett Estate from insolvency and at the same time gave him full control over Sumner's reef.

B. F.'s plan, which all the heirs eventually accepted, involved setting up a new corporation to be called the Dowsett Company, Ltd., with a capital of $150,000. The Dowsett Estate would turn all its property in to this corporation and would receive $90,000 in stock plus 3 percent bonds of the company to the amount of $1.2 million, for eventual distribution to the heirs. B. F. would put up the $60,000 cash required to make the estate solvent, receiving a like amount of stock (six thousand shares) plus the right to vote another sixteen hundred shares, which gave him voting control of the corporation. B. F. would manage the corporation, receiving for expenses not more than $3,000 a year until the corporation's net income exceeded $45,000 a year, at which time he might draw up to $6,000. Payment of bond interest would at all times come second only to taxes.

In terms of immediate cash, this deal seems quite unattractive for B. F. Dillingham. He had to put up a substantial amount of money with no prospect of dividends in the foreseeable future, and the management of the company would be a burden rather than a source of income. But it did give him full control of Kaholaloa during the critical period when he was trying to nail down his plans for that area.

By 1899 B. F. had made his peace with the local government over the west end of Honolulu Harbor and had got the 4,000 feet of dock space that he needed, but that settlement had no bearing on the status of Kaholaloa.

The Republic of Hawaii and after Annexation the U. S. government had used a portion of Kaholaloa as a quarantine station, under lease from the owners. As early as 1896, the minister of the interior had refused to pay the lease rent on the grounds that Sumner's title really included only the fishing rights, with the reef itself belonging to the government. With Annexation, the government's claim passed to the United States, but no legal determination had been made as to the real ownership.

B. F. first brought a suit for ejectment against the quarantine station, but before it was settled he made a trip to Washington in 1902 and agreed on a compromise under which the U. S. government received title to the reef, and the Oahu Railway and the Dowsett Company got title to the tidewater parcel of Kahaohao adjacent to the railroad's docks. The United States undertook to dredge a 600-foot channel between the two sections, filling the Kahaohao mudflats with the dredged material. B. F. had to bring another lawsuit to enforce his option on Sumner's interest, but eventually the deal was consummated and the Oahu Railway and the Dowsett Company each received an undivided one-half interest in 112 acres of prime harbor property.

At first glance the United States seemed to have come away the winner, because the area that the government received far exceeded that of the private companies. But in truth B. F. had bargained away a doubtful legal claim for extremely valuable industrial waterfront property. The whole incident was in fact typical not only of his foresight but of the tenacity with which he pursued a chosen goal.

Advantageous as it proved, however, the Dowsett Company arrangement did require at the end of 1899 $60,000 cash, which B. F. had to borrow. He already owed Castle and Cooke for the merchandise purchase, he had borrowed $160,000 from the estate of S. N. Castle, he owed August Dreier $250,000 on the Eleele deal, he had borrowed $150,000 from the Bishop Estate and $100,000 from Claus Spreckels and Company, the partnership of Dillingham, Thurston, and Carter was heavily in debt, and he held assessable stock of $1.1 million at par, on which probably not even a third was paid in. The obvious answer was to borrow more money, and Frank gave first refusal to the new bank in which he held stock.

When Frank got excited, he habitually turned to letter writing as a release. On 18 September 1899, he wrote twice to Cecil Brown regarding a proposed loan from the First American Bank (which was about to become the First National Bank) and three times to George Macfarlane on the same subject. He asked for $500,000 to pay the Castle Estate notes, take control of the Dowsett Estate, and meet his assessments for the next six months. Obviously the new bank could not carry a loan of that size; he requested them to secure the money through the bank's correspondent, the Anglo-California Bank of San Francisco. Frank himself, on the advice of counsel, was staying out of California to avoid the serving of papers while the Soper–Valentine case was pending.

Unfortunately in one of his letters to Macfarlane he made a suggestion which seems unworthy of his usual ethical standards. He offered Macfarlane, if he could put the loan through on B. F.'s terms, a personal commission of $2,500 in cash and one thousand paid-up shares in Olaa with a par value of $20,000. B. F. must have felt uneasy about this offer himself, as he justified it at length but unconvincingly.

"I recognize," he wrote to Macfarlane,

> that you have done a good work for the whole Country in getting the new Bank started, and while I am under no obligations legally or morally to pay you any thing for such service, still it is a fact that in the accomplishment of that undertaking, all investments and property interests in this country—however good they were before—have been strengthened by the presence and financial faith indicated by that new financial enterprise. It is, it seems to me, due therefore to you and to me, to say, here and now, that a recognition of these facts actuated and influenced my mind and heart, when I made you what would I think, be regarded by the average business man as a peculiarly flush offer, such as under other circumstances and to a stranger might be looked upon with suspicion. But it is needless for me to say I know you know better.

Macfarlane never got his commission, however, as the bank never made the loan as requested. The local bank did lend B. F. $110,000 to pay off the first Castle Estate note, but the Anglo-California Bank, in the person of Ignatz Steinhart, dragged its feet on the balance, stating that for a loan of that size B. F. should incorporate his estate including his life insurance, so that his death would not interrupt the normal flow of business. B. F. accordingly organized The B. F. Dillingham Company, Ltd., to which he transferred a major share of his financial assets and liabilities. From that point on, his financial affairs became even more complicated and confusing.

By the time this company was organized, the Waialua case had been settled, and B. F. was free to travel to California when he wished. Walter was at Harvard, Harold in school at Oakland, Marion at Dana Hall in Massachusetts, and Emma traveling between them. Frank packed up and headed for San Francisco to raise money.

Frank may not have realized it at the time, but that trip marked a milestone in his career. For the next ten years he would spend more time in the mainland United States than in Hawaii. He had already launched, with one exception, every major business project of his life. From that time on, he of necessity devoted his energies not to dreaming dreams and building empires but to trying to scrape together enough money with which to hang on to his projects and bring them to fruition.

# CHAPTER 34

*With the exception of the [bubonic] plague I believe the health of Honolulu is as good or better than usual.*

George P. Denison to B. F. D.
19 March 1900

WHEN B. F. arrived in San Francisco on 5 December he found the financial part of the city in a flap over British reverses in the Boer War. The Anglo-California Bank cut his loan application from $500,000 to $300,000 and B. F. took to his bed with the grippe. On the eighteenth, still sick, he boarded the *Sunset Limited* for New York City and heard just before he left that the bank had rejected the loan entirely. He arrived in New York on Christmas Day, feeling, he said, "not very jolly." "These experiences," he added, "are like skating on thin ice!!! Experiences that I have had enough of and hope never more to repeat."

At least Emma, Walter, Harold, and Marion were waiting for him in New York. Of the whole family, only May was back in Honolulu with her husband.

More bad news met him in New York. A case of the bubonic plague had appeared in Honolulu's Chinatown, followed rapidly by other cases, and the Board of Health had clamped a strict quarantine on the whole Chinatown district. An embargo on passenger trains lasted for four months, costing the O. R. and L. an estimated $50,000 in revenue. In January efforts to burn out the plague spots resulted in the great Chinatown fire which destroyed some 38 acres of close-packed slums.

While the plague directly hurt B. F.'s interests only to the extent of the lost railway traffic, it had a depressing effect on his efforts to raise money, by adding to the general impression of Hawaii as a primitive and uncivilized territory where investment was risky. It also caused a business depression in Honolulu which drove prices down on the Honolulu Stock Exchange and frightened investors in California.

A dramatic view down King Street during the great Chinatown fire of 1900. The Pacific Hardware Company, successor to Dillingham and Company, is on the right, sharing rather unimpressive quarters with Castle and Cooke, Ltd. (Photo by Ray Jerome Baker, Bishop Museum)

B. F. by this time was juggling an extraordinary number of balls in the air at one time: Olaa assessable; Dillingham, Thurston, and Carter; Hilo Railroad; Puna Sugar; McBryde; the Dowsett Company; Pacific Hardware; and so on, including particularly a staggering amount in almost-due loans. To get an idea of what was going on in general, it is necessary to look for a moment at a few of the problems he faced.

B. F. had invested half a million dollars in McBryde Sugar and had taken in addition a large block of assessable stock. Apparently he unloaded the assessable early, but he had acquired his paid-up stock at par and had no idea of sacrificing it.

The first sign of trouble came early in 1900, only nine months after the company's launching. Theo. H. Davies and Company wrote him in February in great distress over McBryde's overdraft with their firm, which had already reached half a million dollars. B. F. suggested a bond issue of a million dollars, and also wrote to W. A. Kinney to advise him to take hold of the situation. McBryde did authorize $750,000 in bonds, and at B. F.'s suggestion gave $325,000 worth of them to the defunct American Sugar Company for their buildings and machinery.

Despite these halfway measures, McBryde quickly slipped back into debt with its agent, the Davies firm. By 1902 Davies was planning to increase the bond issue to $2 million and had asked B. F. to undertake the refinancing. Kinney urged him not only to carry through the refinancing but to take on the plantation agency as well, and Davies agreed to withdraw if the new agents paid up the plantation overdraft.

In spite of all the complications he had got into, B. F. was sorely tempted by the offer. On 13 January 1902 he wrote to Kinney that he had been hoping to "snug up" so that he might be largely relieved from business cares. In any case, he would have to talk the proposition over with Paxton and with Walter Dillingham and would not go into it contrary to their advice or wishes. But on the same day he wrote to Paxton that there was too much at stake to let the safety of McBryde be jeopardized by incompetent financial management, and he was inclined to take up the proposition. This attitude, he admitted, doesn't look much like adhering to our policy of nonexpansion, but it seems to be manifest destiny for us to increase rather than diminish our business responsibilities.

The prospect of tucking another major plantation under the wing of The B. F. Dillingham Company must have excited B. F.'s imagination, because three days later he got off a train in Ogden, Utah, long enough to wire Emma that he believed McBryde to be important to them and hoped that she, Walter, and Paxton would favor the proposition. Emma by that time was the major stockholder in The B. F. Dillingham Company and Frank was still following his old habit of talking over everything with her.

Presumably Emma or Walter or Paxton balked at the idea, as nothing came of it. McBryde staggered along as usual for another few years. As Paxton said, why worry about McBryde, because Davies is in so deep already they can't possibly let go. Meanwhile McBryde stock slipped to a low of $3.50 for a par $20.00 share and became almost worthless as collateral for B. F.'s borrowing.

At the far end of the Hawaiian chain from McBryde, Manager F. B. McStocker had laid hold with vigor and determination on the herculean task of building Olaa Plantation.

When McStocker took charge at the end of June 1899, he found 50 "free" laborers at work (as distinguished from "contract" laborers who were bound to the plantation by the employment contracts under which they came from Japan), 40 acres of seed cane planted, and three horses engaged in plowing. By the end of the year, the plantation had 402 mules housed in newly built stables, and accommodations for 1,800 laborers and homes for skilled labor and superintendents. Employees totaled 1,629, including 1,097 contract laborers, 66 contract Japanese women, 105 free Japanese, 132 Chinese, and a smattering of other nationalities.

McStocker's men had by that time cleared and planted 716 acres of seed cane, mostly the standard Lahaina variety, with Rose Bamboo, Yellow Bamboo, and Yellow Caledonia for the uplands. Almost 6,000 more acres had been cleared, of which close to half had been plowed at least once. Stands of *'ōhi'a* trees had covered a great deal of the land, and the workers had cut these into lengths and piled them up for use as fence-posts, railroad ties, and firewood. The Hilo Railroad later tried to burn *'ōhi'a* logs as a fuel for locomotives, but found that it wouldn't produce enough steam to make the trains run uphill.

Years later H. A. Garlach, a blacksmith at the plantation, wrote to McStocker that "the newcomers do not recognize the amount of hard work that was accomplished here the first six years, in these rocky fields, and heavy timbered lands, but we that have had an active part in this work can always remember it, as one continuous hustle, and rush, from morning to night, everyone trying their best from the Manager and his staff to the common field laborer. We all worked hard and some how or other there was a great deal accomplished and everybody seemed good natured and content with their part of the work."

Things never went easily at Olaa. In one especially wet season McStocker wrote of the portable railway track sinking out of sight and mules floundering up to their bellies in the mud. He used rocks cleared from the fields to build 11 miles of roads for the rainy weather. The plantation stretched for 15 miles; at the upper end he found pockets of clay in the soil and turned them into reservoirs and began the building of flumes to carry the water down to the mill.

Gradually there took shape not only a plantation but a community, a place where people lived and worked and had children and died: one of the seedbeds of modern Hawaii.

When things started to go wrong, McStocker was accused of extravagance, a charge frequently hurled at a manager when the owners back in Honolulu found themselves unable to pay a dividend. He did try to provide better accommodations for the workers than most plantations had offered, but it was a time of labor shortage and labor unrest, and he presumably considered the expense worthwhile. From this distance in time, it looks as though he was trying to do a good job and build solidly for the future.

The mill, originally ordered for Kihei, proved a bright spot. Built near the little town of Keaau, the buildings covered more than an acre of ground, with railroad tracks running through. The mill could handle 1,200 tons or more of cane a day and turn out 160 to 180 tons of sugar; the building had room for a second train of rollers, which would double the capacity. The mill worked well from the beginning and was constantly being refined and improved.

But signs of trouble appeared when the mill got into production. The prospectus had spoken of harvesting 8,000 acres a year and milling 6 tons of sugar per acre, for an annual grind of 48,000 tons, which would cost $30 a ton and sell for $70. McStocker first esti-

The little town of Keaau, by the Olaa mill, celebrates a Japanese Boys' Day in the early 1900s. This community was typical of those that grew near the sugar plantations. (Bishop Museum photo)

mated 5,000 acres at 5 tons per acre, or 25,000 tons; the actual crop of 1902 turned out to be 4,000 acres at 4½ tons, or 18,000 tons. Sugar prices had fallen meanwhile to $52 net. But the real shocker came in the cost of production, which amounted to $57 per ton. Olaa was in trouble.

Puna Sugar never really got off the ground. According to B. F.'s later statement, all that Robinson and A. J. Campbell could do was to provide the land and about $50,000 in working capital. By March of 1900 Robinson could raise no more money on his securities and was "about at his wit's end" to carry on the plantation. At that point he incorporated the venture, evidently to raise more capital. B. F. agreed to help, but by that time he was hardly in control of his own situation. As a result Puna never got its own mill, had to make a contract with Olaa for grinding, and ended up in debt to its agent, The B. F. Dillingham Company. Ahead lay disaster for Mark Robinson and a monumental headache for his old friend Frank Dillingham.

The Hilo Railroad got off to a fast start. Its contract with Olaa called for service to the mill site by November 1900. B. F. sent C. H. Kluegel, a seasoned professional, to lay out the line and superintend the construction. The first locomotive came ashore on 15 May and by the time it was ready to run a couple of weeks later, the tracks were complete to the mill site. By the end of the year, the tracks ran well into the Puna district and 2 miles past the mill toward the volcano, and yards had been built at Hilo and Olaa. The road at this time did not run into Hilo proper but to the Waiakea dock site, with a branch to the Waiakea Mill.

During 1901 Thurston secured a right-of-way from Waiakea along Hilo Bay to Waianuenue Street in the heart of Hilo and also negotiated contracts with the Hilo Mercantile Company and with Hackfeld to haul merchandise from the dock to their establishments. His work was made easier by the failure at this time of a group of men who had been promising to carry out S. G. Wilder's old scheme of a railroad north from Hilo, under the name of the Kohala and Hilo Railway Company.

Thurston was also working on the Hilo Dock Company proposal. He had wanted to bring Matson Navigation, Inter-Island Steam Navigation, Davies, Hackfeld, and Hilo and Waiakea plantations into the scheme, but finally settled for a combination of the Hilo Railroad, Olaa, Puna, and Matson. Stock was subscribed in the amount of $72,000, and the dock was planned for the Waiakea area where Hilo Bay was most protected.

Thurston also negotiated with Captain William Matson an agreement under which Matson got to carry the sugar from Olaa and Puna to the mainland. This agreement caused endless trouble in the years ahead.

B. F.'s financial strategy for the Hilo Railroad resembled that for the O. R. and L.: issue bonds to cover the cost of the physical property, and let the common stock represent the intangible values of the franchise and freight contracts. In 1900 he believed implicitly that the road's earnings would equal, as a percentage of the common stock, those of the Oahu Railway. He had arbitrarily increased the outstanding stock to $500,000, of which he held more than three-fifths, and expected within a couple of years to be paying fat dividends.

But trouble quickly developed on the financial scene. C. M. Cooke deprecated the value of the bonds, declaring that the plantation ought to own the railroad. B. F.'s old friend Charles H. Daly of Oakland told B. F. frankly that the road was bonded too high, far higher than any of the California roads. And B. F. found that he

The Olaa Temperance Society goes for an outing on the Hilo Railroad. In back stands the big Olaa mill, originally ordered for Kihei plantation. (Bishop Museum photo)

could sell the bonds only at a deep discount from par. The B. F. Dillingham Company, Ltd., as agents for the railroad, had to step in and advance money to keep the line running until the time should come when the business from Olaa and Puna would make it profitable.

By 1900 B. F. realized very well the extent of his problems. He spent months in the East trying to solve them at one blow by launching the "Hawaiian–American Trust and Investment Company," to be capitalized at $8 million, which would control McBryde, Olaa, Puna, and the Hilo Railroad. He believed that the successful formation of this holding company would not only get him out of a jam but do a great deal of good for Hawaii by establishing for the first time a New York market for Hawaiian securities.

But waiting for answers was anxious work, and B. F.'s health suffered. On 2 April he took time out to write to Marion:

> Doubtless you have been good enough to think of "mama" and "papa" as *one,* and so we are, and yet we have an individuality in our relations to our children and friends as well as to the world. . . . I know your good mother has instructed you fully in regard to the importance of guarding your health, and so I will only add that you should always remember, that good physical and mental health *exceed* all other earthly blessings. I have been greatly favored in that respect all my life. But since my arrival in S. F. on the 5th of last December, with my best effort to keep well I have found it a difficult matter to do so. I am sitting up again today after ten days in bed with a return of the grippe.

But not everything was bad news and anxiety. Frank and Emma were looking forward to having Walter, Harold, and Marion join them for the Easter holidays. And on 6 April May Frear gave them their first grandchild, Virginia Dillingham Frear, born auspiciously in the same year that her father became the territory's first chief justice.

B. F. also passed the time by pressing George Dearborn, president of the American–Hawaiian Steamship Company, to sell some McBryde and Hilo Railroad bonds for him, offering him freight in exchange and not very subtly pointing out the threat of competition from Captain William Matson. Dearborn, however, proved as evasive as Matson himself.

In the end B. F.'s big project, the Hawaiian–American Trust, came to nothing. Hawaii was too far away and sugarcane too exotic an article to interest eastern capitalists. B. F. even made a fast trip to Montreal to talk to Sir William Van Horne, a former president of the Canadian Pacific Railway who had large investments in Cuban sugar properties. Van Horne kept the door open for five months, but never got down to serious bargaining.

Meanwhile, Alexander and Baldwin had become uneasy about the amount of money being poured into Olaa. The Olaa directors had voted to assume the Kihei factory contract at a time when the Olaa assessments had already been set for the first half of 1900, thereby upsetting the financial projections of the treasurer, Jim Castle. As a result the plantation slipped into debt to its agent. A & B objected, pointing out that the $250,000 line of credit provided in the agency agreement was supposed to finance crops and not capital improvements. As early as January 1900, B. F. was asking Castle whether A & B would give up the agency, and Castle was evading the question by asking whether B. F. would sell his holdings at par.

In good times B. F. would probably have had no dispute with A & B, who would most likely have carried Olaa until the necessary assessments came in. A & B was still a partnership, however, the principles being Samuel T. and Wallace M. Alexander in San Francisco, James B. Castle and Joseph P. Cooke in Honolulu, and Henry P. Baldwin on Maui. In that form the partnership was only a year and a half old. The partners were still trying to digest the huge H. C. and S. plantation, and were thought to be heavily in debt to Daniel Meyer, the San Francisco money man who had backed their takeover of the plantation. When sugar prices broke and the plague triggered a depression in Honolulu, A & B hit the panic button and demanded that Olaa pay its accounts in full, at the same time giving B. F. an option to take over the agency by buying the $250,000 of stock which A & B held in the plantation at par plus 6 percent interest for the last year.

B. F. at that point was still working on his Hawaiian–American Trust scheme. A few days later the Republican Party of Hawaii, after sending a man around to B. F.'s office in Honolulu to make sure that he was a Republican, unanimously elected him delegate to the Republican convention in Philadelphia in June. But an urgent wire from Thurston in San Francisco made him drop his activities in the East and catch a train for San Francisco on 12 June. The time was nearing for a showdown on Olaa.

# CHAPTER 35

*While you are developing that property [the Dowsett Company] and bringing it up to the point where it will pay dividends on its present capitalization, you will also be developing your own mind and business capacities.*

B. F. D. to Walter F. Dillingham
15 October 1901

BY the time B. F. Dillingham entrained for San Francisco in June of 1900, he had pretty well made up his mind to dump A & B as agents for the Olaa Sugar Company. Probably personalities influenced his decision, but basically he had laid his own reputation on the line with Olaa and had come to feel that A & B lacked the necessary resolve to carry through the plantation successfully.

B. F. had, of course, a great deal more than his reputation at stake. He had undertaken to prevent any delinquent assessable shares from going on the market by taking them over himself, with the result that by June 1900 he was paying assessments on about sixty-five thousand shares, at the rate of $32,000 a month. Not only was his reputation at stake in Olaa but his entire fortune as well.

Thurston and H. P. Baldwin met B. F. in San Francisco and outlined for him an unhappy situation. A & B had advanced about $200,000 to Olaa; Baldwin refused to go further and demanded to be paid. The plantation owed Honolulu Iron Works two payments on the mill totaling $150,000. Stock assessments were seriously delinquent, and no income from sugar could be expected for more than a year.

B. F. could see that regardless of who had the agency, Olaa would have to issue bonds to pay off its debts and keep it going until returns from sugar started coming in. And in order to buy out the A & B position, he would need a reliable market for Olaa securities so that he could borrow freely against his enormous holdings in that company.

To arouse public interest in his projects, B. F. took an odd but imaginative step which he later credited for much of his success in raising money. He interviewed himself on the subject of Olaa and his other interests, wrote up the interview at great length, and had it published in half a dozen San Francisco newspapers. For publishing the interview, which appeared as the work of their own reporters, the newspapers charged him a total of $2,255. The *Chronicle*, as the most prestigious paper, sent the largest bill. Not surprisingly, B. F. concluded in his interview that Olaa presented a splendid opportunity for investment and would soon be paying fat dividends out of profits estimated for 1905 at $2,500,000.

B. F. continued to negotiate with A & B regarding the transfer of the agency and also regarding the proposed bond issue. A & B proved tough negotiators; by the end of July they were giving the impression that they would stick by the plantation. B. F. wrote them that

> the agency of Olaa has not been of my own seeking but circumstances beyond our mutual control has made it absolutely imperative that either your firm or I personally should assume the responsibility for raising the money necessary. As I am now carrying nearly 70,000 shares of assessable stock, more than half of which belongs to other people, who but for my assistance would have been obliged to throw it on the already demoralized market, I have reached a point where I must refuse to carry it any longer if I am obliged to meet the assessment which will be necessary to call unless the money is raised upon the bonds. Your written notice . . . threw the burden of meeting your demands on me personally as well as the added responsibility of finding ways and means to raise the necessary cash capital. If you turn the agency over to me, notifying me of your acceptance of my offer promptly, I can get the money to carry the plantation through, but not otherwise.

Within a few days of writing this letter on 8 August, B. F. decided to bring matters to a head by taking passage back to Honolulu to talk to A & B in person. Paxton, meanwhile, had decided that he had to talk to B. F., and took ship to San Francisco; they passed in mid-ocean. Such were the difficulties of doing business without a cable.

In the meeting A & B got exactly what they wanted: full payment of their account and par for their stock plus 6 percent interest from May of 1899. B. F. had to give the firm his note for $270,000 for the stock, to be secured by Olaa bonds as soon as they were issued.

From our vantage point in time, B. F.'s action in buying out the agency on terms so favorable to A & B seems rash and foolish. In the years ahead Olaa would need all the financial help it could get. Yet it is equally possible that B. F. analyzed the situation correctly and that if A & B had had the agency during the next crisis, the plantation would have gone down the drain altogether.

It is also an interesting question whether A & B actually had a better understanding than B. F. of what was happening at Olaa. Apparently A & B were as much lucky as smart in getting out when they did. The A & B people (Mr. Castle excepted) were much more cautious and conservative than B. F. They had other problems on their hands, it was an uneasy time in the sugar business, and they probably got out more because of outside factors than because of any lack of faith in Olaa itself.

At any rate, the deal went through in August 1900, and The B. F. Dillingham Company found itself agent for an enormous, half-developed plantation that had yet to grind its first pound of sugar.

Before leaving San Francisco, B. F. had taken steps to place the $1.25 million in bonds which the directors and stockholders had already authorized. On 23 July he gave the Bank of California a four-month option to sell the bonds at a 5 percent discount plus a 5 percent commission in stock. As an inducement to purchase, B. F. offered to exchange bonds for stock on or before 1 January 1903, the stock to be provided by him and Thurston. He estimated in September that sale of the bonds, assessments, and returns from the 1902 crop would pay the plantation's bills and leave a surplus at the end of 1902 of $239,000.

B. F. had some basis for his optimism. In August Dr. Walter Maxwell, director of the experiment station, inspected the plantation and reported it in excellent condition. What he did not report was the age-old fact that farming depends on often unpredictable and uncontrollable factors: weather, pests, and market prices.

Walter Dillingham, meanwhile, had finished his second year at Harvard and made his way to San Francisco, where he picked up some instructions from his father before going home for the summer. He arrived at Honolulu in July, dropped his bags at home, and went to the office, where he found Mark Robinson, Frear, Paxton, and Alfred Carter in a huddle. Walter filled them in on his father's plans and urged them to push the authorization for the Olaa bonds. He, Paxton, and Carter called on A & B the next morning, where they found Joe Cooke disposed to stand by Olaa. Walter wrote his father expressing the opinion that it seemed important to come to terms with A & B and hoping that B. F. had not bound himself to transfer the agency.

Walter by that time was twenty-five years old, having worked for the railroad for five years after finishing high school. His father had treated him as an adult and thrust responsibility on him, so that by the time he went to Harvard he had a considerable degree of maturity. During his two years at college his father had sent him copies of business correspondence and had even sent men to talk business with him. Walter had responded to this indoctrination with enthusiasm.

Now B. F. wrote his son to suggest that instead of returning to Harvard he should stay home and learn the business. Walter pounced on the idea. "I cannot tell you," he wrote, "how much I have enjoyed getting in touch with your business. Such a future as it seems to offer!" He added that he liked Mokuleia better every time he went there.

A few days after this exchange of letters B. F. made his quick trip to settle with A & B. Walter by that time had come to agree with him. "Thank heaven we are to be free of A and B," he wrote. "I do not wonder you have chafed under their would-be management."

At the same time that he took over the Olaa agency, B. F. sealed his bargain with Walter. Walter stayed on in The B. F. Dillingham Company with the title of treasurer and the special duty of managing the Dowsett Company. Neither B. F. nor Walter had any intention of limiting his interests. Within a short time he had made himself well aware of the complications of his father's affairs.

B. F. never made a shrewder business decision than he did when he kept Walter home from Harvard. The assumption of the Olaa agency, piled on top of the organization of the Dowsett Company, enormously complicated his business life and created a pressing need for new talent. Beyond that, B. F. may have had a premonition that in a time of great stress his own strength might fail as it had once before. In 1900 Walter Dillingham was young, eager, smart, personable, and quick to learn, but he was not a seasoned businessman who could step in and lay hold of a complicated situation. Four years later he was probably the only man who could have held together the Dillingham interests during his father's incapacity.

During the same quick trip to Honolulu, B. F. took care of another item of business which was to have far less happy results in the long run.

The partnership of Dillingham, Thurston, and Carter had made Olaa possible by securing the lands on which the plantation was built. Alfred W. Carter had only a one-sixth interest in the partnership, though his cash contribution of close to $72,000 had far exceeded Thurston's $50,000. B. F. had paid in $122,000 as capital and had lent the partnership another $164,000, as well as putting up his credit to obtain further loans for the partnership of close to $300,000.

In September of 1899 Carter accepted the guardianship of Thelma Parker and management of the Parker Ranch. In August of 1900, at the same time that B. F. and A & B were coming to a final agreement, Carter asked to be released from the Dillingham, Thurston, and Carter partnership on the grounds that it interfered with his duties as guardian. B. F. accordingly assumed his share, giving himself a two-thirds interest in the partnership and Carter a three-year note for $150,000 in payment.

Mr. Dillingham appears to have acted more from emotion than from logic in this matter. The Dillingham, Thurston, and Carter partnership owed the banks more than $260,000. The partnership was still committed to paying out a substantial amount on land options yet to come due, without receiving any payment except in the form of Olaa stock. Clearly the partnership needed all the financial strength it could muster, yet without gaining any compensating advantage B. F. overextended himself still further, added to his existing burdens, and released a man who had undertaken to carry a share of the load.

B. F. returned to San Francisco in September with his course for the next few years pretty well mapped out. His main concern would be to provide the money to keep Olaa going until the mill started grinding out sugar. He knew that he could not depend on Honolulu for funds on the scale which he needed, and he had had no success in the East. San Francisco would have to be his primary field of operations.

In San Francisco B. F. had a loose-knit group of friends whom he relied on to help his interests.

For his lawyer there he had William H. Chickering of the firm of Chickering and Gregory. Chickering, who was a few years younger than B. F., had graduated from Amherst in 1871 and had come to Punahou to teach while earning money to go to law school. At Punahou he was immensely popular with the boys, whom he taught the newfangled game of baseball. He sang in the Bethel choir and became a fast friend of Frank and Emma Dillingham. In San Francisco his relations with B. F. were so close that B. F. kept a desk in his office and often used his Oakland home in the wintertime when Chickering stayed in town rather than take the Bay ferries.

In Oakland Frank had another staunch friend in the person of Charles Daly, whom he had been doing business with since the days of Dillingham and Company. He had made Daly a director and mainland representative of the Pacific Hardware Company, and Daly did a good deal of buying for the Oahu Railway as well. Daly could not provide the money that B. F. needed, but B. F. trusted him fully and relied on him to carry out a wide variety of business functions.

As San Francisco agent for the Olaa Sugar Company, B. F. chose a man named Henry F. Allen who had previously acted as agent for H. C. and S. plantation when it was controlled by Gus and Rudolph Spreckels. Allen had an extremely high standing in San Francisco financial circles, but he was not young and his health was poor. Moreover, he cared more about preserving the wealth he had accumulated than about increasing it through speculation. He made it quite clear to B. F. that in accepting the Olaa agency he would neither invest in the plantation nor advance substantial sums of money.

The other member of B. F.'s inner circle, incredibly enough, was that arch conservative, Charles R. Bishop. After he sold Bishop and Company and moved to San Francisco, Bishop had allied himself with the Bank of California, where he held the title of vice-president; the Bank of California extended a line of credit to his old bank in Honolulu, Bishop and Company, now in the hands of Samuel M. Damon. Over the years Bishop had come to appreciate B. F. Dillingham's energy, ability, and bold ideas, and during the early 1900s he provided B. F. with a major share of his financing, both directly from the Bank of California and indirectly from other institutions where he had influence.

To a considerable extent Bishop filled the void left in B. F.'s life by the death of S. N. Castle. B. F. felt toward the older man the same filial respect and affection which he had felt toward Mr. Castle. He also heeded his advice no more than he had Mr. Castle's. Mr. Bishop had a magnificent capacity for worry; over the years he had never ceased his admonitions to "snug up," pay off obligations, get out of debt. Oddly enough, when the crash came and B. F. got into difficulties which he could have avoided by taking Bishop's advice years before, Bishop never lost faith in him and remained his loyal supporter.

With Bishop's help, B. F. was able in October of 1900 to borrow enough to take care of his immediate requirements. In writing back to Albert Raas, one of his aides in Honolulu, he spoke of the steady though not rapid success he had had since the publication of his newspaper interviews, to which he attributed his progress. "It seems," he wrote, "as though I can do with the banks and trust companies almost anything I propose."

By December B. F. had sold $334,000 in Olaa bonds and placed an additional $576,000 worth as collateral for a loan of $500,000, leaving $340,000 unsold. Paxton estimated that by selling the remaining bonds the company could avoid calling further assessments until the following July.

No doubt feeling pleased with the results of his work, B. F. went home for Christmas. The railroad was doing well, now that the plague had ended, and the directors in November had voted a dividend of 1 percent ($20,000) per month, more than half of which

The Stangenwald Building on Merchant Street in Honolulu, where The B. F. Dillingham Company, Limited had its offices. The grassy area in the foreground is now the site of the Financial Plaza of the Pacific. (Photo by Ray Jerome Baker, Bishop Museum)

went to the Dillingham interests. The B. F. Dillingham Company needed more room; B. F. approved the leasing of the fourth floor of the new Stangenwald Building.

One cloud still hung on the horizon: the huge investment required to bring Olaa into production. Chickering was working on a plan to sell the plantation to British investors, but B. F. must have known that in all probability he would have to carry it through on his own.

# CHAPTER 36

*You say the last ten years as I look at it must seem like a dream. I can assure you that it has been a serious reality, little resembling anything like a dream, unless it has been such a dream as few men care to recall to mind.*

B. F. D. to Isaac Dillingham
6 May 1901

FROM the end of 1900 to the middle of 1904 must have been one of the most disagreeable periods in B. F. Dillingham's life. He kept his ship afloat in a bad storm and managed to do a surprising amount of constructive work at the same time, but for the most part he resembled the quarterback on a football team behind in the last quarter, desperately trying to connect on a long pass downfield against a vicious rush by the opposing linemen.

B. F. did not suffer alone. The Hawaiian sugar industry during this time went through one of the most critical periods in its history, and the prices of all Hawaiian securities fell to panic levels.

According to one of B. F.'s San Francisco bankers, the drop in island stocks began in the summer of 1901 when the Oceanic Steamship Company levied an assessment ten days after it declared a dividend. Then Hutchinson reduced its dividend, and Hawaiian Commercial and Onomea passed theirs. Island real estate and stocks had been inflated; now panic took over and the bottom dropped out of the market.

Low prices for sugar were the principal cause of the depression, but the sugar industry was also struggling with a labor problem that arose at least partly from Annexation. The Organic Act had knocked out the contract labor system under which workers had come from Japan, making labor scarce and (by the standards of the day) costly.

In 1902 the situation had become so serious that those plantations which were operating profitably had, all together, a profit for the year of only $2,860,000, while the unprofitable plantations showed a total loss of $2,025,000. Clearly, the entire industry had become marginal. Even the mighty Ewa Plantation cut its dividend in half.

B. F. in May of 1902 called the conditions in San Francisco for raising money on plantation securities "more discouraging than ever before." A month later Paxton wrote B. F. "a private letter . . . not intended for the files" in which he spoke of the present mental strain as "almost too much for me." A default in our obligations, he said, would not only ruin us but everything else as well: "a break of confidence in any large firm at this time would certainly be followed by a panic." Davies and Company, he added, were in the same position with regard to McBryde, for they realized that if they stopped making advances it would mean ruin to the community.

Several of B. F.'s closest associates got into serious difficulties in this period. Mark Robinson got deeply involved through Puna Sugar, and L. A. Thurston defaulted on his Olaa assessable stock. With Olaa paid-up selling at 10—half of its par value—the assessable had very little value at all, and those who held it had to raise money elsewhere to pay their assessments, or default. Even Henry St. Goar, of the well-known San Francisco brokerage firm of Edward Pollitz and Company, failed to pay the assessments on two thousand shares of Olaa he had taken in the name of his wife.

Against this background of distress and panic, B. F. enjoyed remarkable success in raising money in San Francisco. He renewed most of his loans as they came due, sold $709,000 worth of Olaa bonds and placed the remaining $541,000 as collateral for new loans of $465,000, sold about $500,000 of Puna Sugar bonds, sold $850,000 of Hilo Railroad bonds and exchanged another $150,000 for the Hilo Dock Company assets, and in a remarkable operation in the darkest days of 1902 secured a loan of $500,000 from a syndicate of San Francisco banks, who accepted as security stock in Olaa and the Hilo Railroad. Of this amount, $300,000 went to pay assessments on Olaa stock, which otherwise The B. F. Dillingham Company could not have met.

These loans, however, were defensive operations. B. F. as quarterback kept trying for the "long bomb" which would get his team out of the hole. Nothing came of Chickering's attempt to sell Olaa to British investors; in 1902 B. F. tried a different tack by proposing the "Island Railways Company," a holding company for the O. R. and

L. Under this plan, B. F. agreed to give up control of the railway in exchange for cash to protect his other investments.

Mr. Bishop, for one, loved the idea of retrenchment. "The plans of which you advised me," he wrote to B. F., "have my hearty commendation, and the manner in which you bear in mind those who have invested under your management and largely because of their confidence in your judgment and integrity does you honor and is what I, who know you so well, would expect."

Working through the well-known bond house of E. H. Rollins and Sons, B. F. made a serious attempt to carry out this scheme, but miserable market conditions doomed the proposal.

By the fall of 1902, B. F. was working on another idea which ultimately would have tremendous impact on Hawaiian business. From his vantage point on the mainland B. F. could clearly see the weakness of the individual sugar factors, particularly in dealing with the Western Sugar Refinery. He proposed a truly radical solution: merger of all the Hawaiian plantations, with the presumable exception of those controlled by W. G. Irwin and Company.

At any other time such an idea would have drawn derisive laughter, but in the terrible days of 1902 it commanded respectful attention. "It seems hardly fitting and rather presumptuous that I should undertake to bring all the other houses together," B. F. wrote. He had, of course, fought strenuously with A & B over Kihei and Olaa, with Davies over McBryde, and with Castle and Cooke over Ewa and Waialua. But he had fought cleanly and openly and had kept the respect of his opponents. If any man could have made the idea work, B. F. was probably the one.

Eventually the plan in its original form died of inertia. First, as Alexander Young pointed out, came the difficulty of reaching agreement on the relative values of the various plantations. Beyond that, as Lorrin Thurston told B. F., consolidation would never go through unless someone really took hold and pushed it. B. F., chained in California by his financial juggling act, simply could not handle the task.

But B. F. knew that he had hold of an essential principle when he preached strength through unity, and in the following year he brought it out again in a form more palatable to his fellow magnates. This time he proposed a cooperative owned jointly by the plantations to handle the marketing of Hawaiian sugar after acquiring the existing refinery at Crockett, California. By late November 1903, B. F., then in Honolulu, was writing Paxton of his hopes for a "solid legally organized corporation" to be formed by all the sugar factors except W. G. Irwin and Company, which was tied into the Spreckels interests in California. B. F.'s own troubles at that point prevented him from playing midwife at the delivery of the fruits of his missionary efforts, but his son Walter served in his place on the committee which in the early part of 1904 organized the Sugar Factors Company, the predecessor of the well-known C and H sugar refinery and marketing cooperative. It is doubtful that the industry could have survived for the next seventy years without this established outlet for its product, and among all the illustrious names in the sugar business, it was B. F. Dillingham who most effectively preached the need for its formation.

Emma and Walter spent Christmas of 1901 at Woodlawn. Harold was at Harvard, Marion at Dana Hall, and Frank in San Francisco, waiting to go to Washington about the Sumner property and brooding about taking over McBryde Plantation. Three days later Emma wrote to Marion: "This morning's paper had the news that the big *Olaa Mill* had *commenced grinding!* & that is the very best possible news that could go forward to papa. It *ought* to help him very much in his efforts to get money, and lift *a great load from his* head and heart. It has seemed a long time to wait until *this climax,* & I pray the rest of the way will be, as it were, *down hill* & *pay as we go!*"

Poor Emma. "Down hill" was a long way off still, and "pay as we go" a will-o'-the-wisp.

In the light of its size and newness, Olaa probably fared no worse than other plantations during this period. The first crop, that of 1902, produced a slight loss, but the 1903 crop wiped out the deficit and left a surplus of $67,000. The 1904 crop showed another small profit, but events outside the plantation had in the meantime changed the entire aspect of the matter.

After B. F.'s success in selling Puna Sugar bonds in 1901, that company had briefly considered erecting its own mill, but abandoned the idea. Exactly what went wrong is not clear, but within a year the plantation was deeply in debt to The B. F. Dillingham Company, its agent. Robinson and A. J. Campbell held the assessable stock in Puna and could not meet the assessments; Robinson also was being pressed for payment of other loans. B. F. had to keep Puna running, on account of the Hilo Railroad. In the late summer of

1902, when the sugar industry was hitting bottom, Robinson and Campbell turned their stock in Puna over to The B. F. Dillingham Company in exchange for a note of $75,000, and the balance due on the assessable stock was then cancelled against the balance due the Dillingham Company. The Dillingham Company then turned the Puna stock over to Olaa in partial settlement of what it owed that plantation.

Thus Olaa became the owner of Puna, and Robinson and Campbell were wiped out of their Puna venture, except for the note and some bonds Robinson owned. "We have done all in our power," B. F. wrote to Walter, "to turn their [Robinson's and Campbell's] interest over to some one who will do better for them than we can but all our efforts have been in vain. So I hope they will be satisfied tho' I know it will be a hard pill to swallow." B. F. always maintained that by wiping out their liability on the assessable stock, his actions saved Robinson and Campbell from a more serious loss.

But the ghost of Puna would not rest quietly. Olaa's ownership of Puna would stand up only as long as the Puna bondholders received their interest, and Puna proved unprofitable for Olaa to operate.

In their anxiety to sell Puna bonds in 1901, B. F. and Robinson had given repurchase agreements along with certain of the bonds, and now those bondholders wanted their money back. Robinson had no means of taking his share, and B. F. had to find the money for both of them.

In the long run Puna provided some of Olaa's best sugar land, but over the near term it helped to bring the plantation to the brink of collapse by running at a deficit and tying up needed capital.

The crucial factor at Olaa during this period turned out to be not the small annual profits or losses but the steady drain of cash invested in future crops, in capital improvements, in advances to independent planters, and in Puna and the Hilo Railroad. Assessments on stock were supposed to provide the money for these expenditures, but The B. F. Dillingham Company was carrying well over half the assessable stock, and when B. F. made his $500,000 syndicate loan in 1902, he had reached the bottom of his barrel. As the remaining assessments came due, the Olaa Sugar Company marked the Dillingham stock as paid and charged the agents' account on the Olaa books. By 1904 The B. F. Dillingham Company owed the plantation $372,000, with no visible means of repayment except through Olaa dividends. And dividends, which Paxton had hopefully predicted from the first crop, kept receding into the distance. In June of 1902 B. F. noted that on the basis of an expected crop of 20,000 tons, the fall in the price of sugar from the previous year had cost the company $400,000, making the difference between a decent profit and a slight loss.

With so many other problems to worry about, it is hardly surprising that no one got particularly upset at the appearance at Olaa during 1903 of a small insect called the leafhopper, which fed on the leaves of the sugarcane. The experiment station was breeding natural enemies to wipe it out, and it appeared to represent no serious threat.

The Hilo Railroad, meanwhile, had got off to a reasonably good start. By the beginning of 1903 it had a surplus of $32,000, and on the basis of Paxton's estimate for the year ahead the directors established a dividend rate of 1 percent every three months, on a capital which was about to be blown up to $1 million. The increase in capital had no justification except the hope of future earnings, and the payment of dividends at that point was justified only by The B. F. Dillingham Company's terrible need for cash.

For a couple of quarters the railroad paid the dividend. But the railway existed to serve Olaa and Puna plantations, and Olaa was supposed to ship 48,000 tons of sugar a year and Puna another 20,000 or so. With both plantations together shipping around 18,000 tons, the railroad had no way to carry $60,000 a year in bond interest. The local freight between Hilo and the dock could not substitute for two healthy plantations. By 1904 dividends had ceased and the railroad paid its bills only because Olaa kept advancing it money.

B. F. during these years was traveling incessantly. San Francisco was his base on the mainland, but he went on coal business to Seattle and St. Paul, to Washington about his harbor scheme, to New York and Chicago in search of money, and frequently to Boston to see Harold at Harvard and Marion at Dana Hall. Both children gave him cause for pride and pleasure. Harold, who loved to sing and to dance the hula, was immensely popular at college and for his senior year was elected captain of the varsity crew—hardly an empty honor, since it entailed making up the schedule of races, finding a coach, and arranging for training camp. Marion, a special pet of her father's and a great chum of Harold and his friends, graduated in 1902. The following summer she became engaged to the Reverend John P. Erdman, nine years her senior, who was planning to go to Japan with the Presbyterian Board of Missions.

On one of his trips to Washington, B. F. had the pleasure of an interview with President Theodore Roosevelt, who sought his opinion on land and labor problems in the new territory. B. F. and Emma had a taste of high life in the capital, dining out in fashionable homes for two nights running. "The [Fosters'] house *was a dream,*" Emma reported to Marion, "& the crockery used in the *many* courses was *rare* & splendid. I wore both my new gowns & they are entirely satisfactory. Papa was delighted with both."

One of B. F.'s strongest characteristics, an intense interest in new technology, led him during this period to investigate oil as a replacement for coal. As Captain Matson reported, oil was being struck all over the place in California, and the price was ridiculously low. B. F. had serious doubts that it would replace coal, but he hedged his bets by using the threat of oil to drive down the price of coal. He flirted with the Matson–Crocker oil interests, but as always he found William Matson a tough man to bargain with. In the end he agreed to represent the Union Oil Company, for whom he built storage tanks at Iwilei.

B. F., with the help of Thurston, did manage to get together with Matson concerning shipments out of Hilo, in what he described later as about the worst contract he ever made. Matson gave him one thousand shares of stock in the newly formed Matson Navigation Company, and in return B. F. promised Matson through the Hilo Railroad a certain tonnage of outgoing freight. Because of the low sugar production at Olaa and Puna, the railroad failed to meet the quotas; the railroad complained that when a cargo was available, Matson would fail to pick it up. Matson refused to use the railroad dock, claiming that the swells made it unsafe, and charged extra for lightering cargo out to his ships. The problem of an all-weather dock remained unsolved until the railroad persuaded Congress to vote money for a breakwater.

In Honolulu, Walter Dillingham got his baptism of fire early. He quickly discovered that in 1900 the expenses of the Dowsett Company exceeded revenues by about $40,000. With $1.1 million in bonds to pay interest on, the company had no chance of reducing expenses substantially; the best chance for success lay in building up the income.

Unfortunately the major commitment was in ranching, mostly on leased land, a precarious enterprise at best. The company moreover lacked good lands for fattening, the profitable end of the business. Walter began to think in terms of getting out of ranching and developing income from fee-simple properties.

To buy time he sold the Rose Ranch at Ulupalakua. Ewa Plantation leased almost 100 acres at Puuloa for cane, and the U.S. Navy bought another 320 acres. Walter planned a waterfront subdivision in the same area, and negotiated a sale to the United States of the leasehold interest in Kahauiki, which became Fort Shafter. He also developed company lands in the Aala area, near the railway depot.

But in spite of these measures, and in spite of funds advanced by The B. F. Dillingham Company, the Dowsett Company defaulted on bond interest at the beginning of 1903. As a result of this default, the Hawaiian Trust Company was able to force a division of the Kaholaloa lands between the Oahu Railway and the Dowsett Company, a division which actually worked to the benefit of both companies. The Dowsett Company went through a reorganization which reduced the bonded debt to a more realistic $275,000, but Walter remained as treasurer and The B. F. Dillingham Company kept the management. Finally, in 1904, at the lowest point of B. F.'s misfortunes, the Dowsett Company again defaulted on its bonds, partly because The B. F. Dillingham Company had repaid itself a part of its advances to the firm. This time, to the disgust of Walter and his father, the Hawaiian Trust Company succeeded in taking over the management of the company, and except for a few acrimonious parting shots, the managerial connection between the Dillinghams and the Dowsett Company ended. The Dillingham Company sold its Dowsett stock in 1915.

On another front, Walter took the lead in building a branch of the Oahu Railway from Puuloa station to Bishop Point at the mouth of Pearl Harbor. The Bishop Estate, in giving the right-of-way through its lands of Halawa, forbade the building of a dock but gave permission for a ferry across to Puuloa, where Walter was planning a subdivision.

Probably no civilian at that time had closer contact with the military authorities in Hawaii than young Walter Dillingham, through his work for the railroad and the Dowsett Company and in a short time for the Hawaiian Dredging Company. Tall, athletic, incredibly handsome, and endowed with great personal charm and presence, he was laying the groundwork in these years for his future collaboration with military authorities on projects of vast dimensions.

The story of Walter Dillingham and the Hawaiian Dredging Company is somewhat peripheral to the life of B. F. Dillingham. Let it suffice to say here that in 1902 Walter started the dredging company with no capital, as a side venture to his work for his father, by leasing the dredge which the railway had bought from the Pacific Coast Dredging and Reclamation Company. By good luck and astute management he built the company up to a point where in 1911 he was able to put up $100,000 of his own money earned through the dredging company to help refinance The B. F. Dillingham Company notes.

As if Walter did not have enough to occupy his time, he served also as manager of the family ranch at Mokuleia and began his long career as Oahu's leading polo player. Through polo he became intimate with S. E. ("Ned") Damon, Sam Damon's son and heir apparent. Perhaps through Walter's influence, Ned was elected a director of the Oahu Railway in 1901, and the often stormy relations between the two families took a turn for the better, to the point where Sam Damon in 1903 invested $25,000 in The B. F. Dillingham Company, becoming its only outside stockholder. B. F. reported that Mr. Damon and he had become "quite chummy."

The railroad during these years remained the bedrock foundation of the Dillingham fortune, but it had its share of troubles, which bas-

A scene at the Honolulu depot in the early 1900s. The Oahu Railway proved to be Dillingham's anchor to windward throughout his financial troubles from 1904 to 1914. (Bishop Museum photo)

ically stemmed from B. F.'s constant need for cash. From 1901 through 1903 more than three-quarters of the earnings went out in dividends, in spite of a constant pressure for capital improvements. Moreover, the railroad was charging no depreciation on its physical assets and no amortization of its franchise and freight contracts. Inevitably the notes and accounts payable again ballooned, reaching a peak of $423,000 and leaving the railroad in a vulnerable position. In 1902 the railroad transferred its banking from Bishop and Company to the First National Bank in exchange for a loan of $300,000, but this move gave only temporary relief rather than a positive solution.

# CHAPTER 37

*My life has been devoted to business, and my nature has been naturally very intense, and I have allowed business to be very absorbing, still following the illustrious example of my Grandfather (your own Father) who used to say "Anything worth doing at all is worth doing with all one's might."*

B. F. D. to his aunt, Mrs. Harriet N. Swift
27 October 1914

THE long-awaited recovery of the sugar industry simply did not materialize in 1903. Prices firmed slightly—Olaa averaged about $56 per ton net return, against $52 in 1902—but not enough to make the business more than marginally profitable.

By the fall of 1903 B. F.'s finances had reached a state of uneasy equilibrium. Olaa was more or less self-sufficient, and the monthly dividends from the Oahu Railway kept his interest payments current, but he had no means of paying off any loan that might be called.

To finance Olaa's crop from the time it was harvested to the time the sugar was marketed and payment received in Honolulu, he relied on San Francisco drafts, usually for four months. The B. F. Dillingham Company would send Henry F. Allen, Olaa's agent in San Francisco, a paper asking him to pay the Dillingham Company a certain sum of money four months in the future. When Allen accepted this draft, it then became negotiable and B. F. could use it to secure cash from Bishop and Company, within a line of credit established by the bank. Several hundred thousand dollars was usually outstanding in this manner.

B. F. had had a running battle about these drafts with Mr. Allen from the time that Allen had become Olaa's agent. B. F. kept pressuring Allen to back the plantation with his personal credit. At one point B. F.'s own attorney, Mr. Chickering, had to tell him that "you have gone beyond reason in this, Mr. Dillingham, and Mr. Allen will not submit to your proposition." As a result of Allen's refusal, B. F. had to draw the drafts not on Henry F. Allen but on Henry F. Allen, Agent for the Olaa Sugar Company. This arrangement left Allen free to dishonor a draft at maturity if he held no funds of Olaa to cover it, and the bank would then have had to look to The B. F. Dillingham Company or to Olaa for repayment of its advance. As a matter of fact Allen did pay a number of drafts out of his own funds, but at least the arrangement left him discretion in the matter.

This distinction in the drawing of the drafts, though it may seem obscure or esoteric, came to have vital importance in the crisis which lay ahead.

In November of 1903 B. F. was in Honolulu, entertaining distinguished visitors including General Arthur MacArthur (the father of General Douglas MacArthur) and Isaac L. Requa of the Oakland Bank of Savings. General MacArthur was inspecting the proposed location of an army camp at Leilehua (now Schofield Barracks) and Requa was looking over the Dillingham properties, in particular the Oahu Railway. B. F. was also conferring with James D. Dole, who had satisfied himself that the Wahiawa area provided ideal conditions for growing pineapples and who wanted a railway line and a cannery in Honolulu. In between times B. F. was pushing his proposal of a marketing cooperative for the sugar factors.

In late November B. F. sent a four-month draft on Henry F. Allen, Agent for Olaa, to Bishop and Company, but that bank declined to handle it on the grounds that its own line of credit with the Bank of California was exhausted, and suggested that B. F. put it through one of the other banks. B. F. sent it to the First National Bank, who were happy to get the business and made temporary arrangements to handle similar drafts through January.

On Wednesday, 2 December, B. F. took General MacArthur and his aide and Mr. Requa and their wives to the Haleiwa Hotel for two nights of relaxation. Before leaving Honolulu, B. F. received word that the Empire Mines Company in California was demanding payment of its note for $75,000 on the due date, 6 December. The following day Walter took the afternoon train to Haleiwa to consult, and at five o'clock on Friday morning Bob Atkinson phoned Walter by prearrangement to get the wording of a cable to send to San Francisco regarding the Empire Mines. And at five in the morning Walter told his father another piece of news which he had thought best to withhold the evening before: The First National Bank of San Francisco (the correspondent bank of the First National of Hawaii) had rejected The B. F. Dillingham Company's draft because it was written on Henry F. Allen, Agent, rather than on Allen personally.

"It seemed to me," B. F. wrote, "that unless I could do something immediately that the weight of this thing would absolutely crush out my vital forces and leave me mentally stranded as well as physically . . . [our business] is in a condition that should not subject the Managers of such property to such experiences as I have had on several occasions during the past three years and I will not continue on in this way if I have to sell out everything I have got and be reduced to the condition I was in when I came to this country."

In this crisis B. F. turned for help to the Damons, who promised support to the limit of their ability. Once their attention was called to the way the drafts were written, however, they adopted the attitude that they would not touch them either unless Allen accepted them personally, even though B. F. maintained that he had pointed out the problem to Mr. Damon a year earlier. Allen remained adamant in this position, and an apparent stalemate developed.

These negotiations occupied the month of December. Even then things might have worked out, as Damon was willing to supply the money needed, for 1 percent of the gross proceeds of the Olaa sugar, if he could find suitable security. Allen was willing to subordinate a portion of his security to the bank. As late as 14 January B. F. was still at his desk, writing Jim Dole that if General MacArthur's visit resulted in the establishment of a camp for fifteen hundred soldiers, he would expect to build a branch line to Wahiawa. "Bishop and Company as well as we," he wrote to Paxton, "have done *our best* to manage a very disagreeable crisis."

Early in the crisis B. F. had gone to W. G. Cooper, the cashier of the First National Bank of Hawaii, to explain that Damon was taking over the Dillingham banking, and found Cooper "most pleasant." By late January, however, Cooper's bank was having second thoughts. In rapid succession the bank called a demand loan of B. F.'s for $25,000 and when it was not paid filed a notarized protest of nonpayment, demanded bills of lading covering not less than 600 tons of sugar as security for the draft on H. F. Allen, Agent, and served notice of immediate termination of the agreements under which it was banking for the Oahu Railway. If the First National was indeed trying to put B. F. out of business, it had taken every logical step in its power.

It is hardly possible at this point in time to disinter the bank's motives. Cecil Brown, Mark Robinson, and Cooper ran the bank; there is no evidence that they wished B. F. ill or sought to profit from his misfortunes. Yet the bank's actions over the next year could hardly have caused him more difficulty if they had. "If they hung out the right kind of sign," B. F. commented sourly, "they would have three balls over the front door"

Frank Dillingham at the beginning of 1904 was approaching sixty years of age. He had run his own businesses for almost thirty-five years, during which time he had never been out of debt. He had lived through panics, depressions, revolutions, lawsuits, plagues, fires, and almost every form of commercial disaster. He had driven himself without mercy, subordinating even his family life to the demands of business. And now as he approached an age when he could expect to relax and enjoy the fruits of his labor, the whole fortune which he had built up with so much work and sacrifice seemed to be slipping away from him. He had reached his breaking point.

Unable either to rest or tend to business, Frank in February took Emma and went on a six-week cruise to Japan and Manila. They returned at the end of March, with Frank no better. "Since father's return from the Orient," Walter reported, "he has been kept away from the office most of the time. . . . We are making a desperate effort to hold things together." On 19 April Frank sailed for San Francisco with Emma and Marion, and shortly after his arrival entered a sanitarium run by Dr. James W. Ward. Probably few people who were aware of his condition expected him ever to resume an active business career.

A creditor's committee, meanwhile, had formed in Honolulu with Alfred W. Carter as chairman and had dug into the business affairs of B. F. and of The B. F. Dillingham Company. They concluded that B. F. and the company together owed almost $3 million and held assets of slightly more than that amount. The committee was, of course, indulging in an exercise in futility when it tried to appraise the assets, as these consisted to a considerable extent of stocks with an extremely narrow and weak market. Moreover, the news of Mr. Dillingham's incapacity and the rumors of his insolvency would quickly demoralize what little market existed for Olaa stock. Outside of the

O. R. and L. stock, which paid regular dividends, his holdings had very little to attract an investor; the O. R. and L.—like practically everything else—was pledged as security for loans.

If times had been a little better, so that B. F.'s investments would have looked more attractive, his creditors would probably have thrown his assets on the market to recover what they could and written off the rest. But because of the demoralized state of Hawaiian securities, they began to talk about some form of trusteeship to hold his enterprises together for the time being.

# Part VI
# HOLDING ON

# CHAPTER 38

*Our good friend Charles R. Bishop was constrained to remark several times to me in a way that I did not consider complimentary—"Dillingham, you are a terrible fellow to hold on." I feel that I can thank my propensity for holding on for whatever I have got at the present time, with all due deference to wiser heads and intended good advisors.*

B. F. D. to W. F. Dillingham
29 August 1914

THE creditors and well-wishers of B. F. Dillingham were reckoning without his amazing powers of recuperation. Even as the committee in Honolulu was wrangling over plans to liquidate his empire, B. F. lay in Dr. Ward's sanitarium in San Francisco gathering strength to return to the wars.

Dr. James W. Ward, who apparently did not have an M.D. degree, practiced homeopathic medicine, whose theories would find little support today among medical doctors. But B. F. knew and trusted him, and Dr. Ward evidently had a great personal concern for his patient, for B. F. began to recover with amazing speed. He entered the sanitarium at the end of April, and by 9 May Dr. Ward was allowing Chickering to send him a brief and cheerful letter about his business affairs. On 13 June B. F. left the sanitarium to continue his recuperation on the campus of Mills College, and on 16 July he ventured into San Francisco for the first time. At the end of July he was objecting to the idea of a trusteeship, and by early August he was working on a plan to salvage Puna Sugar.

Harold Dillingham has left a memorandum telling how in his senior year at Harvard the family spared him knowledge of the seriousness of his father's condition. Arriving at San Francisco in early July

1904, he found his father staying at the Chickering house in Oakland, quite unable to work. One evening there came a knock on the door, as Walter arrived unexpectedly from Honolulu. From that moment, Harold related, hope and courage returned and his father began rapidly to get well.

On 10 August, still in the Chickering house, Marion Dillingham married the Reverend John P. Erdman, who was on his way to Japan

The Dillingham family about 1903. Left to right: May Frear, Harold, Frank, Walter Frear, Walter, Emma, Marion. This picture was presumably taken not long before Marion's marriage in 1904 to the Reverend John P. Erdman. (Courtesy of the Dillingham family)

as a missionary. Twenty-seven years later the first child of this happy union, Harold R. Erdman, married Mr. Chickering's granddaughter, Mary Chickering.

After Marion's wedding, Emma and Walter accompanied the new couple as far as Honolulu, leaving Frank under the doctor's care in San Francisco, with Harold to keep him company. "Tell him [John Erdman]," Frank wrote to Marion, "I have *never* seen any man into who's hands I would have been more willing to intrust the happiness of my daughter."

Frank for the moment was considerably chastened. He had customarily taken a suite at the best hotel wherever he stayed. Now he and Harold shared for the next three months a double bed in the small back room of a wooden frame hotel on Van Ness Avenue. Harold evidently found it more difficult than Frank did, for if the father fell asleep first, his snoring would keep Harold awake for hours. For entertainment they would walk, talk, read, go to church, or do anything that required no money. Happily, their friends in San Francisco stood by them, and they were constantly invited to dine out together.

"I have been gaining in mental and physical strength every day since you left San Francisco," he wrote to Marion in November. "Have had enough to keep me busy, and the cool bracing climate was just what I needed. I weigh now 185. I am trying to keep my weight down, by taking plenty of exercise with dumbbells and otherwise."

There is no sign that this breakdown at the age of sixty affected Frank's powers of reasoning in any degree. His business letters after his illness are just as clear and explicit as before. Toward his family and friends he was perhaps even more tender and affectionate. But it does appear that he became more arbitrary and excitable whenever he was crossed in a business matter, and that he exercised less tact and diplomacy in dealing with those who opposed him. He had always had a low boiling point, but now he could hardly tolerate certain subjects and personalities.

His illness had one other profound effect on his business life. Before his breakdown he had been very much the captain of his ship, and Walter one of his lieutenants. Now Walter had had to step in and run the show for at least six months. From that time on Walter became more and more an equal partner in the family enterprises. His letters to his father show a great deal of deference and solicitude, but they also contain very positive opinions, and his advice quite generally prevailed. From 1904 it becomes difficult to write of the business career of B. F. Dillingham, because his interests became merged into those of his family and decisions became a matter of consensus between him and Walter and later Harold.

In the final analysis, inertia and the distance between Honolulu and San Francisco saved B. F.'s financial hide, as much as anything else.

Those creditors who held O. R. and L. stock as collateral had no great cause for worry and were generally willing to ride out the storm. Those who held plantation stocks were mostly unwilling to swallow the losses necessary in liquidation. The Honolulu creditors devised one plan, the San Francisco creditors another, and neither plan went into effect. Even the First National Bank of Hawaii fired off volleys of demands and failed to follow through on them.

B. F. had many loyal supporters. The San Francisco bankers were almost all friendly to him. In Honolulu Joseph O. Carter successfully held out against an attempt to pirate some of his securities, and W. A. Kinney came down from Kauai to rally his forces. Thurston stood by his friend wholeheartedly, and always there was Walter, working quietly, diplomatically, and effectively.

Those who held Olaa stock as collateral put their trust in Bishop and Company. "Damon is taking a great interest in the effort to see the Dillingham Company through," Walter wrote on 19 April, "and I firmly believe as his pride is now at stake, that he will stand by us."

But two weeks later, before any plan for saving Olaa was adopted, there came a terrible shock which sent the Dillingham fortunes to their lowest ebb.

Out in the green, wet fields of Olaa millions of tiny leafhoppers had been steadily chewing away. Now their hour of triumph had arrived. Where the ravaged leaves joined the cane stalks, black slime formed, and the cane rotted in the ground. "Fields . . . have simply gone as if a blight had fallen on nature," reported the distraught Manager McStocker. He hesitated whether to strip the leaves and expose the tender young bark to the hoppers, or to leave the slimy, rotten mass where it stood. In one stroke he cut his crop estimate from 24,000 tons to 19,661, a net loss of some $300,000.

To Walter, the revised estimate "came like a bolt of lightning." To the Damons it was equally devastating. Ned Damon took ship to San Francisco to confer with the creditors there, accompanied by Allen W. T. Bottomley, a Scotch accountant and Mr. Damon's most trusted adviser. In San Francisco they found H. F. Allen too sick to act, and the other creditors procrastinating about putting up a portion of Olaa's estimated requirements. "Make no more advances to Olaa," Ned cabled his father. "Let creditors sweat." C. Brewer and Company expressed interest in taking on the agency of Olaa, but refused to touch it unless the stockholders were washed out and the bonds traded in for new stock.

In spite of Ned's "hard work and enthusiasm," as Paxton expressed it, the trip produced nothing except the Bank of California's evident backing of the Damons in taking over the Olaa account entirely. Providentially, sugar prices had firmed in late May, practically offsetting the shortfall in Olaa sugar tonnage; the Damons took a deep breath and plunged in.

At the end of June Olaa signed a new agreement making Bishop and Company its agent, and the Damons began to make advances to the plantation under a blanket mortgage incorporated in the agreement. Simultaneously the Bank of Hawaii, dominated by the Cooke family, paid off a loan outstanding from the First National Bank to the Oahu Railway and took over the railroad account. As Walter wrote, "we do not want Damon overloaded, and further I consider it good policy to stand in a little with the Cooke combination, who have bucked us so persistently in the past."

Like any losing team, Olaa Sugar Company got a new manager. The new board of directors, dominated by Bishop and Company, accepted McStocker's resignation before even receiving it, and appointed John Watt in his place. McStocker withdrew with dignity and good grace from the place where he had given heart and soul for five years.

Bishop and Company's takeover came just in time. In California even Chickering was talking of a receivership for the plantation. With Olaa's finances secure for the time being, Paxton could turn his attention to the problem of B. F.'s debts in California.

"I feel very sure," wrote Walter, "that in San Francisco you will not meet such obstinacy, pure and simple, as we found in one or two of the creditors here."

Actually, the San Francisco creditors proved as a whole much more reasonable and cooperative than the Honolulu ones. As Paxton wrote, "They express the greatest sympathy for Mr. D. and the highest regard for him."

In 1903 B. F. had reported meeting Frank B. Anderson, the new vice-president of the Bank of California, and liking him very much. Now Anderson was handling the Dillingham account with his bank and also spearheading the effort to hold the California creditors in line. Anderson became a particularly close friend of Walter Dillingham's and over the years provided invaluable support for the family.

Before attacking directly the question of extensions on his loans in San Francisco, B. F. sought a solution to the sticky problem of the Puna Sugar Company bonds which he and Mark Robinson had sold in San Francisco. About $260,000 worth of these remained outstanding, most of them in the hands of banks to which B. F. owed money, plus $174,000 worth which The B. F. Dillingham Company had taken in payment of advances to Puna. To preserve his own reputation, B. F. had to make some attempt to redeem these bonds.

Puna itself was in a hopeless mess. It owed Olaa over $280,000, and no one could see any chance of its breaking even on its present basis. The bond coupons had gone unpaid at 1 July and the First National Bank of Hawaii was demanding a receivership. The Damons vacillated about keeping it running for the 1905 crop but finally decided to get rid of it "lock, stock and barrel." At the end of August, W. Pfotenhauer, an official of Hackfeld and Company, was appointed receiver.

Against this unpromising background, B. F. convinced the San Francisco bondholders to give him limited authority to handle their interest in the matter, thus gaining a measure of control of $434,000 out of the $500,000 in bonds. Included in this total was $53,000 worth which he had sold to the Pacific Mutual Life Insurance Company through his friend Dr. George A. Moore, president of the company. He now agreed with Dr. Moore to repurchase these bonds at par, and the insurance company agreed to lend him $96,000, out of which he paid for the bonds with interest and had $40,000 left over to pay on account to the First National Bank of Hawaii. As security he gave the insurance company the bonds plus fifteen thousand shares of McBryde stock. This remarkable transaction got him out of a tight spot, as the bank was about to close out his McBryde for whatever it would bring.

With Olaa taken care of temporarily, and the Puna bonds swept under the rug, B. F. worked out a *modus vivendi* with his San Francisco creditors. Because Damon had kept the option of dropping Olaa at any time, the creditors secured by Olaa stock would not give the three-year extension which B. F. sought, but they at least indicated that they would give the new arrangement a year to see how it worked. His other creditors were, in general, more liberal, even in some cases reducing the interest rate. From this experience B. F. drew a conclusion which became an obsession with him: that Damon had forced an unfair and one-sided agreement on Olaa, and that B. F. must get out of Damon's clutches as quickly as possible.

One more serious problem remained: the Hilo Railroad bond interest. Part of the bonds were held in San Francisco, and part in Honolulu; desperate to sell them, B. F. had guaranteed, through The B. F. Dillingham Company, the interest on these bonds. The railroad itself had no money and its principal customer, Olaa Sugar, refused to pay its bills because of the heavy advances it had already made to the railway.

In Honolulu Damon flatly refused to help the railroad unless Walter hypothecated Mokuleia Ranch, the last unencumbered piece of property the family owned. Walter declined to do so, and a stalemate ensued. At the last moment Thurston, the president of the railway, put up some Hawaiian Gazette Company stock and the railroad borrowed enough to pay the 1 October coupons presented in Honolulu. In San Francisco B. F. covered the coupons with the sale of two hundred shares of Waialua stock and a loan from Dr. Ward.

On 27 September Walter was working late at the office in Honolulu, writing his father a letter to say that he had pasted the O. R. and L. stock proxies into the minutes book, whence they could not be removed without tearing the pages. Abruptly, he changed the subject.

> It is now nine o'clock Tuesday evening, and the terrible news of the death of Ned Damon has just been telephoned to me. I understand that he was stabbed and killed at Moanalua. I have telephoned home for Sally and the buggy, and I am going right out to Moanalua. His poor little wife and four babies left behind. I am wondering what this shock will do to Sam. Ned had become such an important factor in the old man's business life. It will be a terrible blow I am sure. We little know what a day or an hour will bring forth, certainly, I little dreamed of this when I was talking with both Ned and Mr. Damon this noon.

Only a few days after this terrible incident, Mr. Damon attended a meeting of the Olaa directors called to consider the matter of the money owed to Olaa by The B. F. Dillingham Company, which amounted to $368,000 and was secured by Olaa stock of an equal value at par. Damon proposed to take immediate steps to sell the collateral at public auction and proceed against The Dillingham Company for the deficiency, an act which would undoubtedly have bankrupted the Dillingham interests.

Walter, Thurston, and a young lawyer named Ernest A. Mott-Smith, who had been helping to adjust the Dillingham affairs in Honolulu, represented the Dillingham interests on the Olaa board, against four men appointed by the bank. Damon's proposal left them aghast. Mott-Smith declared that he would cut off his right hand before he took part in any such action. Walter argued that the debt had arisen from the Dillinghams' efforts to protect the stockholders, cited the Dillingham endorsement of a new Olaa note for $265,000 within the last sixty days, and pointed out that the eighteen thousand shares of Olaa would completely demoralize the market and cause a heavy loss to the creditors, including the Bank of California. In the end Mr. Damon said that he had not considered the Dillingham side of the matter, and let the question stand over until Mr. Dillingham's return from California.

This near-fatal incident strengthened B. F.'s resolve to get out of Mr. Damon's hands.

Walter meanwhile had stripped the Honolulu office down to essentials, giving up most of the floor which The B. F. Dillingham Company had leased and cutting the staff to five men on "Scotch-coolie wages," as he put it. The senior in age was A. W. Van Valkenburg ("Van"), thirty-five years old, followed by a trusted cashier with the improbable name of Mr. Crook. Walter's lifelong friend Bob Atkinson, whom B. F. had helped through Harvard, handled the insurance business. Walter and one clerk completed the roster. Paxton resigned rather than go to Hilo as manager of the Hilo Railroad, but landed on his feet as manager of the Sugar Factors Company.

Walter also reduced The B. F. Dillingham Company's debts by settlements with various creditors. A & B was still owed $65,000 which they cancelled by taking over the security, an equal amount of Olaa bonds. Robinson and A. J. Campbell held unsecured notes totaling about $140,000, for which they took McBryde and Olaa stock at par; Walter settled his mother's claim for $26,000 on the same basis. Alfred W. Carter settled his note for $150,000 by taking over the securities. Altogether, these transactions eliminated close to $400,000 of debts.

But even after this substantial relief from interest charges, the company's income failed to cover its operating expenses and interest payments by a substantial amount. This shortfall plagued B. F. and Walter for the next several years.

B. F. in San Francisco continued to feel better. He put $5 down on a piano to be shipped to Marion in Japan, and talked of going to Mexico to look into the Hidalgo Rubber Plantation. Walter urged him to come home; "we need *you* more than we do the rubber business right now."

"I consider our *whole* business is *entirely* in our *own hands*. . . . we cannot be *held down* by *any cast iron rules* but must manage our affairs in any way and every way that will lead to the settlement we desire to reach," B. F. wrote to Walter. His recovery was complete.

Harold had been studying accounting in San Francisco. At the end of October, Walter cabled him to come home as cashier of the Oahu Railway, and Harold caught the next boat. This fortunate move, which came about because Walter fired the superintendant of the Hilo Railroad and moved the Oahu cashier to Hilo, greatly strengthened the family team over the next critical years. Harold turned out to have a fine head for figures and a gift for financial analysis, as well as a winning personality.

Two weeks later B. F. followed Harold, after an absence from home of most of the year. On the voyage down he caught his breath and wrote Marion a long letter.

> My precious daughter,
>
> . . . it will seem so strange to me not to find you at home when I return. But our family have been scattered a great deal since May and Walter first went away to attend school and College in the "East." . . . My life has been so crowded with anxious thoughts that the years have vanished like a dream, and our precious Children are all grown up and entered upon the duties and responsibilities of real life. . . . you will be glad to know that all my San Francisco creditors have treated me with the utmost kindness and consideration. They have seen me come up out of the grave seemingly, and with my returning health, their full confidence in me and my affairs, and in my ability to manage my business successfully, has returned. I have been able to make further loans in S. F. with which to pay off some pressing obligations to some of my less friendly creditors at Honolulu, which also brings comfort and satisfaction to my wounded pride. I now feel that I am "on deck" again, and with God's continued blessing I expect to prove myself master of the situation and able to pay off every dollar I

owe and have a substantial fortune left. . . . The total amount of sugar made at "Olaa" from the first three crops was 54,000 tons which was sold in New York for an average of say 70.00 per ton. At the present price the *difference* would have been $25.00 per ton, on 54,000 tons = $1,350,000. The leafhopper destroyed at "Olaa" last year 10,000 tons, which at 95.00 per ton would have returned to the plantation after paying freight and all other charges say 80.00 per ton making $800,000 more or a total difference of $2,150,000. That difference would have saved me from a year's illness and no end of anxiety. However, the past is gone. I am truly thankful for the present indications of renewed prosperity. I am not greedy for great gain but naturally I am anxious for such a measure of prosperity as will enable me to get out of debt, or reach a point where financial strain and anxiety will be at an end.

Affectionately
Father

# CHAPTER 39

*We (Emma and I) have traveled together very little in all the years of our married life until the last two years, excepting our trip in 1887. I hardly need tell you she is the best fellow in the world.*

B. F. D. to W. F. Dillingham
June 1906

At the beginning of 1905 B. F. and The B. F. Dillingham Company together still owed close to $3 million. They held a majority of the stock in the Oahu Railway, Olaa Sugar, and the Hilo Railroad, though his debts and those of the corporations severely limited his degree of control. B. F. also had a major investment in McBryde and lesser ones in Kihei, Waialua, and numerous smaller enterprises. Practically everything he had was pledged as security for loans.

For three years—1905 through 1907—B. F. struggled along without making much progress. He did pay off some debts, but at the expense of liquidating some assets. He won some small tactical victories and he avoided giving up more ground, but at the end of that time his position remained desperate.

More than anything else, the state of Olaa Sugar Company held him down. For the entire three years Olaa averaged about $60 a ton return on its sugar, net after marketing costs, and it lost money every year. Olaa's tonnage, moreover, fell from 18,000 in 1902 and 1903 to about 10,000 in 1906 and 1907. The manager blamed this terrible decline on the old reliable Lahaina cane, which had become subject to root rot, and proceeded to replace it with Yellow Caledonia on the lower fields and Rose Bamboo in the Mountain View section. As Olaa operated on a cycle of three rattoon crops, it took time to make the change; even in 1905 the directors could see that no profit was possible before 1908. By that time the plantation had lost altogether about a million dollars, and owed Bishop and Company the staggering total of $1.8 million.

If Olaa was the millstone around B. F.'s neck, his life preserver was the Oahu Railway. The railroad had a rather disappointing year in 1904. Under pressure from the San Francisco creditors, Walter at the end of the year wrote off close to half a million dollars in depreciation and amortization, reducing the surplus to a quarter of a million. But from that time on the road went ahead at an amazing rate.

In 1905 B. F. and Walter decided to build the Wahiawa branch, a courageous decision in the light of conditions at the time. This project involved some 10 miles of road starting near the Waipahu mill and climbing to an elevation of 923 feet at the Wahiawa townsite. Unlike most of the main line this branch required a great number of curves and rather heavy grades.

The branch opened in the middle of 1906 and proved an instant success as the pineapple business boomed beyond all expectations. In its first six months the line produced as much traffic as had been estimated for the first year. Within two years traffic had built up to a

First use of the spur track connecting Wahiawa Depot with Leilehua plains, January 13, 1909. The "Pineapple Limited," as the soldiers dubbed the train, is about to carry the 2nd squadron, 5th cavalry regiment, from the new Schofield Barracks to a waiting transport in Honolulu Harbor. (Courtesy of the Tropic Lightning Historical Society)

point where the railway had to order two 42-ton "Consolidation" (2-8-0) locomotives to handle it. Walter paid for the extension—about $150,000—out of a line of credit at the Bank of Hawaii, and by 1908 the railway had completely paid off its debts except for the bond issue.

The O. R. and L. had been paying $240,000 a year in dividends since 1901, more than half of it to the Dillinghams. By 1907 dividends totaled $360,000 a year, and the road was still charging depreciation and increasing the surplus each year. Without the railway's splendid record of growth, B. F. could never have survived the grim years at Olaa.

B. F. had returned to a late Thanksgiving and a warm homecoming in November of 1904. "Yes it does seem good to be at home once more," he wrote to Marion in Japan. "I cannot tell you how delightful it really is. The many shades of vivid green that cover the landscape in every direction are indescribably beautiful. 'Mother' is so well, and as bright and cheerful as ever. . . . Everybody I know whom I have thus far had the privilege of meeting seemed glad to see me in Honolulu and so expressed themselves in terms and manner indicating genuine sincerity."

By the end of the year the euphoria of homecoming had worn off. Bishop and Company had refused to let Olaa pay the Hilo Railroad's bill, bringing B. F. to a boil again on the subject of getting out of Damon's clutches. On New Year's Day, 1905, B. F. cornered Damon in his office and the two of them, in B. F.'s phrase, exchanged some "home truths." B. F. evidently relieved his own feelings at the expense of agitating Damon, with unfortunate results.

In spite of this emotional outburst, however, the Olaa directors voted five days later to settle The B. F. Dillingham Company debt by taking back Olaa stock at par, in the amount of $372,000. This settlement represented a big step in straightening out the Dillingham affairs.

At the same time Mark Robinson was forced to dump his considerable holdings of O. R. and L. stock, driving the market down below 70. Anderson at the Bank of California wrote B. F. a letter couched in unusually critical terms, wanting to know the reason for the low stock quotation, demanding an explanation of several transactions, and requesting that the O. R. and L. put a representative of Bishop and Company on its board and elect Bottomley its auditor. Rudolph Spreckels, who held a piece of the syndicate loan, refused to give

B. F. Dillingham in 1905, at the age of sixty-one. At this point he had returned to Honolulu after recovering from his breakdown, but still faced monumental problems of debt and lack of liquidity. (Photo by Webster, Bishop Museum)

B. F. his proxy on the Olaa stock and cabled demanding a payment or more security.

So ticklish did the situation seem that Walter went to San Francisco in February. He reported that the difficulties had arisen as a result of the fight with Damon on New Year's Day, and that Anderson had actually intervened on B. F.'s behalf in the matter of the Dillingham debt to Olaa. He also described Anderson as most anxious that B. F. and Damon should find a common ground for working together. While he was undoubtedly reporting Anderson's position accurately, one gets the impression that he was seizing the opportunity to calm his father down a bit.

Walter also called together the Puna bondholders in San Francisco to present an offer from Olaa Sugar to buy the Puna bonds with Olaa stock. The bondholders rejected the offer, but Walter may have been pleased rather than disappointed, because they gave as the reason for their rejection the fact that the plantation was tied to Damon for ten years, although Damon could drop the plantation at any time.

Armed with this argument, Anderson put some discreet pressure on Damon to modify his stance. Damon refused to change the contract, but he did agree to give it up on payment of the balance owing plus $100,000, which represented a considerable concession toward the Dillingham position. But with money tight and sugar prices low, none of the other factoring houses cared to pick up the proposition, and Olaa and Bishop and Company remained locked in an uneasy embrace.

Damon's attitude, particularly with respect to the Hilo Railroad, did become more conciliatory, and the San Francisco creditors calmed down until the next crisis; Walter's trip must be rated a success. At one point, after dealing with an irate creditor in Honolulu, Walter had reported that he spent three-quarters of an hour "stroking him down"; he certainly proved himself a master of the technique.

B. F. back in Honolulu was desperately trying to salvage something from Puna. The receiver for the plantation had advertised a public sale, which B. F., armed with limited powers from the San Francisco bondholders, kept having postponed for ten days at a time while he sought to form a syndicate to buy and operate the plantation. The local bondholders—Mark Robinson and Hackfeld and Company—refused to join with the others, and B. F. suspected that Hackfeld and the First National Bank wanted to force a sale, bid in the assets for a song, take off the cane at a profit, and liquidate the plantation at leisure.

B. F. never got his syndicate together to buy Puna, and C. Brewer finally backed out of what he had thought was a commitment to buy it. In May he got the Olaa stockholders, with Damon and A. W. Carter dissenting, to sweeten their previous offer by trading Olaa stock for Puna bonds par for par, and the deal quickly went through. B. F. exulted that Olaa now controlled 20,000 acres of sugar land in fee simple and 10,000 acres under long lease; he confidently expected it to rival H. C. and S. as the territory's greatest sugar producer.

This resolution of the Puna question left the Hilo Railroad as the number one Dillingham headache. The Dillingham Company's guarantee of the railroad bond interest ran through 1911; the railroad was losing money steadily, and The Dillingham Company was short of income to pay the interest on its own debts. Keeping the road out of bankruptcy required a financial juggling act for years to come.

B. F. and Sam Damon had got past the Puna crisis together, each pledging complete cooperation, but mutual understanding hardly flourished. In June B. F. wrote to Damon to invite him to come to his office to discuss funding Olaa's bonded and floating debt and also to hear his thoughts on the Hilo Railroad. Damon replied that he would prefer to see a letter on the subjects and that if a conference were necessary Alexander Garvie and Bottomley should be present. That ended the exchange.

Walter returned at the beginning of June, exulting that "nothing succeeds like success, and the victory achieved in the Puna matter has been very beneficial to all our interests." B. F. had expected to take his place in San Francisco, but stayed on to negotiate with C. Brewer.

B. F. Dillingham, confronted with the Hilo Railroad situation, instinctively sought a positive solution to the problem: extend the line and tap new sources of business. From the defunct Hilo–Kohala railroad group he picked up the franchise to build north from Hilo, along the North Hilo and Hamakua coasts, where a long string of plantations sent their sugar to market in a costly, inefficient, and dangerous fashion by transferring it, generally by overhead cable, to small steamers lying off the rocky coast. The government road up the coast qualified as a second-class mule track; one plantation manager was accused of laying out his plantation railroad in such a manner that he could use it to get to dinner once a week at the next plantation.

Remembering perhaps the early days of the O. R. and L., B. F. determined to build along the coast in increments, and set as his first target the thriving plantation of Onomea. Onomea was only 6 miles out of Hilo, the line would run through country less horrendous for railroad building than that which lay farther north, and between Onomea and Hilo several smaller plantations would fall into the railroad's lap once the line was built.

B. F. had logic on his side but not the politics of business. C. Brewer and Company controlled Onomea, and the president of C. Brewer was C. M. Cooke. Besides heading C. Brewer and the Bank of Hawaii, Mr. Cooke had put together and now headed the Inter-Island Steam Navigation Company, whose ships picked up the sugar all along the coast. The Brewer directors listened attentively to B. F.'s proposition, deliberated for several weeks, and approved a five-year contract with Inter-Island. "We are met with all sorts of surprises these days," B. F. remarked to Walter, "that are not complimentary to 'high class' business men."

The Bank of Hawaii, on the other hand, was only too happy to work with B. F. on refunding McBryde Sugar. The easy success of this venture perhaps influenced Mr. Damon, as he called on B. F. and "expressed the desire that we might be able to work together in perfect harmony." The two of them visited Olaa together, where B. F. could hardly sleep after seeing the wretched state of the cane. But Damon assured him that he intended to see the plantation through. "His reputation is at stake, as mine is," said B. F. Later the two met in San Francisco to work out the details of the proposed new Olaa bond issue.

Emma meanwhile had sailed for Japan to be with Marion, who was expecting her first child. On 19 June came the joyful news of the birth of Harold Randolph Erdman, B. F.'s and Emma's first grandson. "It was so good and generous of you . . . to give us all another Harlo Boy. There has been great rejoicing here I can assure you," wrote the proud grandfather.

In August B. F. was writing to Marion again: "I have written very

Emma Dillingham carried on her father and mother's ideals of service to others. She served for forty-eight years as treasurer of the Women's Board of Missions, and was a founder and president of both the YWCA and the Daughters of Hawaii. She was particularly interested in the welfare of Hawaiians; she spoke the Hawaiian language fluently and loved Hawaiian music. She loved to give *lomi lomi* to any of her friends who were tired or sick. As a wife and mother she proved a tower of strength, and her husband throughout their married life discussed with her at great length his business plans and opportunities. (Courtesy of the Dillingham family)

fully to your good mother, and enclosed copies of my business correspondence which will give you all a correct idea of the situation and just what I have to accomplish if possible in order to get away comfortably.''

By October he had completed preliminary work on the new bond issue and sailed from San Francisco on the *Korea,* which touched at Honolulu on its way to Japan.

Marion and John were living at Yamaguchi in the extreme western part of Japan. Frank arrived there in early November, just in time to hear Emma and Marion play the piano for a crowd of one thousand celebrating the Emperor's birthday. He found his new grandson all that he had expected, but after a short visit he returned home by way of Yokohama, stopping there to pick up some Christmas merchandise for Pacific Hardware. ''Mother and I are having another 'honey moon',' ' he reported to Marion from Yokohama. By early December he was back in Honolulu, working until eleven at night to get his goods unpacked and marked for the Christmas trade.

But the overriding fact of life at The B. F. Dillingham Company was still the need for cash. At the end of 1905 B. F. induced the O. R. and L. directors to declare an extra dividend of 0.5 percent, payable in January 1906. This move provoked a storm of protest in San Francisco, and one of the creditor banks demanded immediate payment of its loan. B. F. by that time had reached San Francisco on his way to New York, and went to see Anderson prepared to justify the action. According to B. F.'s account, he found Anderson so disagreeable that when Anderson asked him why he had paid the dividend, he simply said, ''Because I needed the money.''

B. F. took the train east, and Walter was left with the job of pacifying Anderson by letter. In Honolulu Damon demanded payment of three B. F. Dillingham Company notes totaling $82,000, and even Walter began to think in terms of a receivership.

The next crisis came early in April when four San Francisco banks demanded payments on account, and it appeared that the time might be at hand that Walter had warned of, when he said that a shock in the money market could wipe them out.

For close to forty years B. F.'s finances had suffered from every revolution and conflagration in sight. This one time he profited from a terrible and wholly unexpected disaster.

The next shock came, not in the money market but along the San Andreas fault. On 19 April San Francisco suffered its great earthquake, followed by four days of uncontrolled fire. When it was all over the city lay in shambles. The banks remained closed for weeks, trying to reconstruct their records, with bigger problems to worry about than trying to collect on the Dillingham loans.

B. F. in New York was chasing what turned out to be a wild goose, in an effort to raise money to extend the Hilo Railroad. When he heard of the disaster in San Francisco, he lined up a group of New York bankers who in a spirit of helpfulness agreed to pick up all his San Francisco loans if the banks there would agree to buy them back again in two years. The plan never went through, ostensibly because the San Francisco Savings Union could not legally make such a commitment, but it evidently made a strong impression on the San Francisco bankers, and the demands for payment were heard no more.

Back in Honolulu, Walter somehow convinced Mr. Damon that he had had Damon's interest uppermost in his mind when he renewed the O. R. and L.'s arrangement with the Bank of Hawaii, to which Damon had strongly objected. When Walter had finished stroking him down, Mr. Damon not only renewed the notes he had called but voluntarily reduced the interest rate.

But the family was still, as Walter reported, "closer-hauled than ever before." Walter had used his personal funds to pay company bills and borrowed from his brother, sisters, mother, and brother-in-law. He talked to Harold at great length, and the two agreed that their father should sell control of the Oahu Railway at $125 a share and get the family completely out of debt.

B. F. was agreeable to the idea, and in fact had already been working on a plan for launching a holding company, the Pacific Development Company, to own both railroads. Talks went on for months, but in August the other parties broke off "temporarily," blaming bad money conditions from the earthquake that destroyed Valparaiso and the tidal wave at Maalaea. B. F. was rather pleased than otherwise.

Temporary relief came from another quarter. When Walter had returned from Harvard, he had been followed by Isaac L. Dillingham, known as Ike, the son of Frank's cousin Isaac, at whose home in Auburndale Walter had lived while going to Newton High School. Ike had gone to work for Pacific Hardware, and B. F. had eventually removed the old management in disgust and given the firm to Ike to run. Ike had done well with the business, but now he saw a chance for a quick profit. He obtained options at about 50 cents on the dollar on most of the Pacific Hardware stock not held by the family, then turned around and sold the business to Theo. H. Davies and E. O. Hall and Company. The Dillinghams got about $60,000 out of the deal, of which half went to pay loans against the stock and the rest carried them through a most critical period.

B. F. meantime, while waiting for answers on his railroad projects, had been enjoying another honeymoon, this time in Massachusetts. Emma's sixtieth birthday was on 4 June, and they celebrated it with an all-day trolley ride through the New England landscape. A week later they were taking a trolley from Worcester to Southboro to visit the graves of his father and mother, and to Holden to see the old Damon house.

By October B. F. was ready to go home. The sale of the railroads had gone up in smoke, and he had not found the money for the Hilo Railroad extension or put over the Olaa refunding, but the San Francisco creditors had given him a two-year extension. Sam Damon went home on the same boat, and B. F. reported that they became "very chummy," sitting side by side at the table. "I think there will be no difficulty in our pulling together hereafter," he wrote.

The middle of 1906 marked low tide for the Dillingham fortunes; from that point they had only one way to go. The year 1907 was like 1894 in the old days of the railroad's struggle, in that the tide was beginning to turn even though no one could see it at the time.

Sugar prices were still low. Olaa harvested a miserable crop which yielded only 10,000 tons of sugar. The plantation suffered its worst annual loss, more than $300,000, and its debt to Bishop and Company crept up toward $2 million. More than a thousand acres of rattoons, the last of the Lahaina cane, gave only about three-quarters of a ton of sugar per acre. But out in the fields the growing cane that would produce the crops for the next few years looked strong and juicy.

Besides its massive debt to Bishop and Company, Olaa still owed $465,000 secured by its own bonds and guaranteed by The B. F. Dillingham Company. Three San Francisco banks holding $415,000 worth of these notes had become extremely restless and were demanding payment. In spite of Olaa's connection with Bishop and Company, B. F. induced C. M. Cooke of the Bank of Hawaii to pick up these loans, a transaction which undoubtedly strengthened the

Dillingham credit in San Francisco. It also indicated the extent to which business conditions had improved in Hawaii, as the plantations generally had learned to live with the prevailing low sugar prices.

Even the Hilo Railroad gave some grounds for hope. Congress had at last voted funds to start the Hilo breakwater, an essential factor in B. F.'s master plan for the Hilo–Hamakua area. Besides making Hilo an all-weather port, the breakwater would give the railroad a nice piece of business for several years in hauling rock. The Hawaiian Mahogany Lumber Company began building 12 miles of private track to connect with the Hilo Railroad at Glenwood, offering the promise of another source of freight. And B. F. got through the legislature a tax exemption for his proposed line north from Hilo.

Evidently B. F. held no rancor against Cecil Brown of the First National Bank, for he went back to Brown in the summer of 1907 for help in floating $700,000 in additional Hilo Railroad bonds to start the extension. Brown accepted the commission on behalf of the bank, but the offering failed and no bonds were issued.

The Oahu Railway maintained its pattern of growth in traffic and in earnings. In July B. F. resumed the offensive against Anderson in the matter of increased dividends, pointing out that in three years he and The B. F. Dillingham Company had decreased their total liabilities by $1.3 million. Interest and life insurance premiums, he calcu-

An old picture of the docks at Hilo, made possible by the breakwater which the Hilo Railroad pushed so vigorously. (Bishop Museum photo)

lated, ran about $175,000 a year. If the banks would let him pay 9 percent on the Oahu Railway stock, it would give him dividends of $170,000, which together with $6,000 income from bond coupons would service the debt and life insurance until the time ripened to sell some of the non-dividend-paying stocks. This time Anderson on behalf of the creditor banks gave reluctant consent and the cash flow problem was solved—with the horrible exception of whatever cash the Dillinghams might have to supply to pay the Hilo Railroad bond coupons.

Within the family, news was splendid. Walter's dredging business was growing beyond all expectation. Walter Frear had received appointment as governor of the territory, and Marion and John Erdman were coming to live in Hawaii, where he would continue his missionary work among the Japanese. In the fall Harold became engaged to Miss Margaret Bayard Smith, of a prominent San Francisco family; their wedding took place the following February.

In September B. F. was staying at the Von Holt camp at Pa Lehua, high in the Waianae mountains, and writing to Charles Bishop about the "inexpressably beautiful" view—a view that included 24,000 acres of sugarcane where there had been dry wasteland before B. F. built the Oahu Railway. B. F. was thinking not of the past, however, but of the future; he wanted the Bank of California and Bishop and Company to underwrite a new Hilo Railroad bond issue.

He also took the opportunity to thank Mr. Bishop for past favors, in words which recall the sentiments he had expressed toward old Mr. Castle: "I want to express to you in some degree the deep sense of gratitude I feel for the great kindness and consideration you have shown me, from the time I commenced business in these islands, but especially for the way you have stood by me during the past eight years. I feel that you have been like a father to me! and I assure you from the inmost depths of my heart, I have meant to show myself worthy of your true friendship and the confidence you have reposed in me." If he were to go, he added, Walter and Harold would be able to carry out his plans.

Frank Dillingham was now sixty-three, and he had lived a life of constant strain and anxiety, until now his clock was beginning to run down. He wrote later that in November 1907, "I was visited with a paralytic stroke on the left side. Although I was not laid up in bed more than a day and a half, still the stroke was sufficient to make me feel a sense of loss of interest in things and people in general. From that condition I improved gradually."

Frank did regain his health to the point where he resumed his usual state of activity, but it is doubtful that his old strength and vigor ever returned in full measure. More and more his life became a struggle against the symptoms of physical decay.

# Part VII
# THE LAST BATTLE

# CHAPTER 40

*I have been such a slave to business for the last twenty years, or in fact all my life, that I have seemed to have very little time to devote to my friends in a social way. I have always had my ideals but somehow or other I have never been able to live up to them.*

B. F. Dillingham
14 January 1904

IF 1907 was the year the tide turned, certainly 1908 was the year the turn became apparent.

Sugar prices rose, Olaa's grind shot up to 17,000 tons, and for the first time since Bishop and Company took over as agents, the plantation showed a profit—a small one to be sure, but still a profit.

The federal government had let a contract to begin work on the Hilo breakwater, and the Hilo Railroad's prospects seemed brighter. The B. F. Dillingham Company took preferred stock in payment of $130,000 of advances it had made over the past four years.

On Oahu, Waialua Agricultural finally paid its first dividend, and Ewa alone paid the O. R. and L. $88,000 in rent. The railroad had a splendid year, paying 9 percent in dividends and wiping out its floating debt.

Kihei Plantation gave up, selling out to H. C. and S. at $10 a share, but at least this brought some more cash into The B. F. Dillingham Company.

With increasing prosperity, the San Francisco creditors grew more insistent in their requests for payment. B. F. managed a number of payments on account, and paid off other loans through Honolulu sources.

B. F. failed again, however, to refinance the Olaa bond issue, and blamed Damon for the failure because Damon had signed a five-year contract with a San Francisco agent who could not carry part of the plantation's debt. B. F. worked himself into a rage on the subject, but for once Damon handled him with some tact and he gradually subsided.

All through the islands there was a feeling of change and progress as business emerged from the doldrums of low sugar prices. Three years earlier Walter had reported with astonishment that Harold had *driven* to Mokuleia on the government road; now such trips were commonplace. Walter turned in his Stoddard-Dayton runabout on a Pope-Hartford model M roadster finished in battleship grey. Governor Frear and May held their first "at home" in their new house, "Arcadia," on Punahou Street, near Woodlawn. The Oahu Railway hooked up with the naval railroad. And at the end of the year Walter landed a huge federal contract to dredge Pearl Harbor.

Sugar prices slumped again in 1909, but prosperity continued nevertheless. Olaa ground its biggest crop—19,000 tons—and showed another small profit. The Rose Bamboo cane had given trouble and

Arcadia, home of Governor Frear and May Dillingham Frear, on Punahou Street across from Woodlawn. On its site was built the present Arcadia Retirement Residence. (Photo by Ray Jerome Baker, Bishop Museum)

was being phased out in favor of the new Demarara 1135 in the Mountain View section.

The Oahu Railway chugged steadily ahead and began to cover the Wahiawa tablelands with a network of branch lines to Schofield Barracks, to the Waipio pineapple fields, to Halemano, and to Kunia. In a day and a half the Dillinghams completed negotiations with W. G. Irwin and Company to refinance the railway bonds from 6 percent to 5 percent, at a savings of $20,000 a year. "Things have been moving in our direction for a change," Walter commented.

F. B. Anderson, by now a fast friend of the Dillinghams, had succeeded to the presidency of the Bank of California, which had assumed in an informal way the role of guarding the family interests in California. At the end of July B. F. was able to send the first reduction of $50,000 on the $500,000 syndicate loan which he had taken out seven years before and another $100,000 followed in November. Two years later Anderson organized a new syndicate, with Walter putting in $100,000 of his own money, to pay off the balance of the old loan.

When he heard of the first payment on the syndicate loan, W. H. Chickering wrote to his old friend B. F. that "I wish you were near enough for me to grasp your hand and congratulate you. Your indomitable pluck has helped me very much and I am mightily glad I knew you."

Even the Haleiwa Hotel, an artistic success but a financial disaster, began to show signs of life. Curtis Iaukea had long since given up as manager; in June 1909 one of his successors wrote to the O. R. and L., which was running the hotel, to ask for a six-week leave of absence "to travel on the mainland." Back came a terse reply from Walter Dillingham: "Consideration of the matter will of necessity be delayed until the report of the auditor is received." Three weeks later B. F. announced that "we have engaged Mr. Clifford Kimball to take charge of the hotel."

Clifford Kimball, known to his intimates as "Hickey," had been a boon companion of Walter's since the days of Newton High School and like Ike Dillingham had followed Walter to Hawaii. The Haleiwa Hotel flourished under his management; he later went on to fame as proprietor and manager of the Halekulani Hotel in Waikiki.

In 1908 Harold and Margaret Dillingham celebrated the birth of their first child, Walter Hyde, Frank's first grandchild to bear the

Dillingham name. The happy grandfather expressed his pleasure in both a sentimental and tangible manner.

> My dear son Harold,
>
> Again let me congratulate you and your sweet little wife Margaret upon the birth of your beautiful son. . . .
>
> None of us brought anything into this world, but it was good for us that we found love and tender care awaiting our safe arrival. I have found five shares of the capital stock of the Oahu Railway and Land Company awaiting dear little Walter, which I have had placed in your name as Trustee. I therefore now enclose herewith Certificate No. 2320 for the five shares referred to. Let me express the hope that prosperity, temporal and spiritual, may be his throughout a long and happy life.
>
> Your affectionate
> Father

Four years later he was writing to this grandson that "you are a very dear little boy to me, and I love you more than I can tell!! . . . I want all my children and grandchildren to be interested in the financial family, and so I am giving you today ten shares [of The B. F. Dillingham Co., Ltd.].

In 1909 Frank Dillingham celebrated his fortieth wedding anniversary and his sixty-fifth birthday. Things were indeed moving in his direction, and in his place most men would have been happy to sit back and let Walter and Harold pull the oars. But Frank was a fighter and builder, and Sam Wilder's old dream of a railroad north from Hilo possessed his soul. Armed with $250,000 from the sale of bonds, he began grading a line north from Hilo in the late summer of 1909.

The Hilo and Hamakua plantations averaged at that time somewhere around 75,000 tons of sugar a year, exclusive of the Davies' plantation of Waiakea, already served by the railroad. Of this tonnage, about two-thirds came from plantations factored by W. G. Irwin or by C. Brewer and Company. The remainder was controlled by Davies and by F. A. Schaefer and Company, whose plantations lay in the area farthest from Hilo. The section as far as Hakalau, where the North Hilo and South Hilo districts met, was dominated by Irwin and Brewer.

B. F. had already received proof of Brewer's hostility to the railroad. Irwin was an unknown quantity. Possibly Matson, who was tied in with the Spreckels–Irwin group, encouraged B. F. to think that he could get the Irwin plantation business, but Matson was notoriously hard to pin down in such matters. Probably B. F. figured that the railway could break even on passenger traffic and outbound merchandise from Hilo and that eventually the plantations would have to deal with him out of self-interest.

At the end of 1909, however, two events radically changed the situation. William G. Irwin decided to retire to California and sold his factoring business to C. Brewer, who thus became agent for Hilo, Hakalau, and Paauhau plantations as well as Onomea, Pepeekeo, Honomu, and Ookala. And Theo. H. Davies and Company withdrew from McBryde on Kauai in favor of Alexander and Baldwin.

Stock control of the Irwin plantations remained with the Irwin–Spreckels–Matson group in California, but C. Brewer as agent had enough influence to make it much less likely the plantations would come to terms with the railroad.

On the other hand, A & B had to pay off the McBryde overdraft at Theo. H. Davies, which suddenly found itself with more than a million dollars of free cash.

B. F. had joined with W. A. Kinney in forcing Davies out of the McBryde agency, but he had somehow remained on good terms with the Davies directors. The scent of a million dollars in cash drew him as nectar draws a honey bee. By May he and Davies had signed a contract for Davies to invest the million dollars in Hilo Railroad bonds and give the railroad a twenty-year freight contract with the Kukaiau, Laupahoehoe, and Hamakua mills. At one blow he had seemingly solved the twin problems of capital and enough tonnage to justify the line.

Also during this period C. M. Cooke retired as president of C. Brewer and was succeeded by E. Faxon Bishop, a nephew of Charles R. Bishop. This change did nothing whatever to improve B. F.'s position. Bishop was thought to harbor a personal grudge against the Dillinghams, and his actions certainly did nothing to dispel the idea.

B. F. accomplished one task in early 1910 that he had been working on for years: the refinancing of Olaa's bonded and floating debt by means of a new $2.5 million bond issue, through Bishop and Company. With the aid of the bank, B. F. himself bought for resale $523,000 worth of the bonds. In connection with the bond sale, he gave the bank his proxy to vote the controlling Olaa stock until such time as the bank's own holding of the bonds dropped below $500,000. B. F. was mellowing; he would never have considered such an arrangement a few years before.

Olaa ground another record crop of close to 20,000 tons, but the profit remained minimal. The Demarara cane looked beautiful but turned out to contain little sucrose; the plantation began to abandon fields in the Mountain View section and to rely more heavily on independent planters as a source of cane. Through it all, Damon somehow kept his faith in Olaa.

On another front B. F. was retrenching. The Woodlawn Dairy and Stock Company sold the last of its animals that Frank loved so much and divided its Manoa property for sale as house lots.

B. F. had settled into a regular routine at Woodlawn, and his health improved. In writing to Dr. Ward, he described himself as going to bed at ten or sometimes at nine, getting up at six, swimming in the tank and riding or driving before breakfast, and getting to the office at eight-thirty or nine o'clock. But he felt the strain of the Hilo Railroad negotiations, and determined to take a vacation before he broke down again.

In March 1910 Walter, long known as Honolulu's most eligible bachelor, finally became engaged to Miss Louise Olga Gaylord of Chicago, whom he had met when she stopped in Honolulu on a trip around the world. Walter had to go to Washington on business with the Navy; from there he went to Italy where he and Louise were married in the villa "La Pietra" outside Florence.

In June Frank and Emma went to San Francisco, then east as far as Stockton, where they boarded the train bringing Walter and Louise west. After four days together in San Francisco, Frank and Emma left the newlyweds and headed east again on their own honeymoon.

Their route took them to Paris and thence by chartered automobile to Brussels, Rotterdam, Amsterdam, Dusseldorf, Cologne, Mayence, Frankfurt, Wurzburg, Nuremberg, Munich, Oberammergau, Lucerne, Interlaken, Geneva, back to Paris, and on to London. "It was a vacation for me," Frank wrote, "such as I never had since I was a child."

A handsome letter from Sam Damon caught up with them along the way, announcing the opening of a Hilo branch of his bank aimed at making loans to the independent planters of Olaa. "If I had one-tenth of your courage and foresight," wrote Mr. Damon, "I might have started there years ago, but the necessity of having funds in hand before I started any business has been ground into my make-up, and perhaps I have slept better in consequence.''

B. F. arrived home from his European trip late in the year. Before leaving he had arranged to have the big house at Woodlawn refurbished for Walter and Louise to use until they found a suitable home of their own; meanwhile he and Emma would stay in the smaller cottage which Walter had been using. The arrangement worked so well that Frank and Emma never did move back into the big house. Frank was the most generous of men, but he was also meticulous in dealing with his family, and kept regular accounts with each one of them. In this case he charged Walter $150 a month rent for the house.

From the beginning, nothing went easily with the Hilo Railroad's Paauilo extension, as it came to be known. C. Brewer even tried to keep the survey party off its plantation lands. It took a year to push the line to Papaikou, only 4 miles from the Wailuku River which marked the northern boundary of Hilo town, and the cost figures were ominous. While B. F. was touring Europe, Harold was quietly raising the estimate to $1.5 million. Walter thought it might run closer to $2 million than to $1 million. But B. F. returned full of optimism and insisting that they should use steel bridges, not wooden ones, even if the total cost ran to $3 million. He did regret, however, the original decision ten years before to use standard gauge, which he figured unnecessarily raised the cost by 25 percent or more.

B. F. went to Hilo for an inspection trip in March of 1911, and remained for months. In writing back to Walter, he called the cost overrun ''rather appalling.'' ''Please ask Harold,'' he added, ''to take charge of my Sunday School class or secure the services of Harry Von Holt or some one else to do so during my absence.''

The Paauilo extension by now had become his chief business concern, as he let Walter and Harold in effect run the rest of the show. Back in Honolulu Walter had to borrow $13,000 to meet the 1 April bond coupons, and Harold was making a discouraging analysis of the cost of moving freight on the Hilo Railroad. The actual railroad department cost for moving one ton one mile, he figured, was 3.0 cents, the interest charges 2.7 cents, and extraordinary charges 1.3 cents, for a total of 7.0 cents; the corresponding revenue amounted to 6.47 cents.

Anyone who has flown down the Hamakua coast can appreciate the difficulties the railroad ran into in building the extension. There is almost no land at sea level; the plantation fields begin at the top of cliffs rising several hundred feet from the ocean. The mills all hug the coast, and the natural route for a railroad lies close to the sea. The problem arises from the tremendous amount of water that has to drain into the ocean from the vast rain-soaked mountain slopes that sweep gradually up from the coast. Over the centuries this water has carved gullies, gulches, ravines, and valleys out of the once flat tableland, until now, instead of one plateau, there are scores of tabletops separated from each other by deep chasms.

In spite of all obstacles, B. F. pushed the line forward, but work went slowly. By the end of June 1911 the line had reached Onomea, but it took another year to reach Hakalau, only about 7 miles farther on. Already in 1911 B. F. was starting to borrow to keep the construction moving.

Olaa in 1911 finally had a good year. The price of sugar was high, and the plantation ground a record 25,000 tons for a profit of $317,000. Sam Damon submitted an optimistic statement at the stockholders' meeting emphasizing the large amount of additional land that could be brought under cultivation as conditions warranted.

"I think it is only just to say," B. F. wrote in 1911, "that the stockholders [of Olaa] owe their present hope and expectation in an ultimate realization of a large portion, if not all, of their present holdings, to Mr. Damon of Bishop & Co."

The year 1911 was a banner one for grandchildren as well as sugarcane. Harold and Margaret, who had already had Walter Hyde, now followed with Harold, Jr. The Erdmans, who besides Harold had already had Emma Louise, now produced Dorothy. And Walter and Louise had their first child, Lowell Smith.

In spite of concern over the Hilo Railroad, Frank Dillingham was at last relaxing. In February of 1912 Walter wrote to Ike that "he [Father] has pretty effectually shed the responsibility and detail of this office, and I think does not worry at all now over any of the matters which were so burdensome to him when you were here." And in April he wrote to May that "Father takes everything in a most matter-of-fact way these days, and you can hardly believe that he is the same man who kept so exclusively to business ten years ago. He and mother pick up for a day or two in the country and Father takes a forenoon or afternoon off whenever his fancy moves that way."

This photograph of the Kolekole viaduct under construction gives an idea of the difficulties that plagued the builders of the Hilo Railroad's Paauilo extension. (Bishop Museum photo)

The railroad trestle in this photograph, identified as the second Laupahoehoe trestle, resembles a scale model layout, but it illustrates the difficulties of building a railroad north from Hilo. (Photo by Kent Cochrane, Bishop Museum)

Most of the San Francisco loans were paid off by this time, and in June the family replaced B. F.'s remaining personal notes with ones made by The B. F. Dillingham Company. "Yesterday we cleaned up the balance of Father's outstanding notes," Walter wrote to Bob Atkinson, "so today for the first time in, I should figure, his business history, he owes no man a dollar."

Frank evidently liked the feeling. "I owe no man anything but my good will," he wrote. He celebrated by giving one thousand shares of Olaa to his sister, to his nephew, and to each of two nieces, and five hundred shares each to his widowed sister-in-law and to Mills College. He and Emma between them gave Walter Frear, John Erdman, Margaret Dillingham, and Louise Dillingham each one thousand shares of The B. F. Dillingham Company. As a further present for his family he set aside $10,000 to build a new house at Mokuleia that they could all enjoy, and this splendid country estate became the center of the family's leisure time together.

Frank began at this time a custom of sending a regular monthly check to each of half a dozen impoverished relatives of his in the East. The checks were not large, but in the New England of that day they undoubtedly made the difference between abject poverty and a degree of comfort.

The big house at Mokuleia, for which B. F. Dillingham set aside $10,000 in 1912. The house has eight bedrooms; besides the living area (behind the columns) with kitchen attached, and the bedroom wing on the right, there is a matching wing on the left, outside the range of the camera. For many years it provided a center for the Dillingham family's leisure time activities. (Courtesy of Harold G. Dillingham, Jr.)

B. F. Dillingham in a jaunty pose, with the rear platform of parlor car number 64 behind him. (Bishop Museum photo)

Frank also continued a program he had started several years before, of making good the losses which some of his less prosperous relatives and friends had suffered on Olaa and other stocks which he had recommended, by buying back the stocks at par plus interest at 6 percent for the years they had been held.

Frank also paid the noted artist George Burroughs Torrey $4,500 to paint his portrait and Emma's, noting with satisfaction that Torrey's usual fee would have been $6,000.

Against this pleasant background of prosperity and largesse, the Paauilo extension intruded in somber fashion. In February B. F. wrote to one of the men who had helped to finance it that he expected to reach Paauilo in one year, and that costs were exceeding estimates by 50 percent. "Neither you nor I," he added, "nor any other interested party in the Hilo Railroad realized until the last year, the magnitude of the work we had undertaken." Three months later he echoed those sentiments: "This was a very much bigger undertaking than I realized at the commencement."

# CHAPTER 41

*Dear Walter, never forget or lose confidence in the Alwise Providence whose Hands guide all of our affairs. If we continue to keep ourselves clean and straight, and use our heads and hearts as God would have us, trusting in Him we may have full faith we shall be prospered and blessed in measure and degree best for us. . . . with inexpressible love*

*Father*

B. F. D. to W. F. Dillingham
30 January 1914

By December 1912 the cost overrun on the Paauilo extension had blown up into a full-fledged crisis. Walter was leaving on a trip to the mainland, and on the eve of his departure Damon and Bottomley presented an ultimatum, presumably that the Dillinghams would have to raise the money to complete the line before the bank would make any further advances. B. F. became terribly agitated, and Emma feared for his health.

With Walter gone, the burden of protecting the family's interests fell on Harold, who figured that close to half a million dollars additional was needed to finish the road to Paauilo. Clarence Cooke at the Bank of Hawaii was unable to help, and Theo. H. Davies declined to put up any more money. Harold cared more about his father's health than he did about the railroad, but he felt that his father would not rest until the road was completed.

It seemed "terribly unfair and unjust," Harold wrote, "that the added burden should come at his present time of life . . . his reserve force has been taxed so many times in the past that it is an unknown question in my mind how much there is still remaining."

But the old gentleman still had some bounce left. He suffered through a couple of sleepless nights, but when he had heard the worst, Harold was still able to jolly him up. "Father has kept up his spirits wonderfully," he reported, "and is certainly an object lesson for courage. . . . all will be well if the uncertainty and pressure don't last too long."

In January B. F. loaned the railroad $75,000 of his own money, and deposited Olaa and Hilo Railroad stock with Bishop and Company to serve as security against a loan application which Walter was making to the San Francisco banks. "Don't worry," Walter wrote, "I'll get the money some way."

But 1913 started off with a series of blows that shook the Dillingham interests as they had not been shaken since 1906.

First, the Philadelphia Breakwater Company, which held the current contract for extending the Hilo breakwater, went into bankruptcy, stopping progress on the breakwater and depriving the railroad of desperately needed revenue from hauling rock.

As a partial substitute for the Brewer business, B. F. had been courting F. A. Schaefer and Company, who controlled the Honokaa and Pacific sugar mills. In the middle of January Schaefer signed a five-year contract with Inter-Island Steam Navigation for shipping all their sugar, effectively killing B. F.'s hopes to build the railroad through to its logical terminus at Honokaa.

At the end of January, James Castle and his son Harold sailed from Honolulu for the mainland. An hour after their sailing, news came by wireless from Hilo that fire had wiped out Mr. Castle's Pahoa lumber mill and 8 acres of cut lumber, at a reputed loss of half a million dollars, thus depriving the railroad of another major source of revenue.

In the face of these setbacks, Walter in San Francisco maintained a hard line on the railroad question, arguing that the family were in a position to carry it through even without the Brewer business and that the financial people expected them to make a success of anything they tackled. By the end of January he had arranged a new syndicate loan of $150,000 to help finish the line.

Harold at home was less certain, because his figures told him that even with the Brewer business the railroad could not pay $300,000 a year in interest and still make a big success. He had heard indirectly that Faxon Bishop's price for working with the railroad was a million dollars in railroad stock, and Harold was willing to pay it, but he knew his father would hit the ceiling if he thought the idea came from Harold. Harold believed that they should make a deal with Brewer at almost any price and then sell out.

But the worst blow came from Pearl Harbor, where Walter and the San Francisco Bridge Company had been building a huge dry dock for the Navy. On 17 February, with very little warning, the pressure below the dock blew out its entire floor, leaving the dock in shambles and completely wrecking some two years' work.

"Mr. James Castle sends his most sincere sympathy and Aloha," Harold reported to Walter, "and I believe was perfectly honest when he stated that he felt far worse over our misfortune than he did over his own."

Walter at that point was playing polo at Pasadena, but he had something even more serious to occupy his mind. News of the dry dock, he wrote, "would have been a severe blow to me but for the fact that I was so deep in anxiety as to the health of little Lowell. . . . a most virulent case of pneumonia. . . . but for his wonderful little constitution we would not have him with us today."

Lowell recovered quickly enough, but the dry dock did not. Questions of responsibility for the disaster, of payment for the work that had been done, and of the redesign and rebuilding of the dock took most of Walter's time for the next two years. In September he left Honolulu for Washington, where he spent the next fourteen months prying a settlement out of the reluctant Navy Department. Meanwhile the burden of running the Dillingham affairs rested largely on Harold and their father.

In the meantime, after three good years, sugar prices had slumped again. Olaa in 1913 suffered through the lowest average return per ton of sugar since its first crop in 1902; in spite of a bumper harvest, the plantation lost money. Even more ominous was the passage of a new tariff act providing for a gradual return to free sugar, which seemed to threaten even lower prices in the future. Olaa stock, according to B. F., fell to 50 cents a share following the passage of this act.

Other plantations suffered also. Oahu Sugar and Waialua cut out dividends, and Ewa was rumored to be about to follow suit. Pioneer Mill cut theirs in half. McBryde passed the dividend on its preferred stock, resulting in W. A. Kinney suing A & B, Walter Dillingham, and The B. F. Dillingham Company.

Kinney's suit, however, achieved an unexpectedly favorable result by softening the hostility between A & B and the Oahu Railway, who had been on the verge of a shooting war over the question of what lands were covered by the Kahuku plantation lease. Harold Dillingham and Clarence Cooke served as peacemakers, and amity was restored.

The Hilo Railroad had finally reached Paauilo in April of 1913, at a terrible price. Against its first estimate of a million dollars, the 34-mile extension had cost $3,642,000. The grading had involved moving 2,100,000 cubic yards of material. The track ran through 3,200 feet of tunnels, including one at Maulua half a mile long which ended at a bridge and a blind curve. The longest bridge was 1,006 feet long and 106 feet high, and the highest was 220 feet high and 520 feet long. Some bridge foundations stood in the open sea and extended as much as 30 feet below water level, necessitating the use of coffer dams in construction. The line represented a marvelous piece of engineering and was one of the most expensive railroads, mile for mile, in the United States.

In the late fall of 1913, Frank Dillingham received word that his sister, Abbey D. Newton of Worcester, Massachusetts, was dying, and he and Emma set out to see her once more. From shipboard he wrote that they expected to reach Worcester in ten days from Honolulu. "That will be going some," he commented. It was his last trip to the New England he loved so much. "Cheer up," he wrote Harold from Massachusetts, "and thank God we are not the Philadelphia Breakwater Co."

Before leaving Honolulu Emma penned a note to her daughter Marion.

> I cannot find words to express the happiness in my heart, since, with the completion of your home, *three* of our precious children are domiciled within the boundaries of Woodlawn. We are truly a happy family. . . . it is for my happiness that I wish to give you for a Christmas present, your house and lot. . . . To be able to do this is keener joy to me than can be expressed. . . .
>
> With fondest love
> Your Mother

Time was rolling inexorably on, bringing changes that were not always welcome. "This new Federal Income Tax law," Harold wrote, "is a fright, and has been worrying the banks and many individuals all over the country."

B. F. now had a car and a chauffeur, and he believed that since

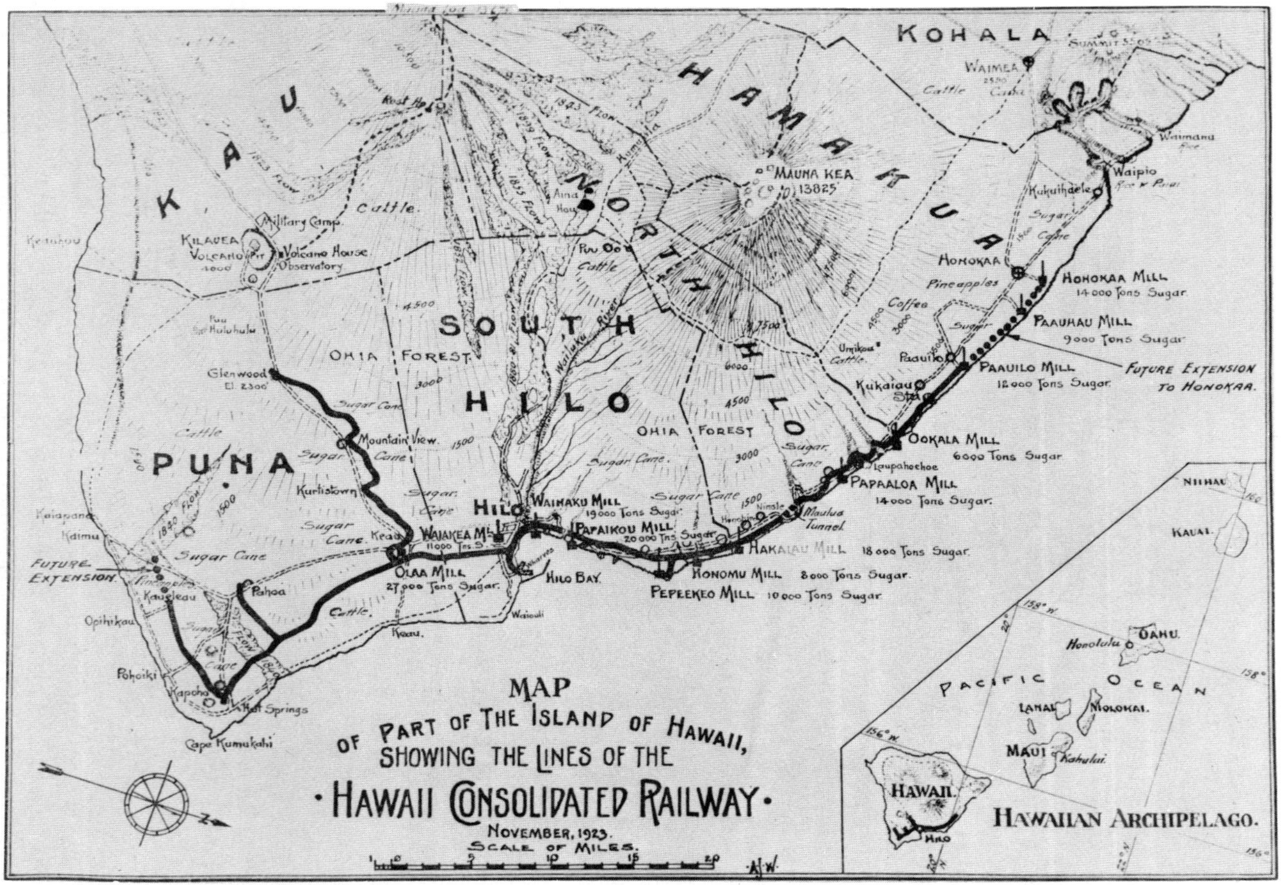


This 1923 map shows the lines of the Hawaii Consolidated Railway, unchanged from those of the Hilo Railroad. The ''future extensions'' were never built. (Bishop Museum photo)

automobile owners in Honolulu paid about $20,000 a year in taxes, the money should be segregated and used for proper maintenance of the roads. Perhaps with a sigh, he consigned for auction one Victoria, one trap, and one pneumatic tire buggy.

For sugar, 1914 started off worse than the year before. Then came August and war in Europe, and suddenly sugar was $125 a ton. B. F. called it the salvation of Olaa and McBryde, but he thought more about the terrible suffering from the war than about the profits in Hawaii. B. F. was seventy, and he was beginning to look at his business interests from a little distance.

But the Hilo Railroad still troubled him. In January Harold estimated that it would lose $117,000 for the year ended 30 June 1914. The money was lacking to pay the 1 April coupons. Bishop and Company agreed to meet the coupons but demanded endorsement by The B. F. Dillingham Company and five thousand shares of railway stock. By this time, of course, the Dillingham guarantee of the bond interest had expired, but the family decided to meet the bank's terms rather than let the road default.

B. F. would not let go. Harold wrote the sad story to Walter: "Poor Father . . . in his old time way sat at his desk hours at a time trying to make figures that would put a different complexion on the whole situation. . . . The result was that he wore himself down so that his progress down hill mentally and physically was perceptible from day to day, so that he reached the point of actually breaking down in tears in his office."

When his father refused to go to the volcano for a weekend, Harold knew that he had to do something drastic. Joe Cooke proved receptive and agreed to try to negotiate a contract between Brewer and the railroad. Harold told his father that it was on condition that he stay out of it, and the old gentleman went happily off to the volcano, returning, Harold said, "as well as ever." "I spend practically every evening with him at home, trying to jolly him up," Harold added.

Harold never did get the Brewer business, though he proposed to give Brewer $1.7 million in railroad stock if Brewer would pay off $150,000 in notes which the Dillingham Company held against the railroad, secured by the stock. By the middle of August, with sugar prices soaring, Harold was resigned to letting the railroad go into receivership.

Harold's tactics undoubtedly saved his father from another breakdown. Something along the way, possibly the terrible war news from

Europe, reconciled B. F. to losing the railroad, and by December he was writing how well he felt and how soundly he was sleeping.

"When you meet Harold," he wrote to Walter, "you will probably recognize a man of as much ability as any business man you have ever known. His growth in capacity and business ability since you have been East has been remarkable. . . . his modesty and humility of spirit are always evidenced by his conversation and general manner."

The Hilo Railroad thrashed about a while longer in its death agony, but reorganization was inescapable. The Dillinghams gave up their common stock, representing control of the road, and agreed to accept preferred stock in a new corporation in exchange for their notes and preferred stock of the Hilo Railroad. Their actual cash loss, if the new preferred stock should prove worthless, was serious but far from catastrophic. By early 1916 the Hawaii Consolidated Railway, Ltd. had taken over from the old corporation, and the Hilo Railroad had passed into history.

The Hilo Railroad was a failure, but a magnificent failure. When the railroad was founded, along with Olaa Sugar Company, Hilo was a village sitting on the edge of a jungle. The huge plantation with its thousands of workers, and the easy access provided by the railroad, did more than anything else to build Hilo into a town. The railroad was responsible for the first dock being built, and later it was the railroad which persuaded the federal government to build the breakwater which transformed Hilo into a real port city. Later still, the Hilo Railroad first forged a usable link between 30-odd miles of coastline and the new port. The town of Hilo and the neighboring countryside flourished in the early twentieth century primarily because of B. F. Dillingham's founding of Olaa Sugar and the Hilo Railroad.

At the end of 1914 Walter returned from Washington, where he had finally secured the settlement he wanted from the navy. With both his sons on deck, Frank was ready to retire. In January he resigned as general manager of the Oahu Railway, though he kept the title of president until his death.

Frank's health was poor in the spring, but he rallied and went with Emma to California in July to recuperate. He improved so much that they were able not only to see the Panama–Pacific Exposition but also to take a long motor trip through southern California, returning to Woodlawn in time for Christmas.

B. F. Dillingham with his sons (Walter on left) around 1915. Mr. Dillingham's style in his later years resembled that of Teddy Roosevelt. (Courtesy of the Dillingham family)

One joyful task remained for Frank. He had long since asked his sons to make certain bequests after his death, whenever the family finances permitted. With increasing prosperity—Olaa paid its first dividend in 1916—he found himself able to do it within his lifetime. In June and July of 1916, he made substantial gifts to Punahou School, the YMCA, Palama Settlement, the YWCA, Leahi Home, and Mills School. But his real monument remained the thousands of times he had given kindness and help to those around him.

As Harold wrote, "Kindness, consideration and generosity were fundamental with him. Through all the years of adversity, he was ever mindful of those who needed help. . . . Courage and persistence—no man had more. . . . a devoted husband and father, with faith in himself and his fellow man and in the future both temporal and eternal. . . . often imposed upon, loyal to principle and to those associated with him. His word was his bond. . . . money was only worth while for the good it could produce."

The year 1915 marked the fiftieth anniversary of the broken leg suffered by the young mate off the packet *Whistler,* an accident which set in motion such a strange and unpredictable chain of events. To celebrate the occasion, Walter Dillingham early in 1916, shortly after his father's return from California, gave a men's luncheon at the Oahu Country Club. Frank's two sons came, of course, and his two sons-in-law, along with such old friends as Curtis Iaukea, Sanford Dole, Will Castle, W. O. Smith, P. C. Jones, and Fred MacFarlane. From the railroad came Harry Von Holt, George Denison, Charley Kluegel, John Hughes, and Fred Smith, and from The B. F. Dillingham Company Van Valkenburgh and Bob Atkinson.

It was a sentimental occasion. Frank since his illnesses preferred not to speak in public, but he had written out a short talk and asked Harold to read it. In it he reminisced in gentle vein about his life as a young boy, about the hardware business in Honolulu, and about the founding of the railroad. As he sat there surrounded by his oldest friends, listening to Harold's voice, he could look back to his father's farm with its yoke of oxen and one horse; to the *Southern Cross* crashing around Cape Horn in a gale; to the little store on Fort Street where he clerked for Father Dimond; to Emma singing in the Bethel choir; to the barren tract of land below Punahou which he and Emma had turned into a home and a garden; to the high excitement and bitter disappointment of their trip to London; to the "first ride," when little *Kauila* had disgraced herself by showering black soot on the passengers. In his lifetime sail had given way to steam, trains had become commonplace, oil had replaced coal, and automobiles had begun to push carriages off the road. Nowadays, Frank often had himself driven up Pacific Heights, just above the country club where he now sat; from there he could see ships tied up at the railroad docks loading sugar and pineapple, and to the west thousands of green acres which had produced nothing but *kiawe* and cactus in the years before the railroad, while out on the Ewa plain the great pumps sucked water out of the earth to give life to the land. This had been his life work: more than any other man, he had brought life and prosperity to that part of Oahu which stretched from Pearl Harbor all the way to Kahuku.

At the very end of the talk which Harold read, Frank Dillingham summed up what he believed after a lifetime of struggling and building.

"We are left to realize," he wrote, "there is nothing definite in life upon which we can establish our hearts, except the realizing sense that the great Father of the Universe holds us all in his keeping, and we must look to him for final deliverance."

# EPILOGUE

BENJAMIN Franklin Dillingham died on 7 April 1918, after a prolonged and stubborn battle against cancer and hardening of the arteries, and was buried in Nuuanu Cemetery. His beloved Emma followed him on 20 August 1920 and lies buried by his side.

Their four children, after long and useful lives, were also buried in the family plot at Nuuanu.

Change is the only constant in life, and the enterprises that represented B. F.'s life work have had their share.

Of the five plantations which sprang up where B. F. built his Oahu Railway, only two remain. Honolulu Plantation lost a large share of its lands to the military during World War II and went out of business when peace returned. Kahuku Plantation, on leased land and chronically unprofitable, closed at the end of 1971. Ewa Plantation, once legendary for its dividends, failed to renew its lease with the Campbell Estate in 1970 and was absorbed into the Oahu Sugar Company. Oahu Sugar, long one of Hawaii's premier plantations, now cultivates a greatly expanded acreage, as part of Amfac, Inc. Waialua Agricultural Company, now a part of Castle and Cooke, Inc., has long since worked out its initial problems and become one of Hawaii's strongest plantations.

American Factors, Ltd. bought the agency for Olaa Sugar Company from Bishop and Company in 1918 for $230,000, and in 1925 the Dillinghams sold the last of their stock to Amfac at $10 a share. For many years Olaa remained the sick man of the industry, but agressive management has recently turned it around into an efficient producer. The plantation has been rechristened the Puna Sugar Company and is now a part of Amfac, Inc., the successor corporation to H. Hackfeld and Company.

The Hawaii Consolidated Railway struggled along for many years without achieving much financial success. The great tidal wave of 1945 destroyed its line through the town of Hilo and washed out a number of steel bridges, and the road was never rebuilt. Several parts of the highway north from Hilo follow its old roadbed.

B. F.'s greatest enterprise, the Oahu Railway, flourished into the

1940s. After B. F.'s lease expired in 1939, the Campbell Estate dealt directly with the plantations which had been subleasing its lands from the O. R. and L., but the railway continued to prosper. The railroad had its finest hour during World War II, when it proved indispensable to the army and navy on Oahu. In 1943 it carried more than two and a half million passengers, as well as its normal freight and an immense amount of war material of every description.

After World War II, during which Oahu's highway system was drastically improved, the railroad could no longer compete successfully with trucks and buses. The main line closed down at the end of 1947; switching operations between pineapple canneries and the docks continued for a few more years before final abandonment.

In 1961 the remains of the O. R. and L. merged with the Hawaiian Dredging Company to form the Dillingham Corporation, of which the current chairman of the board is one of B. F.'s grandsons, Lowell Smith Dillingham.

The B. F. Dillingham Company, Ltd. continues as a holding company. Its current president is Bayard H. Dillingham, another grandson of B. F. Dillingham.

# SOURCES

THIS book rests largely on unpublished material in the Bernice P. Bishop Museum, Honolulu. The Dillingham Corporation has donated to that museum a vast collection of letters, documents, accounting records, maps, photographs, and miscellaneous papers from the files of the Oahu Railway and Land Company; the Hawaiian Construction Company; the Woodlawn Dairy and Stock Company; Dillingham and Company; the Pacific Hardware Company; Dillingham, Thurston, and Carter; the Haleiwa Hotel; the Mokuleia Ranch and Land Company; and the Hawaiian Dredging Company. The collection also includes financial records, documents, business correspondence, and miscellaneous material of B. F. Dillingham, a vast correspondence carried on by Walter F. Dillingham, and journals and letters of the Smith family. The B. F. Dillingham Company, Ltd. has donated to the same museum its documents, minutes, accounting records, and correspondence up to the year 1924, including letters written and received by B. F. Dillingham while traveling in 1900 and 1904. While this material (other than that of the Smith family) focuses on business, it involves also a great deal of personal matter. The record has many gaps, particularly in the early years, but on the whole it presents a quite detailed account of Mr. Dillingham's activities. Because of the sheer bulk of the material, however, and the large number of different files and the sometimes haphazard methods of filing, it is often difficult to locate a particular piece of information.

The author has supplemented these archives in the Bishop Museum with source material in the library of the Hawaiian Mission Children's Society (H.M.C.S.) and in the Hawaii State Archives, with Honolulu newspapers and magazines of the period, and with published works, a list of which is appended. Descendants of B. F. Dillingham have provided other material, as noted below.

Unfortunately, very few letters have turned up from Mr. Dillingham to his wife. They were separated for long periods and he undoubtedly wrote her frequently and at great length, but the bulk of the letters must be presumed lost.

Mr. Dillingham left a brief account of his life up to the middle of 1895. Mrs. Edward O'Neill kindly supplied the author with a copy of this memoir, together with notations by his oldest daughter, Mrs. May Frear. This memoir forms the basic source for his life up to the time of his marriage and an important source for the period from 1869 to 1885. Although he wrote the memoir late in his life, the facts as he gave them have checked out very consistently with other sources.

For his family background I have relied on a visit to his birthplace, as well as on the genealogy of his family prepared by Philip Schuyler de Luze in 1905. The Register of Probate in Worcester County (Massachusetts) Court House has the probate record of his father's estate, which sheds light on family conditions at that time.

May Frear has written the story of the Smith family in "Lowell and Abigail," privately printed in New Haven in 1934. At that time, however, Mrs. Frear was planning a book on the life of her father and therefore omitted most material pertaining to her father and mother's life together. From the Smith family letters and journals (now in the Bishop Museum), she had generous excerpts typed for the pleasure of her family, and Mr. Bayard H. Dillingham kindly supplied a copy. The original documents were scissored up in the course of transcription and are difficult to use. As far as can now be determined, Mrs. Frear omitted little of interest to the present subject. These letters have proved fundamental in reconstructing Mr. Dillingham's courtship and family life up to about 1885. The Hawaiian Mission Children's Society also has several interesting letters written by Emma Smith both before and after her marriage. Mrs. O'Neill furnished the author with several invaluable letters from Frank Dillingham to Emma, including the earliest known letter of his, dated 28 January 1867.

Mr. Dillingham's earliest surviving business records date from 1880 and are fragmentary enough to leave many questions unanswered. His own memoir is helpful, and the Castle papers in the H.M.C.S. library shed a great deal of light. *H. J. Agnew* v. *B. F. Dillingham* (Equity 10) in the State Archives gives a great deal of information on both his business and personal life in the 1870s, while *J. H. Wood* v. *B. F. Dillingham* (Equity 543) contains a complete record of the Nuuanu dairy imbroglio. The Bureau of Conveyances in Honolulu has a record of his real estate transactions, starting with the lease in 1878 of the premises of 37 Fort Street.

Mr. Dillingham's surviving business papers gradually become more complete in the 1880s; most of the information comes from the B. F. D. document files, with almost no letters remaining from this period. Starting in 1884, the Woodlawn Dairy records are fairly complete and quite useful. Mr. Dillingham's memoir ends in 1885, the year that Abigail died, and for the next several years information comes mostly from the B. F. D. document and miscellaneous files, from the Castle papers, and from the Bureau of Conveyances.

Knowledge of Mr. Dillingham's trip to London in 1887 depends largely on the journal which he briefly kept and the letter book in which he made copies of his business correspondence, and on several letters of Lowell Smith among the Smith papers. This letter book of B. F. D.'s represents the earliest surviving substantial amount of his correspondence.

Mr. Dillingham's business correspondence after his return to Honolulu continues in a bound volume of letters, 1888–1889; unfortunately, many of them have deteriorated. The Castle letters are still useful, and also the Woodlawn Dairy records. The Honolulu newspapers become a valuable source, particularly for legislative action. Starting in 1889, the O. R. and L. records, particularly the minutes books, correspondence, and miscellaneous files, are invaluable. The printed annual reports of the railroad give a good outline history of the enterprise. A document entitled "Financial History of the O. R. and L., 1888–1907," prepared by the Audit Company of Hawaii (found in box 9 of the O. R. and L. miscellaneous files), is particularly helpful.

Starting in 1890, Mr. Dillingham adopted the practice of having his outgoing letters typed and preserving the carbons. His letters for 1890 and 1891 are found in box 5 of his correspondence. Unfortunately, his letters for almost the rest of that decade are scattered among the files of the O. R. and L., the Hawaiian Construction Company, and various miscellaneous and illogical places, and many have undoubtedly been lost. Information for the years 1892–1899 comes largely from the O. R. and L. correspondence and miscellaneous files and from the B. F. D. documents and miscellaneous files. In general, from 1890 on, the Dillingham files in the Bishop Museum contain such a wealth of information that Mr. Dillingham's career can be traced almost completely from them alone.

Two of Mr. Dillingham's major projects, however, the Olaa Sugar Company and the Hilo Railroad, later passed out of the family hands and their minutes books and financial records went also, though much of their correspondence remains in The B. F. Dillingham Company files. In the case of Olaa the original minutes book has not surfaced, but Olaa's successor, the Puna Sugar Company, has a great deal of early correspondence, as well as the printed annual reports of the company. The Bishop Museum has the original minutes book of the Hilo Railroad (with annual reports attached), under agreement with the Hawaiian Trust Company, Ltd., but the correspondence has disappeared, except for what remains in the Dillingham files.

Mrs. Harold G. Erdman supplied information on the life of her grandfather, William H. Chickering.

In addition to the sources mentioned above, the author has relied on a considerable number of published works, of which those most helpful for his purposes are listed below:

Adler, Jacob. *Claus Spreckels: The Sugar King in Hawaii.* Honolulu, 1966.

Ai, Chun Kun. *My Seventy-nine Years in Hawaii.* Hong Kong, 1960. (Factually inaccurate with respect to Mr. Dillingham.)

Alexander, Mary Charlotte, and Dodge, Charlotte Peabody. *Punahou 1841–1941.* Berkeley, 1941.

Baldwin, Arthur D. *A Memoir of Henry Perrine Baldwin, 1842 to 1911.* Cleveland, 1915.

Baker, Ray Jerome. *Sketches and Maps of Old Honolulu.* Honolulu, 1950.

Brundage, Lucile A. *Alfred W. Carter, Hawaii's Dean of Cattlemen and Notes on Hawaiian Livestock.* Kamuela, Hawaii, 1971.

Castle, William Richards, Jr. *Life of Samuel Northrup Castle.* Honolulu, 1960.

Comstock, Henry B. *The Iron Horse.* New York, 1971.

Conde, Jesse C. *Sugar Trains Pictorial.* Felton, CA, 1975.

Conde, Jesse C., and Best, Gerald M. *Sugar Trains.* Felton, CA, 1973.

Cutler, Carl C. *Greyhounds of the Sea.* New York, 1930.

Dalzell, George W. *The Flight from the Flag.* Chapel Hill, N.C., 1940.

Damon, Ethel M. *Sanford Ballard Dole and His Hawaii.* Palo Alto, CA, 1957.

——. *Samuel Chenery Damon.* Honolulu, 1966.

Daws, Gavan. *Shoal of Time.* Honolulu, 1968.

Dean, Arthur L. *Alexander and Baldwin, Ltd. and the Predecessor Partnerships.* Honolulu, 1950.

Feher, Joseph, et al. *Hawaii: A Pictorial History*. Honolulu, 1969.

Greer, Richard A. *Downtown Profile: Honolulu a Century Ago.* Honolulu, 1966.

Hawaiian Mission Children's Society. *Missionary Album.* Honolulu, 1969.

Honolulu Star Bulletin. *Men of Hawaii, The Story of Hawaii and Its Builders.* Honolulu, 1925.

Hungerford, John B. *Hawaiian Railroads.* Reseda, CA, 1963.

Kent, Harold W. *Charles Reed Bishop, Man of Hawaii.* Palo Alto, CA, 1965.

Kuykendall, Ralph S. *The Hawaiian Kingdom,* 3 vols. Honolulu, 1938–1967.

Loomis, Albertine. *For Whom Are the Stars?* Honolulu, 1976.

McCandless, James S. *A Brief History of the McCandless Brothers.* Honolulu, 1936.

McGrath, Edward J., et al. *Historic Waianae.* Norfolk Island, Australia, 1973.

Mulholland, John F. *Hawaii's Religions.* Tokyo, Japan, 1970.

Schmitt, Robert C. *Demographic Statistics of Hawaii, 1778-1965.* Honolulu, 1968.

Sullivan, Josephine. *A History of C. Brewer & Company, Limited.* Boston, 1926.

Taylor, J. T.; Welty, E. M.; and Eyre, D. W. *From Land and Sea.* San Francisco, 1976.

Thrum, Thomas G. *Hawaiian Almanac and Annual.* Honolulu, 1875–1924.

Thurston, Lorrin A., and Dole, Sanford Ballard. *Memoirs of the Hawaiian Revolution and Writings of Lorrin A. Thurston.* Vols. 1 and 3. Honolulu, 1936.

Tilton, Cecil G. *The History of Banking in Hawaii.* Honolulu, 1927.

University of Hawaii, Department of Geography. *Atlas of Hawaii.* Honolulu, 1973.

# INDEX

Waimea Bay
Waimea
RAILWAY
OAHU
Kawailoa
HALEIWA HOTEL
Waialua Bay
Waialua
PUULKI
Mokuleia
Kaena Pt.
Sugar Plantation
Schofield
Barracks
U.S. Military
Makaha
Sugar
Plantation
OAHU
Robinson
Oahu
OAHU
WAIPAHU
Hoaeae
Honouliuli
Ewa Sugar
Plantation
RAILWAY
Ewa Mill
Sisal
Barber's Pt.

# OAHU RAILWA